BERNARD O'CONNOR

AGENT FIFI

AND THE WARTIME HONEYTRAP SPIES

AMBERLEY

First published 2015

Amberley Publishing
The Hill, Stroud
Gloucestershire, GL5 4EP

www.amberley-books.com

British Library Cataloguing in Publication Data.
A catalogue record for this book is available from the British Library.

ISBN 978-1-4456-4650-3 (hardback)
ISBN 978-1-4456-4651-0 (ebook)

Typesetting and Origination by Amberley Publishing.
Printed in the UK

Contents

Foreword

On 17 September 2014, I received an email from Steven Kippax, a historian who had set up a group for people interested in the Special Operations Executive (SOE), a top-secret organisation during the Second World War. He drew my attention to an article in *The Telegraph* entitled 'Revealed: identity of Fifi, the stunning wartime spy'. It was about recently released documents in the National Archives in Kew that revealed previously unknown details about 'Fifi', an agent provocateur used by the SOE to test how willing the men and women they had trained to be secret agents were to divulge details about their training, their cover stories, their family background and their mission behind enemy lines.

I had previously researched and written numerous books about the agents' training, their missions and RAF Tempsford, the secret airfield in Bedfordshire from where most were flown out on moonlit nights and dropped by parachute or landed in remote fields in occupied Europe. In most contemporary sources, the term 'agent provocatrice' was used to stress the gender.

M. R. D. Foot, in his 1984 history of the SOE, mentioned them wanting to test the agents' security while they were at their training schools and at safe flats in the West End of London in the intervals between training courses. 'Did they talk in their sleep, and if so in what language? There was a devastating blonde codenamed Fifi who made it her business to find out.'[1]

David Stafford, another SOE historian, commented that all the secretaries seemed to know about 'Fifi'.

> She was the Agent Provocatrice, gorgeous and enticing, who went *all the way* (at least for male trainees, what facilities there were for female trainees remains a mystery). Significantly, none of them actually *met* the legendry Fifi, nor has she ever surfaced with her story. Perhaps she has passed on, or now resides in south-coast respectability eager to forget her risqué past. More likely she never existed, her slinky seductress ways merely conjured up in Beaulieu's ingenious minds as a dire warning to their students. This certainly, will be one SOE secrets never revealed.[2]

Expecting widespread interest, Jonathan Cole created a blog for the National

Archives website entitled 'Our Special Agent: "Fifi" and the Special Operations Executive'. In it he stated that 'until Fifi's file was released, she was considered a legend of SOE, a symbol of seduction – not surprising, since she's said to have bedded trainee agents to find out whether they talked in their sleep.'[3]

The British media ran stories, including the *Daily Mail*'s 'Meet Agent Fifi, sent by British spymasters to test out trainee agents before they were sent to occupied Europe', the *Independent*'s 'Revealed after 75 years of secrecy: "Fifi the glamorous WW2 special agent who tested British spies' resolve" and the *Sunday Telegraph*'s 'Licensed to thrill: Christine Chilver, Britain's Second World War special agent'. I also found similar stories in the United States, Indian and Australian media.

I was able to download Fifi's personnel file from the National Archives website and, using my background knowledge of SOE, the newspaper articles, contemporary biographies and other files in the National Archives, I have been able to piece together her story. While researching her story I found references to other agent provocateurs, female infiltrators and a number of double agents engaged in top secret deception operations. Their stories appear in the final chapters.

It has been rather like an archaeologist trying to find artefacts that shed light on a few years in the past, but in this case I have had to dig in different sites. The resulting account has understandable gaps in it and some pieces may have been wrongly placed, but I trust the story holds enough water to quench your thirst for knowledge about secret operations during the Second World War.

I need to acknowledge the research done by Mary Berbier, Glenda Cooper, Terry Crowdy, Barbara Davies, Patricia Grant, Ben Macintyre, Joan Miller, Clare Mulley, Noreen Riols, Anita Singh, Gregory Walton and Rayyan Sabet-Parry. I would like to thank David Armstrong, Trevor Butterworth, David Harrison, Fred Judge, Willem Mugge, Phil Tomaselli and Roger Tobbell who have been particularly helpful with background information on Britain's intelligence services, the SOE in particular. Jim Cunningham kindly checked copies of *Housewife* magazine in the British Library. Special appreciation is given to Steven Kippax, a mine of information on SOE, who helped me to access personnel and other files in the National Archives in Kew. Jonathan Cole and the rest of the staff there need to be acknowledged for making the SOE files available and creating an online catalogue one can search from one's armchair. The Imperial War Museum in London and the Military Intelligence Museum in Chicksands also hold valuable records relating to the Intelligence Services. Paul Tonge very kindly provided photographs of Fifi.

Bernard O'Connor, 2014

1

Fifi's Background

Documents in her personnel file in the National Archives in Kew, London, show that Marie Christine Chilver, known in her adult life as Christine, was born on 12 September 1920 in London, the daughter of a Latvian mother and the *Times* correspondent in Riga, the capital city of Latvia. Her father took over his father-in-law's timber business in Riga and, from 1920 to 1939, the family lived in a villa a few miles outside the city. Educated at home by French and English governesses, Christine also learned some German from a German maid. She saw little of her father as she was growing up as he spent a lot of his time in the office or away on business.

When she was twelve, her father took her and her governess to Tallin in Estonia and she spent the summer at Kuressaar. In September 1934, she spent a week in Stockholm with her father and, on returning from Sweden, her father rented a flat in Riga, where she attended a German school. When she was fifteen she was sent on her own to spend the summer of 1935 at a 'pension de famille', near La Lavandou on the Côte de Morts, to improve her French. She then spent another six months at school by which time her German was described as literal and colloquial. In spring 1936, she continued to study English and the following summer she went back to England and stayed as a paying guest with English families, first in Devon and then in London.

In spring 1938, she was sent to Paris to attend the Cours de la Civilisation Française at the Sorbonne. She returned to Riga at Christmas and was at home in September 1939 when Germany and the Union of Soviet Socialist Republics (USSR) used the secret Molotov-Ribbentrop Pact to invade Poland. At the end of November, the USSR invaded Finland. Fearing an attack on Latvia, her father decided to send her to England, where she prepared for the college entrance examination to read Modern Languages at Somerfield College, Oxford.

However, her father died on 20 January 1940, before Christine could take her examination, and, due to what was reported as financial problems, she went to France in May to continue her studies at the Sorbonne. One imagines she met up with friends she had made while earlier in Paris.

With the threat of the USSR invading Latvia, her mother took her other daughter to Sweden, where, as British refugees, they were looked after by the

British Consulate in Stockholm. Germany invaded Denmark and Norway in May 1940 and the Netherlands, Belgium, Luxembourg and France in June. In the same month, Latvia was invaded and the Russians confiscated all private property, including her family's.

By the end of June 1940, the Germans had taken control of the north of France and Christine, as a British citizen, was interned in a women's prison camp at Besançon, in the east of the country. Although over 330,000 Allied troops were evacuated from Dunkirk, tens of thousands who had been surrendered or were injured and in hospital were similarly imprisoned. She is reported to have escaped from the camp and made her way to Lyons (Lyon), in the unoccupied zone. While in the British Consulate, which was being administered by the Americans, she met Flight Lieutenant William Simpson, a British pilot who had been shot down in France on 10 May 1940. As his hands had been very badly burned and he had an eye injury, he was receiving treatment in a Lyons hospital. In his autobiography he detailed how

> once or twice I had heard that there was an internment camp full of British women somewhere in the occupied zone of France. I knew that British women had been rounded up in Paris and elsewhere in the occupied zone. It was not until I met Chris, however, that I realised what a ghastly place it was. Chris and I met at the Consulate, and I was immediately struck by her appearance. She was only twenty, but had the assurance and bearing of a woman of at least thirty-five, combined with the physical perfection of youth. Tall, with a wealth of long, fair hair billowing around her shoulders, she was a perfect physical specimen of Scandinavian womanhood.[1]

Christine told him about her family background and her experiences in England and France, including details about her imprisonment.

> One day all the British women in Paris were rounded up by the Germans and put on a train bound for an unknown destination, which later turned out to be Besançon, in eastern France. On the way the women were not allowed out of the train, which had no corridors, although the journey lasted for many hours. Many of them were ill or weak, and a few died before reaching their destination. The internment camp turned out to be an old army barracks, falling rapidly into decay. The women were forced to sleep on the stone floor of the big cold barrack room. Their bedding consisted of straw-filled palliasses [rectangular cloth bags] and dirty grey army blankets. There was no privacy of any kind. Nuns straight from a lifetime spent in the seclusion of a convent slept side by side with women of the streets. Old women were mixed with young girls in their teens. Mothers were there with their babies. The mixture of types of women there was as varied as the coloured pattern of a kaleidoscope. The food was appalling. Potato soup, grey bread and ersatz coffee formed the basis of their diet. Sanitary arrangements were equally bad. The lavatory was outside, and there was never any hot water. Many of the women fell sick and some had died. Most of the windows of the barrack room were broken, and only a few of them had been boarded up. The building was infested with rats, and lice were everywhere. The monthly ration of a small

square piece of soap of inferior quality was of very little use in the struggle for cleanliness. When their clothes had worn out the women were issued with disused stocks of the old blue uniformed worn by the French poilus [First World War infantrymen]. They were not even clean, and Chris told me that her particular uniform had a huge bloodstain on the trousers. In spite of all the horrors of the camp, the morale of the women was marvellous and cases of complete breakdown – apart from physical illness – were few. She herself managed to escape after four months, and by the time I saw her she had completely recovered from all ill-effects. But she was exceptional, both physically and mentally.

This was only a part of the whole story that Chris told me herself one afternoon while we were sitting together on the side of the lake in the Parc du Lion d'Or.[2]

One of the women inmates, Rosemary Say, known to her friends as 'Pat', spent several months sharing the same room with Christine. Many years after the war, with the help of her daughter and son-in-law, Say published *Rosie's War,* an account of her time as an internee and refugee. in which Christine is mentioned.

When she was nineteen, Pat went to study in France and was working as an au pair when the Germans invaded. She and Christine were on the same train to Besançon and Christine must have given her a fictitious story about her time in England as Pat commented that they had 'fewer problems than many of the others in adjusting to life there. Our education at English boarding schools was to serve us well after all.'[3]

Christine rose to the challenge of being interned and showed organisational skills and feminine charms in order to improve conditions for the women.

Each room had to select a *chef de chambre*, who would liaise with the German authorities. I proposed our ideal prefect-type, Christine, who was unanimously elected.

'First off, we need to put together a rota for collecting food.' She said as we huddled round the stove. 'It's daft for us all to go down individually and queue. Especially in this weather – we're all freezing. Let's choose two people who can collect each day and they can bring the soup to the rest of us …'

Christine had the job of waiting in line for the fuel chits. These would be exchanged for logs and coal to keep our old stove going. We soon discovered however, that no amount of fuel could really warm the room. The winter of 1940–51 was one of the coldest in living memory. Even in the rooms that didn't have a large hole in the ceiling, icicles would form inside the windows at night.

Repairing the hole was our immediate concern. Christine had an ingenious solution, she would get it fixed by the German guards, her accomplice being the beautiful Marie. 'Point out the hole in the ceiling to our guard,' she said to her. 'After that, just whimper and smile sweetly.' Marie couldn't understand much English, so Christine helped her by putting on a sickly smile and staring coyly up at the ceiling.[4]

Four German guards came in and Christine cajoled them into repairing the hole. Christine was reported as having the measure of the German Schwester (sister) who was under the camp Kommandant's instructions to look after all the rooms on her floor. Each morning she ordered the women to do drills, make their beds in military fashion and obey every instruction immediately.

> We were equally determined not to jump to her orders. We soon found out she was frightened of the Kommandant, who would bang on his desk with his fist and shout at her, accusing her of making trouble. After one of her more ridiculous orders, Christine threatened to report her alleged persecution to the Kommandant. Schwester Ruth rapidly backed down and together we agreed a truce.[5]

Christine helped the old and the sick; for several days she assisted one of the older ladies get down four flights of stairs in the middle of the night so that she could get to the outside toilet and then helped her back to her palliasse, exhausted, dehydrated and freezing. She also had a good sense of humour, which helped cheer up the others.

> One freezing morning, a group of us were sitting in the large and draughty outhouse. We had been there for a couple of hours, surrounded by piles of potatoes, carrots and swedes. We were supposed to be peeling them and it was an almost impossible job. They were black with frozen earth and in varying stages of decay. Our hands were frozen, it was difficult to tell if you were peeling earth, vegetable or human skin.
>
> 'I've had enough,' I cried, jumping up. 'I'm going to see the Kommandant to complain.'
>
> 'Now wait,' Christine said, stopping me. She was as practical as ever. 'If you're going to make a fuss then I'm going to hide some of the carrots first. Just what we want for our tea, girls. Frozen, raw carrots. Lovely. Now we'll be able to see all those little bed bugs in the dark, Pat.'[6]

When the Kommandant arrived she persuaded him to provide them with two braziers. Although they helped raise the temperature, the women nearly choked by the fumes as there was no chimney to let out the smoke. When the RAF started bombing the area, there were not enough blackout curtains to cover all the windows. She managed to persuade the women to take turns giving up a blanket each night when they were ordered to use one to ensure the last one was covered. They didn't want to be bombed by their own men.

Anthony Brooks, who had also been imprisoned in France, mentioned in a post-war interview for the Imperial War Museum that Christine nursed other prisoners and used her friendship with Besançon's doctor to help British prisoners of war escape into unoccupied territory.[7]

How and when Christine escaped is unknown, but when she reached Lyons she befriended Simpson and they spent many hours wandering around the markets, going to the cinema, drinking in cafes and, to find out what was really happening in the war, reading Swiss newspapers and listening to the BBC's French service.

With the help of officials at the American Embassy, Simpson was given permission by the Germans to leave France. Christine volunteered to be his travelling companion and act as his nurse as long as her departure coincided with the dates marked on her Spanish and Portuguese visas. As Simpson had an injured eye, one hand in bandages and the other useless, it would have been impossible for him to travel alone.

On the evening of 10 October 1941, they took the train to Grenoble where they changed to a wagon-lits (sleeper) to take them to the Spanish border. Whether that fact that Simpson was a twenty-seven-year-old married man travelling with a beautiful twenty-one-year-old blonde with a different surname raised French and Spanish eyebrows is unknown. There was no mention of any romantic involvement, with Christine taking a professional view about feeding him, giving him a body wash and helping him to dress and undress.

The only money they were allowed to take with them was 500 French francs. However, three Americans who were travelling with them insisted on buying them first-class tickets to Barcelona and paying for them to stay at the Ritz hotel, but in separate rooms. Here they were able to eat unrationed food, drink good wine, listen to a band playing and have their first hot bath in months.

Despite the British Consul promising them a flight to Madrid, being British citizens, they were not allowed to use the German airline and seats on the Spanish and Italian airline flights had to be booked well in advance. Consequently, they were forced to take the train to Madrid. On the day their three-day police permit to stay in Barcelona expired, Christine had to get up early to queue for tickets and managed to get them half an hour before the train left. The two other passengers in their first-class compartment were suspicious of them. Simpson reported that

> at first I think they took us for Germans. Chris would pass as a German anywhere, with her long, fair hair, bright-blue eyes and Germanic build, and I was carrying a copy of the German paper *Signal*. When they found out later that we were English they seemed quite disappointed.[8]

Accommodation had been booked for them at Hotel Mora, where all British refugees stayed while awaiting exit papers from the British Embassy. Amongst the staff were members of a newly-formed secret organisation known as MI9 (Military Intelligence). It was created on 23 December 1939 by Major (later General) Crockatt, with the role of providing financial and other assistance to Allied troops, downed aircrews, escaped prisoners of war, resistance fighters and other evaders who wanted to reach England. Their officers worked undercover in the passport office of embassies and consulates in Berne, Madrid, Barcelona, Lisbon and Gibraltar.

As Simpson was a pilot, he reported to Wing Commander Dickson, the Air Attaché, who insisted that he and Christine stay in his home. That evening they watched the 1941 film *Target for Tonight*. As MI9 gave priority to returning British military, they were provided with tickets in separate compartments on the following night's sleeper train to Lisbon. Civilians were assisted in getting to Gibraltar, where, after interrogation by MI9 officers, they had to await a berth on one of the ships going in convoy to England. A telegram was sent to Lisbon and London informing them of Simpson and Christine's imminent arrival.

After a few days in a transit camp at Caldas da Sunha outside Lisbon, where they were able to eat good food, smoke English cigarettes and read

British newspapers, Donald Darling, the MI9 representative, arrived in a Dodge to take them to a night club for their last night in Portugal. The next day they were put on a K. L. M. Douglas airliner under charter to the British Overseas Airways Corporation, which flew them to Bristol airport. They landed on 21/22 October 1941, with no family or friends there to welcome them, When an ambulance arrived to take Simpson to a nearby hospital for an eye operation, he reported that 'Chris, feeling the anti-climax of our arrival even more than I, wished me "Bonne chance" and disappeared'.[9]

All refugees arriving in Britain in the first few years of the war were taken to the London Reception Centre in the Royal Victoria Patriotic School in Wandsworth, London. Later in the war, female refugees were sent to Nightingale Lane, another interrogation centre in Clapham. Here they spent several days undergoing a 'legalisation' process of being interrogated by MI5 security officers, primarily to determine whether or not they were German, Italian or other enemy agents, but also to obtain from them any information about what conditions were like in the countries they had been living in. They were asked about their family background, their education, qualifications and work experience, where they had been on holiday and their own and their family and friends' political persuasions. They were also asked about any people they knew who were involved in resistance work, as well as identifying collaborators, people who were working with the Germans. The Ministry of Economic Warfare was also interested in obtaining up-to-date industrial intelligence, particularly those companies actively collaborating with the Germans who would be targeted for sabotage or RAF and, later, USAF bombing missions.

An MI9 officer would try to ascertain as much as they could about how they escaped, what routes they took, how much they paid and the contact details of people who helped them, as well as what the current prices were for goods and services, rationing, train timetables, etc. This intelligence was to help them to further support escape organisations operating behind enemy lines and their undercover officers in Switzerland, Spain and Portugal. The organisation was later given responsibility for helping prisoners of war to escape.

They were quizzed about what they knew about military conditions, the location of anti-aircraft batteries, army barracks, ammunition factories, munition dumps, where the German troops socialised, where their controls were, etc. This intelligence was forwarded to the Army. They were asked for any information about shipping in the ports they might have visited, particularly the submarines that were attacking the Allied convoys and where submarine crews were barracked and socialised. This intelligence was passed to the Royal Navy. Any up-to-date details on the Luftwaffe, aircraft factories, airports and airfields were forwarded to the RAF.

Detailed reports were kept on each refugee, which might include their own written testimony. It is quite possible that Christine's report is to be found in a folder in the National Archives in Kew. The result of their interrogation often led to the refugees being provided with employment: soldiers re-joined their regiments, pilots and aircrew rejoined their squadron, some joined the armed forces of their government-in-exile and others were recruited to work with the British intelligence services. Christine was one of the latter.

2

Background to Britain's Intelligence Services

There has been a long history of governments employing people to collect military, political and economic intelligence and undertake secret, clandestine work. In 1907 the British Government created a Home Section, headed by Vernon Kell, who was given the responsibility of investigating espionage, sabotage and subversion within Britain and overseas.

Two years later, the Committee of Imperial Defence established the Secret Service Bureau, which was known to those involved as the 'Secret Service', the 'SS Bureau' or even 'SS'. A separate section, known as the Foreign Service (MI6), headed by Mansfield Smith-Cumming was responsible for overseas security while the Security Service (MI5) dealt with issues within the United Kingdom.

MI6 officers were sent to work in British embassies or consulates overseas. Their official jobs might have been military attaché, air attaché or naval attaché, but they might also have been involved with overt and covert collection of intelligence that could be passed back to the government in London. Passport Office staff were sometimes engaged in similar clandestine work and, where appropriate, local people might be paid to supply intelligence or undertake secret operations.

Following the outbreak of the First World War, there was a need for closer liaison between the War Office and the various military intelligence organisations. The Foreign Service had to work with the Military Intelligence Directorate, and was known as MI1c. Cumming managed to separate the Foreign Service from Military Intelligence and his organisation became known as the 'Foreign Intelligence Service', the 'Secret Service', the 'Special Intelligence Service' or just 'C'. From 1920, it was more widely known as the Secret Intelligence Service or SIS, with its headquarters at St Ermin's Hotel, opposite New Scotland Yard, London. Within the SIS there was the 'D' Section, people employed to undertake undercover operations, dirty tricks, sabotage, etc.[1]

Following the outbreak of the Second World War, British diplomats were evacuated from Czechoslovakia and Poland, dramatically reducing the British government's intelligence capabilities in Eastern Europe. Many of their local agents were left without financial support or a base to forward their intelligence. The embassies of neutral countries like the USA or Switzerland acted on Britain's behalf.

Guy Burgess, a D-Section officer who was later found to be a Soviet agent, suggested that a special school be established to train agents to be infiltrated behind enemy lines to support those left behind, gather intelligence and encourage resistance. His idea was acted upon and in late 1939 the British government requisitioned Brickendonbury Manor, a large country house with several hundred hectares of parkland outside Hertford, about twenty-five miles north of London. His idea that it should be called the Guy Fawkes School was rejected. Instead it was called the D School, the 'D' said to stand for destruction. Its commanding officer was Frederic Peters RN, with Burgess as his second in command. The man responsible for its syllabus was Kim Philby, another SIS officer who had been Burgess's friend at Cambridge University and who was also a Soviet agent.

As well as physical training, weapons training and espionage skills, sabotage was included in the syllabus as one of a number of means of attacking the enemy. One of Brickendonbury's first sabotage instructors was George Hill, who had worked for the SIS during the First World War and the Russian Revolution and had written a number of books on his sabotage activities. Maybe he told his students Lenin's saying that 'an ounce of resistance is worth a pound of hope'. What was taught included what had been learned about the tight-knit communist cell structure and guerrilla tactics of the Irish Republican Army.

Following the German invasion of Norway, Denmark, Holland, Belgium and France, over 330,000 Allied troops were evacuated from Dunkirk at the end of May 1940. On 10 June, Mussolini sided with the fascists and declared war on Britain and France. The British intelligence community had to come to terms with their diplomatic staff returning home after being forced to leave embassies and consulates, as well as losing their contacts in occupied countries. The British government found itself in a quandary.

On 18 June, General Charles de Gaulle, the leader of the Free French forces who had escaped to England, made a speech on the BBC French Service telling the people of France that they had lost the battle but they had not lost the war. To assist not just the French but people in other German-occupied countries, Hugh Dalton, the Minister of Economic Warfare, suggested the establishment of another secret intelligence organisation. With the agreement of Sir Stewart Menzies, the new head of SIS; Sir Alexander Cadogan, the head of the Foreign Office; and the heads of the Armed Forces, the Special Operations Executive (SOE) was formed on 22 July 1940. Winston Churchill, the British Prime Minister, ordered it 'to set Europe ablaze'. Headed by Sir Frank Nelson, SOE was divided into three branches: SO1 for underground propaganda, SO2 for unacknowledgeable operations, sabotage and supporting the resistance groups in enemy-occupied countries and SO3 for planning. D Section became part of SO2.

SOE staff were mostly recruited from men working in the City who had lived and worked overseas and were fluent in languages. Its headquarters were offices at 64 Baker Street in the Marylebone district of Westminster.

A Requisitioning Section then set about acquiring properties for SOE use. Country Sections were created for Scandinavia, Poland, Czechoslovakia, Denmark, Holland, Belgium, France, Iberia, Italy, the Balkans and the Middle East. Administrative staff were taken on and, generally speaking, all communications used a system of code numbers and symbols for each individual. Given the secret nature of their work, like the SIS, all SOE staff and students had to sign the Official Secrets Act

The SOE was given responsibility for getting information out of occupied Europe; finding out where the Germans were garrisoned, how many there were and what their vulnerable points were; and identifying the people who could be counted upon to actively engage in helping to liberate their country. The SOE was also tasked with sending in wireless sets and wireless operators to enable communication between London and the resistance movements. They took over from SIS in the training of agents and arrangement of their infiltration behind enemy lines and helped the partisans in occupied Europe to attack the German forces in whatever way they could, finding out what weapons, ammunition, food, clothing, medicines, money and other supplies were needed; what training they needed; and locating safe dropping grounds for supplies and agents, safe houses and trusted people who would help. They also took over the propaganda section.

As well as recruiting foreign-language speakers from the business community, SOE also drew from the armed forces, government organisations and refugees who had fled to Britain following the invasion of their country. The latter were identified following their compulsory interviews with officers from Military Intelligence at the London Reception Centre.

In Britain, potential SOE agents, having signed the Official Secrets Act, attended a two- to three-week assessment course at Special Training School (STS) 5. This was the symbol used for Wanborough Manor, near Guildford in Surrey, where students were only allowed to speak the language of the country the SOE hoped to send them to. After June 1943, they would have had a much shorter five-day assessment at Winterfold Manor, near Cranleigh in Surrey. Known as STS 4 when it was used for training Dutch and Belgian agents, it was renamed STS 5 when the Standard Assessment Board took it over.[2]

The SOE had its own training section, known by the symbol M/T. Their instructors not only taught but also reported on the students doing basic military and physical training, learning how to live in an occupied country, Morse code, elementary map reading and weapons training. They were also given psychological tests to determine their suitability for specific roles like organisers, couriers, wireless operators, weapons instructors or saboteurs.

Based on their instructors' reports, those considered suitable were then sent on a four- or five-week paramilitary training course in one of ten shooting lodges near Arisaig in Inverness-shire, north-west Scotland. Each had its own number, ranging from STS 21 to 25 including some as, bs and cs. The syllabus included physical exercises to build up strength and stamina, which included rock-climbing, mountaineering and forced marches over the difficult Scottish countryside, whatever the weather; fieldcraft (outdoor survival); how to use first dummy and then real explosives to blow up bridges, railway lines, locomotives and boats; how to jump off trains safely; how to use British and German weapons; grenade throwing; more Morse code; advanced map reading and orienteering; advanced raiding tactics; burglary, key cutting and forgery; knife work, rope work and boat work; as well as unarmed combat and silent killing, termed at the time 'the art of ungentlemanly warfare'.[3]

If they were successful after this course they then underwent, depending on the weather, a three- to five-day parachute training course at Ringway aerodrome, near Manchester (STS 51), where they learned how to jump and land properly from increasing heights. Most were given three jumps from a basket attached to an air balloon and then two drops from a Whitley bomber, one of them at night.

Having passed this course, they were sent for a month to what was called the Group B finishing school. This was based in one of eleven remote country houses in the grounds of Lord Montagu's estate at Beaulieu in the New Forest, near Southampton. Houses were numbered STS 31 to 38. The main headquarters was in The Rings (STS 31) with the organisation run initially by Lieutenant Colonel J. W. Munn. When he was transferred to run a similar school for the Office of Strategic Services (OSS) – the American equivalent of the SOE in Whitby, Ontario, in April 1941 – he was replaced by Major Stanley Woolrych, the chief instructor. The administration was run by Adjutant, later Major, Alan Wilkinson. There were five sections in the syllabus: agent techniques, exercises, enemy organisations and order of battle, propaganda and codes and ciphers. Depending on what role SOE had chosen for the agent, there were lessons in choosing and describing dropping zones; setting up and training reception committees; learning correct procedures for parachute drops and landings; more about codes and ciphers; further map reading; microphotography; disguises; how to use and arrange messages on the BBC; ways of recognising and making forgeries; the use of new weapons; safe and lock breaking; withstanding interrogation and torture; spy-craft (constant vigilance, organising dead letter boxes and safe houses, using a cut-out); recognising the uniforms of enemy counter-intelligence officers and how to deal with them; learning their cover story (a mix of fact and fiction) off by heart; and missions to different towns or cities with special tasks.[4]

Those that failed the course, for whatever reason, were not allowed to return to their previous employment. They were sent to what was called 'the cooler' for the duration of the war. There were two in Scotland, the Craigerne Hotel for officers and Inverlair for the others. There was also Tyting House, St Martha, near Guildford.

Those identified as potential wireless operators were sent on an intensive Morse Code course at Fawley Court, near Henley-on-Thames (STS 41 from 1940 to 1942, then renamed STS 54a), and then to Thame Park, near Oxford (STS 52). This course could last for as few as sixteen weeks, but for some it took nine months and included a two-week practice exercise in Belhaven, near Dunbar in Southern Scotland (STS 54b). After their training, they were based at Grendon Hall, Grendon Underwood, near Aylesbury, Buckinghamshire (STS 53b), where they encoded and transmitted messages to wireless operators in the field and decoded their incoming messages.[5]

Those considered potential saboteurs were sent to Brickendonbury, which from August 1940 specialised in industrial sabotage. In the SOE's history of the Training Section, it stated that

> The object of the school was to train men of different nationalities as instructors and recruiters who would be equipped and returned to their own countries in order to raise organisations to counter enemy interests and commit acts of sabotage. In addition, the establishment acted as a general purpose school and undertook the special operational training of raiding parties. The syllabus covered a variety of subjects ranging from political theory and propaganda to demolitions and weapon training, including also the technique of secret service work.[6]

The SIS staff at Brickendonbury were transferred to other duties. Parts of the grounds were turned into a demolition-research area, and factories and scrapyards over a wide area were searched for suitable machinery and plant to experiment on. The North British Locomotive Company loaned them a model of a steam engine on which to show students exactly where to place their explosives.[7] Later the students had opportunities to blow them up. As well as industrial areas, electrical installations, power stations, dams, airfields, canals and railways, telegraph networks were studied and targets identified for sabotage. At the end of this course, students were sent on some cleverly designed schemes to assess their skills.

Once their training was finished, the agents were briefed for their mission in one of a number of SOE flats in London. Until their travel arrangements were finalised, they were accommodated at holding schools. Each nationality had their own. The British used Grendon Hall before it was used for wireless transmissions. The Danes used Audley End, near Saffron Walden in Essex (STS 43) before the Poles took it over; the Dutch and Belgians used Winterfold (STS 4) until 1943; the Norwegians and later French and British agents used Gaynes Hall near St Neots (STS 61).

SOE rented a luxury flat in Orchard Court in London where agents were briefed for their mission, had their cover stories checked and were provided with appropriate clothing for the country they were being sent to. There was a liaison section with the RAF to arrange flights for the agents. A squadron was set up and equipped with Whitley Lysanders and Whitley bombers to parachute supplies and drop or land agents. Initially it was based at North Weald, near Brickendonbury, then, as SOE operations increased, it was transferred to Newmarket racecourse; when RAF Tempsford was completed in early 1942, the squadron moved there and was supplied with modified Halifax and Stirling bombers and Hudsons. While most agents infiltrated into Western Europe were parachuted or landed by plane, some were sent by boat, motorboat, felucca (a type of traditional fishing boat) or submarine.

The containers dropped to the resistance were packed initially at Gaynes Hall, about half an hour's drive from Tempsford. In April 1942, the packing operation was transferred to Holme Hall, near Peterborough, and Gaynes Hall was used as a 'Holding Station' for the agents.

3

D/CE: SOE's Security Section and Fifi's Recruitment (1940–1941)

In Christopher Murphy's account of SOE's Security and Special Operations, he detailed the origins and development of the Security Section. While MI5 dealt with national security, in October 1940 SOE created its own small-scale security section, known by the symbol D/T, headed by Lieutenant Colonel Edward Calthorp. Their offices were nine buildings away from SOE's headquarters in St Michael's House, 82 Baker Street, a property previously owned by Marks and Spencer. Despite being confided to a wheelchair, Calthorp liaised with SIS and the police over security matters and, with the assistance of Captain E. R. W. Breakwell, Edwin Whetmore and 'Jack' O'Reilly, helped identify potential students for the different Country Sections.

In July 1941, Air Commander Archibald Boyle was appointed head of SOE's Intelligence and Security Directorate. Given the symbol AD/P, he separated liaison with SIS from security and appointed Major General John Lakin, known by the symbol D/CE, as head of a new Security Section with Whetmore as his deputy. The Security Section was subsequently known as D/CE.

Lakin had been a distinguished soldier and had previously worked for MI5, so continued his liaison with them on operational security; meanwhile, Whetmore took responsibility for SOE's physical security and liaised with the Army and the Home Office. When Whetmore was transferred to Gibraltar in July 1941, thirty-six-year-old Lieutenant Commander John Senter, RNVR, was appointed Director of Security, known by the symbol D/CE 1. After getting an MA in History and an LLB from Edinburgh University, he practised at the Bar in London. Despite having no foreign languages, he had travelled in France, Switzerland, Denmark and Czechoslovakia and, while in the Navy, visited Gibraltar, Italy, Algeria and Egypt.[1] Major Peter Lee, an intelligence officer with responsibility for SOE's Field Security Police (FSP), described Senter as a 'very shrewd, very tough, self-made barrister. [A] very clever man'.[2] His experience questioning defendants and witnesses in court proved extremely valuable in interrogating SOE's students.[3]

Another member of their section was Captain Norman Mott, known by the symbol D/CE 6. Lee described him as a 'laconic pipe smoker who was never seen to be anything less than cool and controlled, however dreadful the crisis'.[4]

The role of the FSP was to accompany the students attending SOE's training schools, making observations on their performance and identifying any flaws in their characters that could be an issue once they were working in the field. They required 'a natural faculty for assessing another man's character correctly, quickly and without prejudice'.[5] Their attention was particularly focussed on the students' attitudes towards money, alcohol and women. Lee commented,

> If you've got a garage mechanic who's an absolutely brilliant radio operator, and was recruited for that job, [if he] had a very modest wage as a garage mechanic and was then dropped into France with half a million Francs around his belt as the paymaster for the circuit, you had to be absolutely sure that that chap would not suddenly start going into expensive hotels and taking out beautiful girls ... you had to be absolutely sure. You had to know exactly how they reacted when they'd had 'one over the eight'. My NCOs [non-commissioned officers] used to spend as much time as possible with them, especially when they were on leave after the courses were over, to see how they behaved with women ... because, after all, intelligence services in any country use women as agent provocateurs.[6]

Later in the war, the FSP officers were known as conducting or accompanying officers, many of whom spoke foreign languages and acted as interpreters during the agents' training. Some accompanied the students in Group A training schools in Scotland, the parachute training school at Ringway, specialist training courses at other country houses and the Group B finishing school at Beaulieu. Here they participated in all the students' activities except the few days when they were sent on a ninety-six-hour practice exercise to one of the provincial towns or cities. Once the students were allocated a mission overseas, they accompanied them to the Holding School and then to the airfield or port they were to leave from.

Every week they provided the school commandant with a detailed report and a copy was sent to Lee, known by the symbol D/CE 3, who forwarded a copy to the head of the relevant Country Section. These reports were considered of great assistance as students were more likely to talk to conducting officers than to their instructors or commandant. Lee described his work as being a branch of the Red Cross. 'We really had to try and make it possible for the agents to do their dangerous work and come out of it alive. The only way to do that was to have a very, very keenly developed sense of security.' At the end of the war, Senter's report on Field Security commented, 'They set out to make each trainee as security conscious as possible, in his own interest and in the interest of the organisation as a whole.'[7]

The intelligence collected by field security police, some of which the agent provocateurs were later to obtain, included

Personal Details.
(a) Physical description and fitness
(b) Family history

(c) Education and civil occupation

(d) Previous civil/military history

(e) Languages

(f) Political views (if any)

(g) Motivation in joining

(h) Areas known in foreign countries

(i) Loyalty to allied cause

(j) Hobbies and outside interests

Character.

(a) Courage moral/physical

(b) Determination

(c) Emotional stability

(d) Power of application

(e) Mental alertness

(f) Honesty/truthfulness

(g) Selfishness/unselfishness

(h) Resourcefulness

(i) Temperate or intemperate attitude towards Drink, Women, Money, Talk

Relations with Others.

(a) Is the trainee a good or bad mixer

(b) Private contacts and correspondence

(c) Reaction to discipline

(d) Organising ability, powers of leadership

(e) Reaction to security instruction

(f) Behaviour off duty.[8]

Negative reports were sometimes ignored by the head of Country Sections. Murphy reported one case of an unnamed Belgian mechanic who had been trained as a wireless operator. The conducting officer described his security as 'absolutely appalling, exhibiting a fondness for drink, no responsibility with money and a tendency to pick up the most awful women'. Lee sent the report to Hardy Amies, the then-head of the Belgian Section, who disregarded the warning and sent the man anyway. He promptly picked up a peroxide blonde, took her to the Palace Hotel in Brussels, which was 'absolutely stiff with Gestapo people', and was caught. According to Lee, eighteen people were shot as a result of his lack of security.[9]

This could have been Jean Cassart, who was dropped on 3 October 1941, although he was trained as a saboteur. Foot said that he talked so much about his experiences to fellow resistance workers that word spread that an officer had arrived from England with instructions from the government-in-exile to establish fighting groups and engage in sabotage. In fact, he undertook much demolition work before being arrested with his wireless operator a week later in a Brussels hotel. There was no mention of a blonde or people being shot as a result, but Cassart escaped and made his way back to England.[10]

Arnoldus Baatsen, cover-named Bouwman, was a Dutch agent whose behaviour raised concern with his conducting officer. He was reported in November 1941 as having been on a weekend's leave in Cambridge and taken a Miss Cooper to the Salisbury Hotel in Hertford, who he introduced as a friend from London. Lee described him as having 'gone sour' and recommended him being sent to 'the cooler'. This was the SOE term for a remote country house in Inverlair, northwest Scotland, where agents who had failed their course were kept in isolation for the duration of the war, making mountaineering equipment for SOE's operations in Norway. Major Charles Blizard had faith in Baatsen and prepared him for a lone sabotage mission. Lee expressed concern to Senter that a foolish, theatrical and boastful man with a poor security record should be considered suitable. Senter raised the issue with Brigadier, later Major General, Colin Gubbins, then head of SOE's Operations and Training. Blizard ignored Gubbins' warning that the importance of the mission justified the risk and Baatsen was sent to Holland on 29 March 1942. As the Abwehr, the German military intelligence service, had already captured one of SOE's Dutch wireless operators and were playing his set back to London, Bouwman was arrested by a German reception committee as soon as he landed. They knew exactly where and when he would be dropped. During his interrogation he reportedly 'poured out to his captors a torrent of detail about where he had been trained, and how, and by whom'. [11]

SOE used an additional method to assess student's security by using men as agent provocateurs. Whose idea it was to employ female agent provocateurs is unknown. In an interview for the Imperial War Museum, Lee said that 'intelligence services of any country use women as agent provocateurs' and thus it was imperative that male students were tested 'to see whether they were susceptible to women's charms'.[12]

Lee and Senter's liaison with the Training Section at Beaulieu meant that they knew that students were sent on ninety-six-hour schemes without a conducting officer. Provided with the cover names the students had been given, their description, the name of the contact and the hotel where they were to rendezvous, this was an opportunity to employ a woman who could try to use her feminine attributes to 'pick up' the students and test how willing they were to divulge any details about what they were up to. The more they revealed, the poorer their security, and a severe talking to would follow. In some cases, the plans for their missions had to be revised.

When details of Christine's interrogation at the London Reception Centre revealed that she spoke German, French and English and had lived in France for over a year, she was considered as a potential recruit for SOE's Security Section.

The first document in her personnel file was a telegram dated 17 October, 1941 from DF, the symbol used by SOE's Clandestine Communications Section, to FA, an unidentified officer in the French Section.

A. WE HAVE RECEIVED NEWS THAT FLIGHT LIEUTENANT SIMPSON YOUNG SCOTS BOMBER PILOT STATIONED IN FRANCE SINCE SEPTEMBER 1939 SEVERELY BURNED WHEN SHOT DOWN MY TENTHS 1940 OVER BELGIUM AND HOSPITALISED IN OCCUPIED FRANCE LOSS NINETY PERCENT USE OF BOTH HANDS HAS BEEN ALLOWED TO

LEAVE FRANCE AND IS NOW ON WAY HOME TO ENGLAND MORALE EXCELLENT STOUT STUFF

B. IF ALREADY IN LISBON PLEASE OBTAIN PRIORITY AND INFORM US DATE AND TIME OF ARRIVAL ENGLAND

C. WE ARE ANXIOUS HE SHOULD NOT BE QUESTIONED BEFORE ARRIVING HERE[13]

A copy was sent to Senter and presumably Major Nicholas Bodington, known by the symbol F/B, the deputy head of F Section. This was SOE's independent French Country Section headed by Lieutenant Colonel Maurice Buckmaster, known by the symbol F. There was also the RF Section, headed by Lieutenant Colonel Dismore, which liaised with General Charles de Gaulle's Free French forces. One of Bodington's responsibilities was infiltrating agents into France and exfiltrating them and other evaders. On 29 October, he contacted Senter about Simpson.

I had an extremely interesting talk with the above and he gave me a number of names, some of which I suspect to be those of 'C' agents.

I am drawing up a report of our conversation which he would like to carry on as soon as his next operation allows him to be seen.

He has been in contact with Virginia Hall [an American agent operating in Lyons] and I think his information should prove most valuable for the future.

He is extremely anxious to be useful and not to remain what he describes as a 'battered body' and I have no doubt that from time to time he will be able to give us useful tips with regard to the Lyons area.[14]

Simpson clearly gave details about Christine during his debrief and in his discussion with Bodington, as later that day Bodington sent Senter a second note.

When I saw F/Lt Simpson yesterday he did not seem entirely happy on the question of Miss Chilbur [*sic*] who came out with him. He expressed surprise at her healthy look and her well-kept appearance for a woman who had just escaped from an internment camp.

He described her as being one of the most expert liars in the world and extremely intelligent, but at the time he could not get the measure of her.

In view of his other excellent activities in Lyons during his stay there, I think his judgment may be relied upon.

This does not constitute a charge against Miss Chilbur, but I think this lady should be kept under observation.

She has left her address in Regent's Park Road and there is some mystery about her residence at the address which she left, i.e. Linden Gardens. The house-keeper there denies all knowledge of her. We are still trying to contact the lady and will let you have further news.

I asked Miss Chilbur to make a detailed report about the Besançon internment camp and her escape from it, as also on her impressions of people in Lyons, but I naturally cannot obtain this until I discover her real whereabouts.

> P.S. Since writing the above I have ascertained that she is at Flat 40, 73, Linden Gardens, telephone Bayswater 5184.[15]

Her report was not included in her file. A fortnight later, Senter contacted Lieutenant Colonel Hinchley-Cooke, a German-speaking interrogator at MI5, about 'Miss Chilbur'.

> There arrived in this country on or about the 24th October, a F/Lt. Simpson, R.A.F., who had been evacuated from France as a grand mutile. He had been very severely burned and had lost the use of his hands.
>
> He was accompanied from Lyons where he was in hospital, by one Miss Mary Christine CHILBUR who had got in touch with him at Lyons, and who had functioned as a nurse to look after him on his journey from Lyons to this country.
>
> Contrary to expectations F/Lt. Simpson was most unfavourably impressed with Miss CHILBUR. F/Lt. Simpson had done excellent work in Lyons in spite of his great physical disablement, and his judgment appears to be sound.
>
> Miss CHILBUR has an English father and a Latvian mother. The latter is at present in Sweden.
>
> According to her own account she went to Paris in 1940 to study French at the Sorbonne. She speaks excellent German.
>
> She is now at 73 Linden Gardens, Flat No. 40, telephone Bayswater 5184.[16]

Whetmore also contacted Hinchley-Cooke about her and in his response to Senter, communicated via Major G. H. Langdon, he was informed that she was Miss Marie Christine Chilver, not Chilbur, and that she had been thoroughly interrogated and cleared by his department. 'If Simpson had more solid grounds for suspicions, he would like to know what they were.'[17]

Senter also contacted Bodington before replying to Langdon informing him that he was unable to pursue Simpson's concerns as he was 'not one of us, but our people in Lisbon took some part in getting him home because they thought he might be of interest'. However, a subsequent memo from AD/R, one of Boyle's staff, reported that

> F Section had learned from a returned agent that she was not to be considered trustworthy as in August 1941 she was in touch with someone in Lyons who 'though appearing to be pro-Ally was actually a German agent. It seems that when Miss Chilvur [sic] returned to England she was very suspicious and startled at questions being asked her; she was especially shaken when she was questioned in German rather unexpectedly.
>
> It is thought that this lady is now working at the BBC and F is rather anxious that this should be brought to the appropriate authorities. ADR[18]

A handwritten note underneath read, 'Ask F for more details in writing. D/CE [Lakin] will take the matter up with MI5. Details of her work with the BBC have yet to come to light but one imagines that it involved using her language skills.'

On 6 December, Senter informed MI5 that he did not think it was worth pursuing Simpson's concerns about her so she was free to enjoy her first Christmas and New Year in England, presumably with friends that she had made at the BBC and in her neighbourhood.

Lakin used the results of his investigation to produce a report giving her nationality as British and date of birth as 12 September 1920 in London. It then read, 'D/T [Calthorp] advised: 4912 [Christine's SOE number] has offered her services for some form of active work under conditions of danger in which her knowledge of the German and Lettish languages will be useful.' After detailing the family history that Christine had given her interrogators, it went on to state that

> M.I.5 have investigated her case and clear her completely from a security point of view. She has been interviewed by a member of 'C' organisation, who described her German as absolutely first class and her intelligence much above the ordinary.
>
> Would this lady be of any interest to you? If not immediately you may like to have her particulars for your records. Please contact her through me if necessary.[19]

There was then a gap in her file until March 1942, when Captain Baird, known by the symbol D/CE.5, informed Bodington that Christine had been cleared by MI5 but added that if any further concerns about her security came to light, Lakin would be prepared to reconsider.[20]

Subsequent documents show that she got a job in the Press Department at the Ministry of Information, doing French and German translations and writing articles for Foreign Propaganda. During this time she was living in Bloomsbury.[21]

Unknown to Christine, 'Pat' Say had also managed to get back to England. She had been transferred to Vittel prison camp, from where she escaped and, with MI9's help, travelled through Spain to Portugal. She reached England in April 1942 and was interrogated at the London Reception Centre. She claimed to have heard about the SOE while she was in London and volunteered to work for them. They considered her to be a potential agent but she refused to be sent back to France, arguing that there would be many people who would recognise her. Fluent in French, she was given a job in the F Section as Bodington's secretary with the symbol F/B. Sec. There is only one page in her biography about her work for SOE. Having signed the Official Secrets Act, one imagines she did not want to reveal too much. She was transferred to work in Madrid in 1943.[22]

There is a gap in Christine's file between 6 March and 11 September 1942. Whether there were any documents relating to this period or whether they were redacted is unknown. Normally, when pages are redacted there is an official stamp indicating when they will be opened to the public, but in this case there was nothing. One document referred to her passport expiring on 18 June 1942, so one imagines she would have been very much involved in obtaining a new one. Another suggests that she contacted Say's parents to give them news about their daughter.

In August 1942, Makin's ill-health led him to be transferred to Edinburgh where he supervised SOE's Norwegian operations until his death in February 1943. Senter took his place as Directory of Security, and Lieutenant Colonel the Honourable Thomas Roche was transferred from SOE's General Intelligence Section to become head of General Security and deputy head of the Security Section with the cover name D/CE.[23] .

One imagines that Lee and Senter's concerns about the Country Sections ignoring their negative reports on agents' security and sending them anyway, only for them to be caught and their intelligence extracted under torture, must have led them to consider using Christine as an agent provocateur.

4

Fifi's Role as SOE's Agent Provocateur (1942–1945)

The Security Section's discussions about Christine must have taken place before the second week of September 1942, when Roche informed Group Captain J. F. Venner, the head of SOE's Finance Section, known by the symbol D/FIN, that

> we spoke yesterday about the female agent. Her name is Christine Chilver.
>
> [Paragraph redacted.]
>
> She will not be vetted nor will she be recorded. I am sending D/CE.Recs [Miss S. Hanbury] a card with her name on a note that she is not to be employed without reference to me.
>
> She will be taken on as from 14.9.42 at the rate of £300 a year. I have in mind that she should come on 3 months' probation, as the work is entirely experimental.
>
> So far as possible, she will not become known to any member of the Organisation other than Miss Slade [probably an SOE administrator] and myself.
>
> As arranged yesterday, I shall draw direct from you for her salary and expenses. May I please have the cash to cover the period 14–30 September, as I assume you would wish her paid in advance?
>
> The above arrangements have been reported to and approved by AD/P [Boyle].[1]

It is worth noting that because SOE was a secret organisation, none of its staff had to pay income tax. On the same day, a note was added to her file stating that Roche advised that her name had to be added to the 'blacklist' and that she was not to be employed without reference to him. Senter later acknowledged that he personally engaged her to work for him in the Security Section. Five days later, Roche informed Boyle that

> 1. This lady has had been engaged on three months' probation as an agent provocateur. [Redacted under Freedom of Information exemption 40. Closed

until 2026.] Her funds have run out and she was looking for a job. 2. [Redacted] formed the impression that she has quite unusual gifts of intelligence, courage and assessment of character. After consultation with you and D/FIN, it was agreed that she should be taken on a three month's trial basis as an agent provocateur to see to what extent she could penetrate 96-hour exercises.

3. I recalled that there had been some talk about her when she arrived with F/Lt Simpson and I spoke to F about her yesterday afternoon, leading him to suppose that I had been asked for information. He said that she was undesirable and pro-German and that F. B. Sec. had been forbidden by her parents to associate with her on that account. I then spoke to F.B. who said he had formed the impression when he saw her last autumn that she was untrustworthy and that agents of his, Marie [?] and Olive [?], had warned him about her, denouncing her, I gathered, as a German agent. I said I was very anxious to know the extent and substance of his information, since she had been [redacted] under very close observation for some months and had been extremely highly commended for the quality of her work and her loyalty. I asked whether F.B.'s information was so circumstantial that he could not accept the statement I had just made. He said that on the contrary, he was quite prepared to believe that he and his sources had been mistaken and glad to hear that she had turned out well.

4. This morning I saw F.B. Sec. and asked whether it was true that she had been forbidden by her parents to see Miss CHILVER and whether that was on account of the latter's pro-German inclinations. F.B. Sec. immediately said she had not seen Miss CHILVER again, as they had spent five months together in prison at Besançon in the same room. She said that Miss CHILVER had got out of France and had called on F.B. Sec.'s father to have news of F.B. Sec. F.B. Sec.'s father had taken against Miss CHILVER and disbelieved the news (which was in fact true). Miss CHILVER was the only one of F.B. Sec.'s friends whom her parents did not like her to see. It was not prohibition and F.B. Sec. had in fact avoided seeing her on account of the work which she, F.B. Sec. was doing here. I asked F.B. Sec. whether she had, in her association with Miss CHILVER, detected pro-German tendencies. F.B. Sec. said, on the contrary, in the only incident that she could think of, Miss CHILVER had taken a very brave line against the Germans at Besançon. She said Miss CHILVER was difficult to make out and was not liked and was regarded as being more German than English because of her education and upbringing at Riga. F.B. Sec. said her only real objection to Miss CHILVER was that she was somewhat over-secretive.

5. I spoke quite frankly to Max Knight [M.I.5's agent handler] on the above. He told me that the French were always denouncing as spies people whom they could not understand, that Miss CHILVER had been under extremely close supervision and also her communications of every kind had been watched for months, that he was satisfied as he originally told me, that she was anti-German and loyal to this country. He did not think that even in the event of a German occupation would she give away information to save her own skin and he fully agreed with F.B. Sec.'s tribute to her courage and resourcefulness.

6. I reported on the above to you and we agreed that the facts must be put before D/CD[O] [Major Gubbins]. I saw D/CD[O] this afternoon, and told him the whole story. He entirely agreed that, as far as possible, we must keep

from members of the Organisation the information that we are using this agent-provocateur and that if the French Section came to hear of it and objected, that would be his affair. He agreed that one would not expect a person capable of being a spy to be a loveable character and attached particular importance to hearing that her communications out of this country had been so closely scrutinised. I undertook to report on her work after the probationary period, before the question of her going to S.T.S. 31 [The Rings, SOE's headquarters at Beaulieu] came up.[2]

The Security Section came up with a cover story for Christine which was closely related to the truth. She had to memorise it should she ever be questioned.

Name: Christine Collard.
Born: 12. 9. 1920 in Paris
Nationality: French
Profession: Journalist

Father: Jean-Pierre Collard
Born: 25. 9. 1880 in Paris
Nationality: French
Profession: Timber merchant

Mother: Mari Kezlevesky
Born: 31. 8. 1888 in Petersburg
Nationality: Russian [changed to Russian-French in a subsequent document with her date of arrival in Britain as 10 October 1939]
Studied French at the Sorbonne, Paris from 1910–1914. Married Collard in 1914 and acquired French nationality.

Collard fought in the last war, as a Captain in an Artillery Regiment. He was demobilised in 1919 and spent the following year re-establishing his position in French timber import. He succeeded in making several contracts with French and Belgian timber and shipping firms. In 1920 the Collards left Paris and Collard established himself in Riga as a timber merchant. Marie Collard died in 1923.

Christine Collard was brought up in Riga. She was educated at home by French and English governesses and also had a German Fraulein. Collard had taken a villa, several miles from Riga and Christine saw little of him, since he spent most of his time at his office in town.

In 1932 Christine accompanied her father to Estonia; she spent the summer at Kuressaar with her governess, while Collard was in Tallin on business.

In September 1934, Christine spent a week in Stockholm with her father. On returning from Sweden, Collard took a flat in town, and Christine was sent to a German school.

In 1935, Christine went to France, alone; she spent the summer holidays on the Côte de Morts, at a pension de famille near La Lavandou.

Returning to Riga in autumn 1935, she went to school for another year; she left school in spring 1936 in order to continue her studies in English.

In 1937 Christine spent a month (June – September) in England, as a P.G. [paying guest] with English families, first in Devonshire and then in London.

In Spring 1938 she was sent to Paris, to attend the Cours de la Civilisation Française at the Sorbonne. She returned to Riga at Christmas 1938 and remained at home until the beginning of the war, when Collard decided to send her to England, where she was to read Modern Languages at Oxford.

Collard died on January 20th 1940, before Christine could take her Entrance Examinations to Oxford University. She could not continue her studies, for financial reasons, and was obliged to find work.

She got a job at the Ministry of Information, doing French and German translations. She lived, at that time, in Bloomsbury. In 1942 she was transferred to the Press Department of the M. of I. [Ministry of Information] to write articles for Foreign Propaganda.[3]

Having gone through it, she submitted a list of questions that she wanted clarification on: 'Relations with Quartier Général (de Gaulle's general staff)? Any papers to certify profession and employment (Press Pass)? Actual subject of series of articles to be written? Department publication or professional articles are destined for? Is the Press Department also in Russell Square? What are French passports like and do French subjects have to carry passports in England? Is Tujorier [*sic*] in England? Police enquiries in provinces – employment references? Ration book, registration at shops, check-up on registration of ration books and of ration cards? Course pour Français?' Presumably the answers to these questions were given to her verbally.

A typed letter with no signature, no addressee and no date was the next document in her file.

On Friday, 18th September, I saw Mr. Cyril Radcliffe, K.C. Director General of the Ministry of Information. I explained that the point I wanted to raise was so confidential that I was not prepared to mention it to anyone except himself. I told him that in connection with the training of personnel in this country we operated 96 hour exercises and that it had been decided to employ a female agent provocateur to test the security of the students.

We had found a young woman [redacted]. She was only 22, looked foreign and would, in fact, have foreign cover. I was anxious that she should, if possible, have Ministry of Information cover employment in order to allay curiosity as to why a woman of this age had not been called up [to join the Armed Forces].

Radcliffe considered the matter sympathetically but warned me that he might not be able to help. The English public was very sensitive to the idea of people snooping and he suggested that, from the nature of the agent's role, she might attract attention.

He will advise me.[4]

According to *The Telegraph*, Christine's true identity was only known to three people. Who they were was not stated, but her personnel file suggests that there were more than Gubbins, Boyle and Senter. Roche must have known, and at least two others, as on 24 September, Major Jack O'Reilly (D/CE 4) wrote to Major Richard Warden (D/CE 7), another officer in the Security Section who liaised with the Royal Patriotic School.

> Concerning your Marie Christine CHILVER, British-born subject, attached herewith are documents which completely change the identity of this woman. She is now to all intents and purposes, Christine COLLARD, French nationality, freelance journalist, and residing at 31 Gloucester Place, W.1. Her new documents consist of:-
> 1. I.B. 23
> 2. Aliens' Registration Certificate No. 1069020.
> 3. National Registration Certificate DWPK 251/7, duly endorsed.
> 4. Ration Books, Clothing coupons, etc.
> For the purpose of making this a water-tight affair, COLLARD's documents were issued with an address at 43 St. George's Square, S.W.1. [non-existent], but which brings the live office of origin registers within the Westminster area of the Food Ministry, who are aware of this Organisation.
> For the purposes of her new activities, her address is given as 31 Gloucester Place, W.1. and her documents have been re-made out with the change of address.
> Perhaps you will have her Alien's Registration Card passed to M.I.5. for any endorsement that may enable or facilitate COLLARD to travel, but as a French citizen she is entitle to the same privileges as a British subject, other than, of course, certain defined regulations, such as change of address, which must, of course, be registered with Police. This is only necessary when an alien leaves her registered address for an extended period, which is not likely to happen in this case.
> It is essential, of course, that great care should be taken of these documents, as no doubt COLLARD will revert in due course to her British nationality. I do not know what this case is all about, but in the best regulated society one is liable to trip up, and if you consider it necessary, you might give COLLARD my name and address in the event of her coming under Police notice.
> In any case, Chief Inspector Robinson will guard his record in his private safe, and it necessarily follows that any Police enquiry would reach him, and so in turn, be passed to me. JCR[5]

The same day, Warden sent a memo to Roche with information about Christine having met up with someone whom MI5 had concerns about.

> Attached please find Belgian notes written by Christine. As far as I can make out, FRANCOTTE alias BOUVIER, is a man who has been interviewed by us, appears to be extremely able, has produced some very excellent reports on North Africa but for some reasons (suspected by T. [Hardy Amies, the head of SOE's Belgian Section] as being villainy of the deepest type). 'C' did not like him awfully and advised T not to employ him. For the rest, after reading volumes

about the Belgian set-up in this country, I gather Christine has produced a very reasonable piece of work and has summed up the Belgian situation accurately. [This, presumably, would have been work that she had done whilst working for the Ministry of Information.]

Apart from the fact that BOUVIER has a slight taint according to 'C'. I do not think the authoress has been mixing with undesirables and 'C' cannot apparently substantiate their accusations so it is probably best not to tell her to finish the friendship although he is, I gather, both intelligent and deep and if there is going to be a leakage we must face up to it that this is a potential one. RW. [A scribbled note underneath the following day read, 'God help us all.']⁶

This did not deter Senter continuing with his plans for Christine. On 25 September, Warden asked Roche to supply her with £10 to cover her expenses for her first excursion, to Leicester, which required her to leave at noon on the same day. She was asked to keep a careful record of all her purchases, which needed to be submitted to Warden.

Whoever was responsible for choosing the accommodation and the bars and restaurants for the rendezvous must have not only have been very well travelled but someone with an incredible memory. While it could have been a team from the Security or Training Section, it would have been one of the least demanding jobs during the war.

There was no mention of her having to make contact with anyone so it was probably an opportunity for her to travel independently, find accommodation and survive in a new city for a few days.

She appeared to have been somewhat bored when she arrived in Leicester as in an undated, handwritten note addressed to John, presumably Senter, she wrote,

Here is the merriest report I've ever produced. I did my best to sort things out, but could not get them typed. So this is just a rough draft of the notes, which I feel has to be accompanied by an appeal to your indulgence. If you cannot make head or tail off the stuff, I shall re-write it all!

Enclosed, expenses list and hotel bill, plus the cash I had left over. The things that look like artistic attempts from a kindergarden are supposed to be map sketches.

Yours sincerely,⁷

She must still have been at a loss for how to enjoy herself on her own, as she wrote another letter the same evening.

Dear John

Humble self very humbly installed at the Humby Hotel (8, Crest Green, Tel. L. 205041). You know: plush curtains, fried fish smell, and aspidistras. How it came about? After 'doing' eleven hotels – all the 'licences' ones in the city plus several lack-aday ones – I had the choice between trying the Grand and taking this. So here I am, looking at the wallpaper (!) and wondering what's going to walk out of the cracks.

This afternoon: digs hunting and first snoop round – 5 hours footing, very gay – Greeting? Well, R.L. Stevenson [a – the man] has already written the essay on the Enjoyment of Unpleasant Places; what more can I say?

I shall stay put unless I get contrary directions. Please don't expect me to come home with a brainstorm or a glamour lick: I'll be glad if I get back at all.

It's great fun.

Yours sincerely,

Christine.[8]

While Christine was away, the Ministry of Information sent Senter the reasons why they had decided not to provide her with cover. 'There are too many people up and down the country, not excluding members of my own regimental staff, whose curiosity might be attracted by a person acting in such circumstances and it would be too difficult for me to give any explanation if some incident did attract attention for me to be ready to take any risks on the matter. I think, therefore, that we must stand out on this.'[9]

By the time she returned, on 30 September, Warden had made sure her Aliens' Registration Certificate had been endorsed by MI5 to allow her to visit 'protected areas'. These were parts of the cities that had tighter security, like docks and certain industrial and military sites.

Little did she know that she had been followed while she was in Leicester. Mott, known by the symbol D/CE.6, was allocated the task of agent provocateur, making contact with her to assess how well she kept to her cover story. On his return on 1 October, he submitted his report on Mademoiselle X to Roche.

Report on Visit to Leicester

28th to 30th September, 1942

I caught the 3.00 p.m. train from St. Pancras on Monday 28th September and arrived in Leicester shortly after 5.30 p.m.

On arrival, I telephoned the Humby Hotel and was relieved to be able to stake a claim on their sole remaining room – B. and Bfast. no or. mls. [bed and breakfast, no ordinary meals].

I located the place after half an hour's prowl through, I should imagine, most of the blind alleys of Leicester in a particularly penetrating drizzle.

I was pleased to note when I signed the Hotel resister that Mlle X had also done so a few entries above and after depositing my gear and executing a few running repairs, I examined the two lounges in the hope of encountering the lady but without success. As it was by then 6.30 p.m and no meal being obtainable in the Hotel, I went into the town to forage. I hope that I am treading on no toes if I interject at this point that Leicester is in my opinion second in dreariness and grublessness only to Doncaster. However, dinner over, I returned to the Hotel and again examined the lounges and again drew a blank. I spent the rest of my evening in exchanging small talk with the other inhabitants and examining the security-mindedness of the dozen or so U.S. troops who were spending the night there.

I put in a rather late appearance at breakfast the following morning but there was still no sign of Mlle X. I played out my time by consuming vast quantities of toast and marmalade and was finally rewarded by the appearance of the lady. A minor hotel drama then being enacted (involving the non-appearance of one of the three regular residents, a R.A.F. Lieutenant, in spite of repeated bangings on his door and three telephone calls from his H.Q.) and of course, the bloodiness of the weather, provided ample material for a conversational gambit. By the time Mlle X. had finished her breakfast, things were proceeding well according to plan and we adjourned to the lounge to continue our conversation.

This covered a very large field and by quarter to eleven, we had settled the details of the post-war reconstruction of Europe and, indeed, the World, had discussed the internal situation in France, (it appeared that she was French) had travelled over much of Europe, (I regretted that I had unfortunately not visited any of the Scandinavian countries and learned in return that although she was French by birth, she had spent much of her time in travel and had lived in the Baltic countries, particularly Latvia) and had agreed very well regarding the National characteristics of several races.

At this point, I realised with rather a shock, that I was due in the Town at eleven to scrutinise some reports which were being prepared for my approval, so like a conscientious Insurance Official I made my excuses and departed after learning that she was going to do some scribbling and would then most probably toddle round the Town to keep warm.

I did indeed visit the offices of the London and Scottish Assurance Corporation by whom I was employed in 1927 to 1930 but saw no-one I knew, so I re-commenced my quest for food. After lunch I returned to the Hotel but drew a blank: I had hoped to fix a dinner and Cinema date! I read a little and then spent an hour or two absorbing culture at the Museum, after which, another comb out of the Hotel and another blank.

Again the eternal search for food, a stroll round, a wash and brush up and another descent to the lounge. Mlle X. did not put in an appearance and in fact I learned later that she had discovered how to operate the gas fire in her bedroom and had spent the evening up there writing. I did however, have a fairly profitable evening's conversation with the spiritual leader of the regular inhabitants, discussing the boot and shoe trade, 'my best bomb stories', Leicester as a residential centre etc. etc. During the course of the evening the conversation by a happy chance (!) drifted round to the examination of the other residents. Apart from the somewhat obvious fact that our good lady was French, and as far as he could make out she dabbled in journalism, he was not very interested. He warmed up a lot better in speculating on the possible causes of the Lieutenant's indisposition of the morning! The other regular inhabitant was a grey and rather vague old lady, who I gathered had a private sitting-room of her own – at all events I did not encounter her except for a brief moment at breakfast on the first morning, so I have no idea what she thought about our friend. The Staff was not promising for questioning. Apart from the Proprietors (Mr. and Mrs. Coddington-Buck – the name seems to account for the profusion of assegais, daggers, swords, shields and tom-toms plastered all over the house and the Burmese lanterns and Buddhas in the garden.) who did not reveal themselves to me, the only others were two maids, one harassed and inaccessible and the other cheerful but not right bright. I did essay a cautious query to the latter but as she did not seem too sure who or what I was talking about, I gave up any further idea of further information from that source. in fact, so far as the staff and other residents were concerned, Mlle X. quite clearly had excited no sort of undue attention whatsoever.

I pushed off to bed and returned to the attack this morning at breakfast, when our lady joined me at my table.

We had another session in the lounge after breakfast, when amongst many other things, vocations and aims in life were brought under review and I learned that she had always enjoyed writing and in fact was a free-lance journalist and considered that as an occupation it was almost ideal, as one had so many opportunities of travelling around, studying people and things and in general, sharpening one's appreciation of the surrounding scene in the search for copy.

In due course, I left for the office to put the finishing touches on the final reports and paddled back just in time to see her setting forth for the station. At her suggestion I collected my traps and we travelled up together, arriving at St. Pancras just before 4.30 p.m. I left her at the entrance to King's Cross Met. Where she thanked me for having helped her to pass part of a dreary sojourn pleasantly and added that if we were to meet again would be in more congenial surroundings than the Humby Hotel in Leicester. I mentally equated the latter with Porchester Gate and decided that her hopes would in all probability be fulfilled.

To sum up, I certainly formed a most favourable impression of Mlle X. for employment with us. During the whole of our conversations her cover story was perfectly maintained in spite of the fact that I did all that I could to draw out flaws and inconsistencies. I hope that it was not obvious to her that I was in fact testing her, I flatter myself that our pow-wow followed an easy and inconsequential course and I shall be most chagrined if I hear from you that she complains of a foxy fellow who third degreed her.

D/CE.7 [Warden] asked me whether I thought her appearance perhaps too striking. On the whole I do not think it at all a disadvantage. She is very talkable-to and an intelligent and well-informed conversationalist, which should be an advantage.

I am afraid that there is not much more that I can add and I trust that you will consider the above information to be sufficiently well worth £2.17.11 to approve the attached Expense Voucher.

I should perhaps add that I did not contact either the C.C. [Chief Constable] of Leicester or your civilian contact, as the necessity did not arise. I had however intended to call on the C.C. before leaving to let him know that all had gone off smoothly but we spent so much time in arranging Europe, that I had no opportunity.[10]

Mott's assessment must have impressed his superiors as to Christine's suitability, and her details were passed to Flying Officer Cyril Miller. Aged forty-three, he had been appointed by Boyle in September 1942 to work in the Security 'grill room'. At what became known as 'Bayswater', he began interrogating agents prior to them being infiltrated behind enemy lines to give them a taste of what to expect should they be caught by the Gestapo or Abwehr; he also interrogated those agents who had returned from the field, especially those who had escaped from captivity. Before the war he had been a barrister, specialising in maritime and international law, and had been adviser to the Ministry of War Transport. Boyle considered that his knowledge of law and good cross-examination skills would be useful. Miller later acknowledged that his legal training 'enabled him to weigh evidence and form a conclusion as to whether the person who he was interrogating was telling the truth or not'. He had lived in Paris for nine months, spoke French well and had been on the clandestine warfare course at Beaulieu before he met Fifi.[11]

Given the symbol D/CE.G, Miller was to be involved with Christine's work for the Security Section. Signing the letter as Cyril, he provided Christine with instructions for her first exercise on 25 October.

Dear Christine,

The form is as follows-

12.30 p.m: 25.10. Meet me at Euston Station. The Manchester train goes from Platform 15 which is on the extreme left of the station (as you face it). I shall be in plain clothes at the entrance to that platform near the telephone boxes. Be on time so that we can talk before the others arrive. Take a 3rd return ticket.

When Wilkes arrives you will try to get into the same carriage, by following him down the platform.

His description is –

Height: 5'3"

Apparent age: 30/35

Build: Slim.

Complexion: Fair, and cheerful expression.

High forehead, eyebrows well apart, slight limp

He may be with three others and will probably be with one other whose description is–

Height: 5'8"

Apparent age: 25

Build: Strong

Complexion: Dark

Black hair and eyebrows meeting in the middle, thick black moustache, strong beard, left ear larger than the right.

These two will be operating in Manchester; the other two in Liverpool. You will concern yourself with the Manchester couple and especially Wilkes.

If we miss them on the train or are unable to contact them, we will travel up together.

p.m. Arrive Manchester. You will go to the Grand Hotel, Ayton Street. Incidentally this is not where I showed you last night but it is quite near the station. I shall be at the Midland Hotel. A room has been booked for you in the name of Collard at the Grand for Sunday, Monday and Tuesday nights.

26.10. 11.00 a.m. Meet me at Duncan and Foster's Café, St. Peter's Square. If either of the other two are in the Café we will not recognise each other, but will meet at 12.45. p.m. at the Waldorf Bar at the corner of John Dalton Street and Deansgate. It will be O.K. for us to meet at Duncan and Foster's unless I am smoking a cigarette when you come in at 11.a.m.

6.00/7.00 p.m. W [Wilkes] will be in the Bar of the Midland Hotel. He has been instructed to effect contact with a person who does not in fact exist. You will try to get into conversation with him on the lines we have discussed. You can mention vaguely such Railway Officials as the Passenger Traffic Manager, Goods Traffic Manager, though I cannot at the moment give you their names but keep off the Chief Inspector of the Goods Department.

27.10. Meet me at the same time and place, with the same alternative rendezvous.

In case of any emergency or difficulty either phone me or leave a message for me (Mr. Miller) at the Midland Hotel.

I hope we shall have some success; but in any event your report on W's behaviour in the bar of the Midland will be of value.

Upon our return to London, probably Wednesday, will you be good enough to let me have your written report as soon as possible.

Yours ever,

Cyril. (Sketch of main streets enclosed)[12]

Christine's first report was duly written up and sent to Miller, a copy of which was in her file. There was no indication that she managed to sit in the same compartment on the train so she had to resort to plan B.

Wilkes was supposed to be in the bar of the Midland Hotel, Manchester, on Oct. 26th, from 6 p.m. to 7 p.m. in order to contact a person who does not really exist.

At that hour there was in the Midland Bar only one man whom the description of W. would have fitted approximately. He appeared to be between 30 and 35 years of age, height about 5'4"; fair complexion and fair hair. His ears did not seem very large, nor had a noticeable limp. He was dressed in a blue-grey, belted overcoat, grey suit, grey socks, and black shoes.

At 6 p.m. he was sitting at the bar with another man, who might have been Lambert. Description: height about 5'6"; age about 25; hair dark and wavy; thin black moustache, no beard; (his face looked freshly shaved) eyebrows: dark and well apart; high forehead; slightly snub-nosed. He was wearing a dark coat. As the bar was crowded, he could not be studied very closely; it was impossible to observe any differences between the left ear and the right.

Both men looked very nondescript and inconspicuous. They had chosen two bar-stools in a central, 'strategically good' position and were able to see everyone in the bar, by turning their heads very slightly or by looking into the mirror opposite them.

Their behaviour was discreet; they neither turned round, nor stared at people, nor looked up every time someone entered. They showed no signs of nervousness, such as glancing around, fidgeting or looking at the time. They did not talk much; only a close observer could have decided whether they were together or not. Their conversation seemed to be in English, although, owing to the general chatter, it was impossible to overhear them. Lambert (?) was heard to order some whiskey; his English seemed to be fluent and almost free of any accent.

They did not pay much attention to the other people in the bar and particularly showed no sign of interest in women. In fact, they gave the impression of endeavouring to keep to themselves, which might have been due to shyness, but merely to the fact that they were expecting to meet someone. A conversation with the barman, which gave several clues readily accepted by other bystanders, was completely ignored by them.

In general, they looked most uninteresting, made no impression at all, and appeared rather difficult to describe or to remember. Their faces bore no expression whatever, except a blank air of restful boredom. Judging by their faces, clothes, and manner, it would have been difficult for any observer to guess their nationality, profession, social standing or personality.

Lambert (?) left the bar at about 6.45 p.m. Wilkes (?) stayed on until 7 p.m. and then sauntered out; hardly anybody looked up as he left. In the crowd it was difficult to distinguish a limp or any peculiar way of walking.[13]

The real identity of Wilkes and Lambert was not given to Christine. If she got them to tell her their real names, it would have broken their rule of tight security. In this case they told her nothing, a very positive result for them.

A week later, Miller submitted his report to Roche with a request that it not be sent on. Presumably he did not want a copy sent on to Woolrych, the commandant at Beaulieu, and their Training Section, which was responsible for coming up with the schemes. This was Christine's first exercise and it was a test, allowing her to learn from her mistakes. In time, as she improved her techniques, her reports would be passed to Beaulieu so that they too could learn from her insight, not just from her character assessment of the students but also her comments on the organisation of the exercises. Miller's report referred to Christine as F. Presumably by then he had decided to call her Fifi. He was also prepared to reveal the real names of Wilkes and Lambert, the latter of which he spelt as Lambat.

Report on 96 Hour Exercise Manchester and Liverpool 25/29.10.42
1. Scheme devised by Beaulieu.

The above area is in the hands of the German Forces; four agents are despatched to the area from their H.Q. at Beaulieu with instructions to carry out a recce [reconnaissance] of the rail communications in the area with the view of subsequently despatching saboteurs to disrupt them. No ports, docks or industrial premises were involved in the scheme, the Agents' duties being confined to collecting information as to the rail communications in the area and submitting a report to S.T.S. [Special Training School]. Two of the agents were detailed to work in Manchester and two in Liverpool.

All four Agents were to proceed from Beaulieu as follows:-
Leave Southampton Sunday 25.10 0951

Arrive Waterloo 12.13.
Leave Euston 13.15.
Arrive Manchester 18.05.
Arrive Liverpool about half an hour later.

The Agents operating in Manchester were described by Beaulieu as follows:-
Wilkes (real name Wyns)
Height 5'3"
Apparent age 30/35
Build – Slim
Complexion – Fair
Other characteristics – High forehead, eyebrows well apart, even teeth, small hands, full head of hair, possibly limping slightly.
Lambat (real name Le Doex)
Height – 5'6"
Apparent age – 25
Build – well built.
Complexion – Not stated.
Other characteristics – Black rather curly hair, black eyebrows meeting in middle, thin black moustache, strong beard, slightly turned up nose, spaced teeth, left ear larger than right.

The Agents operating in Liverpool were Denton (real name Dansart) and Chester (real name Charles); for the reason appearing below their descriptions are not given in this report.

Beaulieu was requested by phone on Thursday 22.10 to send to me the full Brief of operations given to each Agent, so that suitable occasions of contact could be laid on. Normally D/CE.2[14] only receives a 'Pro forma' giving the names and descriptions of the Agents together with a brief statement of the general nature of the proposed activities upon which he advises the local R.S.L.O. [Regional Security Liaison Officer]. Each Agent however is given, before his departure, a Brief which defines in considerable detail the activities which he is to pursue, and the localities and times at which he is either to make contacts or to be present, and also given the names of certain 'safe' persons whom he may contact.

In the present instance this Brief was not received in London until after I had left, it was posted from London on Monday 26.10 to R.S.L.O. Manchester but was not received by him in time for me to make use of it before leaving on Wednesday. I was informed by Beaulieu, however, before leaving that an occasion for contact with F. had been arranged, namely that Wilkes had been instructed to be in the bar of the Midland Hotel, Manchester from 1800/1900 on the 25.10., there to contact a person who did not in fact exist.

Part of the 96 hour scheme is that Agents should find their own accommodation and, having done so, should wire their H.Q. the address.

The 'safe' contacts given to the Manchester Agents, whose names I had before leaving London, were H. Gough, Chief Inspector Goods Dpt., L.M.S. and A.E. McKenna, Solicitor of James Chapman and Co.

1. <u>Schemes for operating F. as A/P</u>

It was decided that F. should attempt to contact Wilkes and Lambat on the Sunday train to Manchester, and should also be in the bar of the Midland on the Monday evening and attempt to engage Wilkes in conversation. If the Brief were received by me in time (as it was not) other opportunities of contact were to be devised.

2. Facts.

Sunday 25.10

12.30 I contacted F. by previous arrangement at Euston and left her by the only entrance by which the Agents could reach the platform. At this time the Agents could not possibly have reached Euston from Waterloo even if the train from Southampton had arrived on time. I myself stood some distance up the platform.

13.10. As no one corresponding with the description of any of the Agents had by then appeared, I took F. away and we got into the train as it was exceedingly crowded and there was a danger of our missing it if we had waited longer. Just before the train left a man corresponding with Wilkes' description hurried down the platform and got in half way up the train. I did not see anyone corresponding with Lambat's description. At this time the train was so crowded that it would have been most unlikely that any effective contact could have been made.

1700. Change at Crewe. I again saw the man whom I considered to be Wilkes but none of the others. He appeared to be alone, was dressed normally and inconspicuously, and behaving in a perfectly normal manner. I should not have taken him for a foreigner by his dress or behaviour. There was no opportunity for contact without exciting suspicion.

1900. Arrived Manchester. F. proceeded to Grand and I to Midland Hotel.

Monday 26.10

Forenoon explored Manchester with the aid of a map and arranged to contact R.S.L.O. at his office at Rusholme about 5 miles out of the centre of Manchester in the afternoon. I had arranged two tentative contacts with F. but was unable to keep them.

1600. Visited Major Baxter R.S.L.O. at Rusholme. He was extremely helpful and appeared to be pleased to have personal contact with an S.O.E. Officer connected with the exercises. He had not yet received the addresses of the Manchester Agents nor their Briefs. He suggested that, unless it was of importance to Beaulieu [that] exercises should be carried out simultaneously in Liverpool and Manchester, they should be carried out in one of these towns singly, as he himself covers both areas and is short of staff. He also would be grateful for a copy of the Agents' Briefs in the future, as this would facilitate his lying on Police interrogation.

18.15. Returned to Midland to supervise F's contact. The Midland Bar is very small and crowded, it is ill suited for this purpose. There is only one entrance, and, as I was particularly anxious not to be seen by the Agents, I took up position some distance from the entrance from which the view of the entrance was not good.

I refer to F's report on this matter. I had previously ascertained that women unaccompanied were allowed in the Bar. From what I could see F. conducted her part well and made such efforts as she could without being conspicuous to attract the attention of the civilians whom she took to be Wilkes and Lambat. I felt satisfied that I had identified one as Wilkes; his companion I could not identify as Lambat from the description. The behaviour of the two was unexceptionable and they gave no indication to me of being anything other than chance acquaintances having a drink. Although Wilkes glanced occasionally round the room, this was done quite naturally and it was not possible to tell from his demeanour that he was expecting to meet a third person. There appeared to be other unattached girls in the bar, but neither Agent appeared to take any interest in them.

Sunday 27.10

11.00. Contacted F. by previous agreement at Duncan & Foster's Café, St. Peter Square; this is an excellent place for a rendezvous as it affords opportunity for confidential conversation and at the same time all the customers are instantly visible to anyone entering. I received a preliminary verbal report from F. on her attempted contact. She had thoroughly explored Manchester the previous day on my instructions. As I had neither the Agents' Brief nor their addresses I was unable to arrange further opportunities of contact for her.

12.45. Met and lunched with R.S.L.O. He had just received the Manchester and Liverpool Agents' addresses by phone, and had accordingly instructed the Police to lay on an interrogation. He informed me that the Police prefer to catch the intended victim at his address in the early morning before he has left (or in an emergency at night) it was unlikely that the Manchester Agents would be interrogated before Wednesday morning. He also informed me that the Manchester interrogation would not be so well and efficiently conducted as that of Liverpool. He had not yet received the Agents' Brief. I therefore decided not to postpone my intended return to London on the Wednesday, on which day I had arranged to interview Capt. Thomson [?] on an urgent matter.

Afternoon I visited each address.

Wilkes was at the Antrim Hotel 266 Oxford Rod. This is a dingy but respectable private unlicensed Hotel next to the University; it appears to be frequented by University Students male or female. It would be difficult to exercise any continuous surveillance of these premises.

Lambat had found accommodation at the other end of the town in the Mitre Hotel, Cathedral Close. This is a licensed Commercial Hotel, also of a respectable character, which is right opposite the Cathedral. It too would be difficult to keep under continuous surveillance and has three exits.

18.30. Contacted F. at Grand Hotel and received final verbal report.

Wednesday

9.55. Returned with F. to London.

4. Conclusions.

(a) F. I consider carried out such small part as could be assigned to her under the conditions of this scheme efficiently. Her appearance is I think too striking and foreign of English tastes, but in my view she is suitable for use with the Beaulieu students who are nearly all foreigners. She could not however without considerable modification of her dress and make-up be used with success in less elegant surroundings than those of the more impressive and flashy hotels and bars and in my view might well be given the chance of modifying her appearance so as to operate in more humble surroundings. I have no reason to doubt her discretion or security.

(b) The Midland Bar is not suitable for such contacts. It is too small and too crowded and is a resort to which the Natives and the local Army and Air Force bring their girlfriends rather than find them. There are however in Manchester two excellent places in which such contacts are made, the Café Royal Bar in Quay Street, and the Grand Hotel Lounge in Agtown Street. The latter particularly appears to be the resort of the amateur or quasi amateur ladies of the town, who appear to welcome approach with true Northern directness. I suppose that good result might be obtained here with Scandinavian Students.

In Liverpool the only practicable place for such contacts is the lounge of the Adelphi Hotel; although the Bar of the State Café makes an excellent lunchtime Rendezvous and ought to be utilised.

(c) It is a waste of time and money to operate F. on only one contact during an exercise of this kind. I appreciate that Beaulieu have to incorporate a great deal into a relatively short time in these exercises, which are in consequence probably already overloaded. But it should be possible to arrange at least one contact for F. with each Student on each exercise [this could easily have been worked on the present exercise for each of the four students having regard to the short distance between Manchester and Liverpool] and, if we in London were sent the Students' Brief by Beaulieu before the exercise commenced it would be possible in many cases to devise opportunities of contact for F. without specific arrangement having to be made by Beaulieu.

(d) It is a handicap to the official operation of F. as an A/P not to receive the Students' addresses until [as in the present case] two days after the commencement of the exercises. Had these addresses been received earlier, opportunities for contact might have been created by tailing the Students from their lodging in the morning. It is inadvisable that the Students should acquire any information as to our own C/E [?] organisation and therefore the obvious method of putting them in direct touch with the local R.S.L.O. is ruled out, but I feel that if it were impressed upon them that their first duty is to wire their address to Beaulieu and Beaulieu were them immediately to contact us, the delay in future would not be great.

(e) The two Students observed during the present exercise appear to have behaved in an exemplary manner. Their conduct in the Bar of the Midland was natural and inconspicuous. Wilkes was faced with a situation which he did not expect, but from his behaviour throughout no one could have deduced that he was waiting for a contact. The choice of accommodation was in both cases excellent. Indeed I await with interest to discover how, arriving in a crowded and strange town, in the pitch dark, on a rainy evening, without any means of transport, the Students managed to find accommodation at all.

6. Recommendation.

(1) That Beaulieu be tactfully approached with the suggestions –

(a) That in good time before the beginning of an exercise not only the Pro Forma but also the Brief should be sent to us in London.

(b) That on each exercise an opportunity for F. to contact each Student be included in the scheme by Beaulieu, and that attention be paid to the suitability of the locality.

(c) That it is particularly impressed on each student that he must wire his address to Beaulieu at the first available opportunity after installing himself, and that this information is passed at once by phone to us in London.

(d) That in future simultaneous exercises in Liverpool and Manchester should not, unless it is of particular importance, be carried out.

(e) That in future a copy of the Brief be sent with the Pro Forma to the local R.S.L.O. at any rate in the Manchester Liverpool area.

(f) That D/CE should consider whether or not it is advisable that D/CE.6 should attend a Police interrogation during an exercise, having regard to the probability of the latter having to meet Students again on their final Cover interrogation.[15]

Who Wyns, Le Doex, Dansart and Charles were remains a mystery. There were no personnel files in the National Archives for the first three men, which suggests that, if those really were their real names, they were not members of the SOE. There were numerous men with the surname Charles. In which case, who were they? Might the Security Section have employed their own staff to create a more realistic experience for Fifi?

On 7 November, Christine was asked to take part in another exercise in Cambridge, which was much more challenging as it included a large group of students. Miller wrote telling her that

I want you to arrive at Cambridge on November 10th and attempt to contact the students whose descriptions are as follows:-

There are nine of them, and they will be split into groups of three, A, B and C.

Group A will operate on the 10th and 11th November. Their names and descriptions are:-

Nechansky.

Height 5'[?]", age about 30, hair light brown, ears sticking out, oval face and high cheek bones, hair brushed well back; when last seen was wearing glasses.

Bednarik.

Height about 5'8", age 30, thin brown hair, brown eyes, round face, reddish complexion, scar under lower lip, medium build and slightly sloping shoulders.

Leparik

Height about 5'9", age 30, light hair, wrinkled forehead, small eyes set close together, long face, prominent nose, strong build.

Gemrot.

Height about 5'7", age about 30. Dark untidy hair growing well back from forehead. High forehead. Dark eyebrows. Light eyes set close together. Prominent nose and large mouth. Dark complexion. Cheerful expression. Slight build.

Group B will operate on the 11th and 12th. Their names and descriptions are: -

Vane.

Height about 5'8". Age about 26. Brown hair brushed well back, broad forehead. Very light blue eyes. Aquiline nose. Long pointed face with distinct cleft in chin. Expression somewhat gaunt with very full lower lip.

Modransky.

Height about 5'7". Age about 28. Dark brown hair and eyes, dark complexion, broad but prominent nose, very distinct lines in cheek from base of nose spreading round mouth. Very full lower lip. Cheerful but somewhat truculent expression. Slim build.

Group C will operate on 13th and 14th. Their names and descriptions are:-

Kobzik.

Height nearly 6'0". Age about 30. Very distinctive black hair, brown eyes, long thin face, thick dark eyebrows, serious stern expression; lobes of ears are wholly attached to side of face.

Kosina.

Height about 5'6". Age about 25. Very thin brown hair growing well back from high forehead. Thin pointed face, small mouth, somewhat effeminate looking, slight build.

All the above will be in plain clothes. They are Central European nationals. Most speak fairly good English.

They will be available at the following times and places:-

Group A (1200 on 10 Nov. 42 to 1330 on 11 Nov. 42)

Occupation   Location

No.1 [i] 1200 – 1230 hrs. 10 Nov.42   Drink in bar   RED LION HOTEL, PETTY CURY.

[ii] 1430 – 1500 hrs – 10 Nov.42   Looking at books   HEFFERS Bookshop, PETTY CURY

[iii] 1800 – 1830 hrs 10 Nov.42   Drink in bar   BLUE BOAR, TRINITY STREET

No.2 [i] 1200 – 1230 hrs. 10 Nov.42   Looking at books   HEFFERS Bookshop, PETTY CURY

[ii] 1430 – 1500 hrs – 10 Nov.42   Walking   North side of TRINITY ST, and KING'S PARADE starting from TRINITY GREAT GATE proceed to KING'S COLLEGE, pause to look at CATHEDRAL

[iii] 1800 – 1830 hrs 10 Nov.42   Drink   RED LION HOTEL, PETTY CURY.

No.3 [i] 1600 – 1630 hrs. 10 Nov.42   Tea   THE WHIM, TRINITY STREET.

[ii] 1000 – 1030 hrs – 11 Nov.42   Looking at books   HEFFERS Bookshop, PETTY CURY

[iii] 1200 – 1230 hrs 11 Nov.42   Drink   RED LION HOTEL, PETTY CURY.

No.4. [i] 1600 – 1630 hrs. 10 Nov.42   Tea   DOROTHY'S GATE, near band.

[ii] 1000 – 1030 hrs – 11 Nov.42   Looking at books   W.H. SMITH & SONS, Sidney Street next to Woolworths.

[iii] 1200 – 1230 hrs 11 Nov.42   Drink   BLUE BOAR HOTEL.

Group B (1400 11 Nov.42 to 1830 12 Nov.42)

No. 1 [i] 1430 – 1500 11 Nov.42   Walking   From top of JESUS LANE down east side of SIDNEY STREET to WOOLWORTHS.

[ii] 1800 – 1830 hrs 11 Nov.42   Drink   RED LION HOTEL, PETTY CURY.

[iii] 1000 – 1030 12 Nov.42   Walking   TRINITY GREAT GATE to KING'S COLLEGE

No.2 [i] 1800 – 1830 hrs 11 Nov.42   Tea   DOROTHY CAFÉ, first floor, as near to the band as possible (if band is still playing)

[ii] 1000 – 1030 – 12 Nov.42   Looking at books   HEFFERS Bookshop, PETTY CURY

[iii] 1430 – 1500 hrs 12 Nov.42   Walking   KING'S COLLEGE to TRINITY GREAT GATE

Group C (1000 13 Nov. to 1400 14 Nov.42)

No.1 [i] 100 – 1030 13 Nov.42   Walking   From TRINITY GREAT GATE to KING's COLLEGE

[ii] 1430 – 1500 hrs – 13 Nov.42   Looking at books   HEFFERS Bookshop, PETTY CURY

[iii] 1800 – 1830 – 13 Nov.42   Drink   RED LION HOTEL, PETTY CURY.

No.2 [i] 1000 – 1030 – 13 Nov.42   Looking at books   HEFFERS Bookshop, PETTY CURY

[ii] 1430 – 1500 hrs – 13 Nov.42   Drink   RED LION HOTEL, PETTY CURY.

[iii] 1800 – 1830 – 13 Nov.42   Walking   CHRIST'SCOLLEGE to TRINITY along SIDNEY ST. and through WHENWELL'S COURT (entrance opposite JESUS LANE)

No. 3 [i] 12.00 – 13.00 hrs. 13 Nov.42   Walking   KING'S COLLEGE to TRINITY North Side

[ii] 1600 – 1630 hrs 13 Nov. 42   Tea   DOROTHY'S CAFÉ near band

[iii] 1200 – 1230 hrs 14 Nov.42   Drink   RED LION HOTEL, PETTY CURY

I will contact you on Monday evening and give you your address for expenses and also the name of the hotel at which accommodation will have been reserved for you,

Yours ever,

Cyril

P.S. All the Students are on an exercise which involves them contacting civilians in Cambridge with the view of forming a subversive organisation there. Cambridge is supposed to be occupied by the enemy and the Agents are working for the British; they ought not to disclose their activities to anyone other than those whom they have been specifically instructed to contact. This is where you come in. Good luck.[16]

It appeared that illness prevented her from going to Cambridge as instructed. Records show that the R.S.L.O. had to pay the Board Hotel in Cambridge 8s for rooms which they had had to book twice.

In early November 1942, the Allies successfully invaded Morocco, Algeria and Tunisia in an attempt to push the Axis forces out of North Africa. The German response was to occupy Southern France down to the Mediterranean and Pyrenees. This led the War Office to put pressure on the SOE to train more agents.

On 20 November, Miller sent Fifi details of another scheme in Birmingham. This time the agent was a Belgian saboteur.

Dear Fifi, Will you kindly proceed on another scheme?

You will leave by the 11.10 train from London, Euston, on Sunday, 22nd November for Birmingham. I will inform you before you go where accommodation has been booked for you.

The subject this time is named Dukes, age 28, height 5'11", slim build, slight stoop, fair hair and complexion, small head, convex nose with depressed tip. He will be in the Midland Hotel bar, Birmingham, on Monday, 23rd November, 1942, between the hours of 6.30 and 7.30. He has been told that there may be a contact there for him, whether male or female is not known. in fact, no such person other than yourself is being laid on, and you will try and engage him in conversation.

He should not disclose his activities to you without getting the password, which, of course, you will not be given, but there is no reason why he should not converse with you, providing that he commits no indiscretion.

For your information it is assumed that the area is in the hands of the enemy, and his duties as a subversive agent, acting in the British interests, are to take steps towards establishing an organisation in the City of Birmingham for the ultimate purpose of the sabotage of railway communications. He should therefore attempt to recruit people loyal to the cause into the organisation.

I think this scheme gives you more scope than the previous scheme, and is a fairer test of the agent's abilities. You are being given the information which an agent provocateur laid on by the enemy would probably have. I think your suggested cover of a journalist interested in transport would be very useful in the present exercise, but you may adopt such cover as you think most likely to succeed.

The object is, of course, to test the student's discretion and ability. He should, if he carries out his training properly, not attempt to recruit anyone of whose loyalty he is not absolutely assured. The enemy would, of course, be only too anxious to detect the proposed subversive activities by getting one of his own agents recruited into the organisation, and this is your role.

I will give you the usual allowances, and at the end of the exercise would you be good enough to make your report and send in your account in the usual way.

If you can induce the agent to see you again during the exercise, by all means do so, because that is exactly what you would do if you were in the field.

You will return to London on Thursday, 25th November.[17]

Although she was given £10 for the exercise, Fifi did not go. She claimed that she was still unwell. On being informed, D/FIN allowed her to keep the money for the next exercise.

Woolrych, now promoted to colonel, and Captain Gerald Forty, one of the Training Section officers at STS 31, must have discovered from the students' debrief that Fifi did not make contact with any of them and informed Miller. He sent his 'sincerest apologies', explaining that he was away and his secretary was ill and confirmed that 'the A/P will be laid on to the Liverpool

Exercise starting next Sunday. I trust that we shall have some success on this occasion'.[18]

On the same day he wrote to Fifi, glad to hear that she recovered from her illness and hoping that she was feeling fit. He also thanked her for returning the advance of her expenses for the Cambridge exercise and provided details of the next.

> We shall be requiring you to go on another exercise to Liverpool starting next Sunday, the 6th December. The agent in this case is of the following appearance:-
>   Age: 26
>   Height: 5'6"
>   Black hair
>   Complexion: sallow
>   Heavy dark eyebrows, large brown eyes.
>   Thin concave nose.
>   Black moustache.
>   Large mouth.
>   Thick lower lip.
>   Small moles on left cheek and right side of chin.
>   Dark jowl.
> He will be in the bar lounge of the State Café in Dale Street at 12.15 hours, Monday, 7th December.
> You will proceed to Liverpool on Sunday by any train. A room will be booked for you at the Liverpool Adelphi Hotel. The agent's activity will be precisely the same as the last occasion for which I enclose you my instructions.
> I trust you will have a successful exercise.[19]

There were a group of trained saboteurs on this exercise and the one she had to target was known as Tas. On her return she submitted two reports.

> On Monday, December 7th, between 1.00 and 1.30 p.m. Tas was seen passing through the Bar of the State Café several times. It was not possible to contact him then, but as he lunched at the State, I went up to him after lunch and asked him whether he was Mr. Tas. He looked surprised (and later told me his first impulse had been to reply 'No') but I quickly said I had been looking forward to meeting him, to see whether I could be of any help. I sat down at his table and talked fast, explaining I was a journalist writing about War Transport and I 'had been asked' to meet him and to be as useful as possible. I assumed a somewhat patronising tone and pretended to know everything about his job, as well as the whole training system, etc. – he later told me he was sure I was an instructor, particularly as I kept on giving him general advice, etc.
> I am aware that there might be doubts as to whether my method of approaching him was quite fair; the fact that I knew his name obviously must have convinced him my story was true. On the other hand it is quite imaginable that an enemy agent would in a similar case have succeeded in getting the name of his victim. Besides, I understood Tas had been given a password; there was no mention of it. Indeed, it later appeared I had been talking so fast that he had

not even noticed my introducing myself, so that, actually, he had been talking quite confidentially to a person whose only credentials were 'I have been asked to help you...'

Where and how in detail?

We spent the day together – (and Tas must have spent about £2.3.0) On what? Where? – and by the evening I had learnt practically all there was to know about him.

(a) His Instructions and Plans.

Tas told me this was his first exercise. He had almost completed his general training and was probably going to do a month's practical work before being sent on a mission. He would most likely go to Belgium, since he knew that country best. He had specialised in training as a sabotage agent, and therefore found that his exercise (a purely intelligence one) was difficult to tackle.

On arriving at Liverpool he had gone to the Exchange Hotel, but was moving into the Nelson (?) as he found the former too expensive. We went round to both places in the afternoon, to collect his things, etc.

He had been instructed to meet a tall, dark man (blue eyes) at the rendez-vous, I met him instead, and that was actually the only thing he seemed to think odd about my approaching him at the State.

As for working out further strategic plans, he had not thought about things much, so far. He was supposed to go round and see a Mr. Williamson (apparently director of the Majestic Cinema) on Tuesday morning. (The interview was later put off to the afternoon.) Tas had been told that Mr. W. was taciturn and difficult to get round, but some of Tas's comrades had advised him that he should not consider that kind of indication, often deliberately 'fanned' by instructors. However, Tas had every intention of being discreet with Mr. W. to whom he was going to introduce himself as a journalist. He had also thought of 'interviewing' other cinema directors and owners, in order not to make his acquaintance with Mr. W. too suspicious.

Did you see him again or just fade out?

Tas talked about the actual job he had been given (preparing a railway sabotage organisation) as if I knew all about it, and promised to get in touch with me after the interview with Mr. W. to let me know his further decisions, etc.

(b) Personal Particulars.

In the course of our conversation I learnt that Tas was Belgian, but had been brought up in N. France. His home is Antwerp.

His father seems to have been a wealthy business man; he possessed a factory or factories in St. Petersburg (District of Viborg) but his property was nationalised by the Soviet in 1917. (No information)

Tas has relatives in England (London, I believe) – an aunt and a cousin. He has not seen them yet. His parents had, it appears, adopted an English boy during the last war, who is now in the Merchant Navy. (No information)

Tas also has a sister who used to be an agent of the French Deuxieme Bureau. (No record) . She is now in prison in Germany, but as the Gestapo found out only a very small part of her activities she was condemned to 6 years' imprisonment, which Tas considers mild. He has got in touch with her secretly, but has not succeeded in helping her to escape.

He also <u>has a wife, and a small daughter of 4</u> at Antwerp. He mentioned that he was not sure he would be able to resist the temptation of going to see his family when he went over.

Tas himself arrived in England about <u>6 months ago</u> via Spain and Gibraltar. He told me of some cases where he has been able to help De Gaullists in France, how he bluffed the French Fascist Party at Nancy, etc. He mentioned <u>the names</u> of most of the people principally concerned in these matters.

When he goes to Belgium he will probably do operational work, i.e. sabotage and organise guerrillas, etc.

<u>Second report on Tas received 11.12.42</u>.

I met Tas after lunch at the State Restaurant, on Monday, about 1.15 p.m., we had coffee and then proceeded to Recce's (?) Café in Parner Street, where we had another coffee. Between 3 and 4 p.m. we went upstairs to a tea-dance. We left just before 6 p.m. and went round to the Exchange Hotel to collect Tas's luggage. Before leaving we had a drink at the Bar. On depositing his things at the Nelson Hotel, we went to a cinema (approximately 7–9 p.m.) after which we dined at the Adelphi. Tas left the Adelphi about 11 p.m.

Approximate account of Tas's expenses.

He told me his expenses for

Bed and Breakfast at the Exchange 1.11.0

Lunch and Coffee (State) about 7.0

Recces 4.0

Cigarettes 4.0

Drinks (Exchange) 4.0

Cinema 3.0

Dinner and drinks (Adelphi) about 1. 5.0

On Tuesday we lunched at the Adelphi where Tas probably spent over £1.0.0 (2 lunches; 15/- plus drinks, coffee and tips).

Tas is inclined to be generous with tips.[20]

Calmo Milmo's article in the *Independent*, 'Revealed after 75 years of secrecy: Fifi the glamorous WW2 special agent who tested British spies' resolve', identified Tas as José Tinchant.[21] According to his personnel file, he was a twenty-six-year-old Belgian cigar manufacturer, married with a child. He joined the army and was captured during the German invasion. After eight months imprisonment, he learned that his wife had deserted him, his sister was imprisoned, charged with espionage, so, like Fifi, he had used one of the escape lines to travel through France and Spain to Gibraltar, reaching Britain in July 1942. After interrogation at the Royal Victoria Patriotic School, he was recruited by SOE to train as a saboteur. One of his instructors on his preliminary assessment course at Winterfold (STS 4), Cranleigh, Surrey, described him as 'thoroughly reliable. His reaction to security instructions were good and I think he is sufficiently intelligent to know how to use his security instruction'. Other notes indicated he had a girlfriend in London and was keen on drink.[22] Fifi's report, a copy of which was in his file, one detailing what was found when a search was made of his room and another relating to him being caught and questioned by the Police suggested that his security was not as good as hoped. Woolrych's final report stated,

> This student made so bad a showing on his 96 hour scheme that we thought it was useless proceeding any further with his training and proposed sending him back by the next train. Unfortunately so much time was consumed over telephone messages to London that train had left and no trace of student ... Had to admit spent day and half with Fifi, instead of going on with his scheme, and altogether seems to have done very little indeed towards latter although he spent five full days in Liverpool; spent between £16 and £20 but only took £7. Seen from Fifi's report that he made almost complete disclosure to her about himself, recent past and probable mission to Belgium. Note also that he went out of his way to give names of people in case of adventure in France; this fact alone disqualifies him from any contemplated work in the field. We have, of course, bluffed him about Fifi; he came back here convinced that she was a 'plant' but is now by no means sure. As Fifi told him she had, herself been interrogated by police, he must be aware that we can also get information from her through same source. Noticed from enclosed copies of reports and interrogation that he only visited contact once instead of four times prescribed which is indicative of his diligence ... From all the foregoing it will be seen that Tas is obviously not a person to be trusted, and if the Scheme represents all security he has learned in three weeks there is obviously nothing to be gained by continuing his instruction. In any case, he appears to be totally unsuitable for this type of work.[23]

Students considered unsuitable to be sent into the field after having signed the Official Secrets Act and undergone part or all of their SOE training were usually sent to 'the cooler', as previously discussed. Inverlair Lodge, a requisitioned property and estate in Cullough, Inverness-shire, was one such 'cooler'. Known as the Inter Services Research Bureau's No. 6 Workshop, its occupants made mountaineering equipment for the commandoes, props for the training school and looked after the estate. It is said to have generated the idea for TV series *The Prisoner*. Senior officers were held at the Craigerne (now Belavil) Hotel, Newtonmore, Inverness-shire and there was another at Tyting House, St Martha, near Guildford.[25]

Instead of being sent to 'the cooler', Tinchant was interviewed by Miller with the suggestion that he was sent back to his unit and joined a new platoon of special parachutists who would be sent to Belgium just before the Allied invasion of Normandy.[26]

On 8 December, Miller wrote to Woolrych,

Dear Colonel,
  I thank you for your letter of 5th December.
1. May I heartily agree with you that no cause for complacency is given at Beaulieu to students, as I can testify from my own pleasant recollections. On the contrary, the vital necessity of adhering to security rules, even though the agent may have been in the country for many months without being surveyed in so far as he knows, is stressed over and over again during your course.

2. I trust that Fifi will have given us better results on the scheme which is just ending. You shall have her report sent to you as soon as I get it.

3. Unfortunately I shall be on duty next Sunday, so shall have to postpone my visit until the earliest date after Christmas which suits you,

Yours sincerely[27]

In the meantime, another scheme had been planned which required Fifi's services. On 12 December, Miller contacted her.

Dear Fifi,

If you are sufficiently recovered will you be good enough to take part in a further exercise, this time at Leeds.

Will you proceed to Leeds on Wednesday 16th December, where accommodation will be booked for you at a hotel of which I will advise you later.

The student in this case is Hamish Reed:-

Apparent age 30.

Height 6'0".

Build: slim.

Eyes: grey and baggy.

Hair: fair and thick.

Nose: straight, thick tipped.

Mouth: wide and tight.

Ears: small and fleshy.

Large hands and feet.

Will be in civilian clothes and probably untidily dressed.

He will be in the bar of the Midland Hotel, Leeds at 12.30 hours on Friday, 18th, for at least half an hour.

The scheme on which he is to be engaged is precisely the same as the last occasion.

You can spend the 17th in finding your way about the salubrious town of Leeds.

I should like you back by Monday, 21st, and should be grateful for your report by Tuesday, 22nd, as soon as you can let me have it at 16 Hans Road.

I enclose your December salary, plus the usual £10 advance of your expenses.

Many congratulations on your last scheme, and my best wishes for your next,

Yours sincerely,[28]

Her report on Hamish Reed is not included in her file. Who he was remains unknown. On 18 December, Fifi received further instructions from Miller:

This is in the first place to wish you a happy Christmas, but I am not certain you will have a happy New Year because we want you to go on an exercise at that time.

Will you proceed to Wolverhampton on Tuesday, 29th December, by any train you like, and a room will be booked for you at the Victoria Hotel, which is the only hotel, and a very bad one at that, in that revolting town.

The student in this case will be operating under the name of Tobias Skog –

Apparent age   29
Height   5'10 ½"
Build   Strong, but round shouldered.
Hair   Thick, dark and wavy, brushed straight up from the forehead; no parting.
Head   Large
Nose   Broad and blunt tipped.
Lips   Thick.

He will be in the lounge of the Victoria Hotel at 18.45 on 13th [sic – probably 30th] December, expecting to be picked up by a <u>man</u>.

The lounge of the Victoria Hotel is immediately on your left as you go in. it is very crowded. There is a bar which is very seldom open, and then only for a short time, the second on your left when you go in. one of the most repellent features of this city is that on several days there is no drink available at all unless you order it early.

If you have marked success with this student you may remain in Wolverhampton, but if not we should like you to take part in another exercise at Cardiff, proceeding to Cardiff on 1st January (or on 31st December if you are unable to arrive in time otherwise), where a room will be booked for you at the Angel Hotel, unless I advise you to the contrary.

The student in this case will be operating under the name of Gunner [sic] Tingulstad:-

Apparent age   29
Height   6'2"
Build   Lanky
Walks with a long stride
Face   Hollow.
Complexion   Sallow.
Hair   Thick, wavy, brown, brushed straight back with no parting.
Eyes   Dark and sunken.

He will be in the lounge of the Angel Hotel at 18.45 hours on 1st January, expecting to be contacted by a man.

The exercise in each case will be the same as before.

I will send you your advance of expenses in due course, and I trust you will have success.[29]

Before Miller received Fifi's report on the Wolverhampton exercise, on 2 January he produced a list of the arrangements so that, should he be out of office, others in the Security Section would know the procedure. In it he refers to Prue Willoughby, a twenty-four-year-old secretary who had been transferred to the Security Section from MI5 in August 1942. In a later interview with Juliette Pattinson, then professor of History at Strathclyde University, Willoughby told Pattinson that she worked in counter-espionage and that it was her job to book accommodation for the students on their ninety-six-hour exercises.

'This was really meant to be a sort of dummy experience of what they would find behind the lines. What they might find in their sort of lifestyle.' She also contacted the regional office and informed them of the arrival and personal details of the students on their scheme. Local police were given descriptions of the students, which encouraged them to adopt disguises. On the scheme, if they had the misfortune to be caught, they were to stick to their 'cover story' and try to be released without interference by the SOE. However, they could make a telephone call which could verify them and occasion their discharge. Thus, they were able to put into practice what they had learned at the various training schools while NCOs observed them and alerted them to their distinctive mannerisms that displayed a slippage between their real and purported identities.[30]

Peter Lee, in an interview for the Imperial War Museum, said that 'intelligence services of any country use women as agent provocateurs' and thus it was imperative that male students were tested 'to see whether they were susceptible to women's charms'.[31]

One imagines that, despite the war, SOE staff at Baker Street had time off to celebrate the New Year. Having returned from his few days off Miller had the following report typed up.

DRILL FOR OPERATING FIFI.

1. Upon receipt of pro forma of exercises from Training Section discover what contacts have been laid on by B. Group for Fifi.

2. Telephone Prue Willoughby and ask her to advise the local R.S.L.O. of Fifi's arrival and stay in the town, and ask him to book accommodation for her.

3. Upon receipt of information from Prue as to the hotel at which accommodation has been booked write by registered letter to Fifi in the name of 'Christine' addressed to Christine Chilver, 9 Nevern Road, Earl's Court, S.W.5, giving her instructions as to: -

(a) The town to which she is to proceed, and when she has to arrive.

(b) The name under which the student, for whom the contact has been arranged, will be operating.

(c) The description of the student as given in the pro forma.

(d) That the exercise upon which the student will be engaged is the same as before.

(e) That she has to submit her report to you by registered post at your private address as soon as possible after her return to London.

(f) The date upon which she is to return to London.

Enclose with this letter £10 advance of expenses, which is obtained from D/FIN personally. Either you or the secretary must go to D/FIN by appointment with him, to collect the money.

4. Upon receipt of Fifi's report have two copies made immediately by the secretary, send one to Commandant B. Group in envelope marked 'MOST SECRET – TO BE OPENED BY THE COMMANDANT PERSONALLY', and the other to MT.2 in an envelope marked 'MOST SECRET – TO BE OPENED BY MT.2 ONLY'. File the original in D/CE.G files.

5. Return any balance of expenses, together with Fifi's account to D/FIN in an envelope marked 'MOST SECRET – TO BE OPENED BY D/FIN ONLY'.

6. It is particularly important that the Commandant Group B should have Fifi's report at the earliest possible moment, as he depends upon this for the interrogation of the student at the end of his exercise.

A note underneath read, 'Cover Name = CHRISTINE COLLARD <u>French Citizen</u>. Always refer to her to D/FIN or his staff as "our special Agent".'

Prue Willoughby had worked as a secretary in the War Office after graduating in History from Oxford University and then for MI5 in Nottingham until she was transferred to the Security Section in August 1942. In her personnel file was a note from Roche related to her claim for a pay increase from the £183 per annum.

She has a very complete knowledge of their [MI5's] set up and of our 96 hours scheme procedure. She does a considerable part of the routine on her own and in the absence of D/CE.2 [Park] carries on the liaison work except for those parts which require a commissioned officer. Her greatest assets are common sense and reliability. We feel that when D/CE.2 is away she will either deal with a matter sensibly or refer it. I consider that she deserves an increase.[32]

On his recommendation, her pay was increased to £210 per annum, which must have been a welcome New Year's present. On 5 January, she submitted her report on Tobias Skog.

Skog was contacted in the bar of the Victoria Hotel, Wolverhampton, on Dec. 30th, between 6.45 and 7.00 p.m. When, after the usual introductory explanations, he was questioned about his Wolverhampton job, he stated without hesitation that he had arrived on Tuesday and was staying until Sunday, at the Talbot Hotel; that this was his first exercise; and the purpose of his stay was the formation of an organisation for railway sabotage. He gave detailed explanations of his instructions, as well as a full account of what he had so far undertaken; according to instructions, he had telephoned a Mr. H. F. Speake (?) director of a business firm in Stafford Street. In the course of our conversation Skog was to enquire when he could see Mr. Speake, adding that he 'did not like to waste time', to which Mr. Speake was to reply that 'there was not much opportunity to do so, nowadays'. Apparently, however, Mr. Speke had missed the cue twice, giving some other answer, and so Skog, without mentioning the real object of his call, had decided to give up attempts to contact Mr. Speake – Skog further stated he was expecting to be contacted by a man ('a railway expert') in the Victoria bar; he seemed somewhat disappointed with his failures in contacting people.

After some drinks, we had dinner together (for which I paid). Questioned about his training and general Service matters, Skog seemed very much more reticent. He stated that he had been in training in Scotland, with a group of Norwegians, that he was most probably going to operate in Norway, and that he had specialised in sabotage. He was uncertain as to the approximate date or the nature of his first mission. He was extremely cautious about making any statements concerning the Norwegian Forces and appeared to be avoiding questions about the number of men in the Forces, where they were mainly stationed, what their headquarters were, etc. He did, however, mention that the majority of Norwegian officers frequented Oddenine's Bar regularly, and he also gave the name of a (Norwegian) friend he had been staying with in London during the Christmas holidays.

Skog was not too communicative about personal matters either. He seemed reluctant to give the name of his home-town, but stated it was the 4th largest town in Norway, situated on the coast, not far from Narvik. He said he had before the war been working in a shop for sports articles. His parents and his sister were still at home, but he had not communicated with them since his departure from Norway. He left that country over a year ago and got to England via Sweden, Russia, Persia, India and Africa. He arrived in England in April 1942. He did not seem at all informed about political questions concerning the Norwegian Government in Great Britain.

Skog's rather poor knowledge of English makes it difficult to judge him fairly. If, at the beginning, he was more communicative then could be justified by the vague introduction to our conversation, this may be partly due to his limited knowledge of English (which also causes difficulties for the agent, since it is practically impossible to interrogate anyone with tact and subtlety while using quite elementary and simple expression). Skog himself mentioned that he felt very handicapped by a foreign language.

Later on during our interview he seemed to regain some sangfroid and to think the situation over critically. It was only then that he began to ask questions, some of them rather intelligent and suspicious, e.g. whom he was talking to, whether the names of any of his instructors were known to me, whether I knew by whom his instructions were issued etc. He appeared reassured by some evasive explanations. When questioned about his further plans for the exercises, however, he did not make any definite statements; it would be interesting to know whether he was being evasive and suspicious, or whether he simply had not decided upon any further plans. He politely accepted a general offer of further help, and I asked him to telephone me at my hotel, if he wished, in the course of the following day, but he did not get in touch with me again.

It seems a pity that he should not have shown that somewhat stubborn, monosyllabic discretion from the start. He seems reticent and uncommunicative by nature. Although his slight knowledge of English is a great handicap, I get the impression that he would be hardly more talkative in his own language like the majority of Nordic people, he seems peculiarly inarticulate, and is, therefore, difficult to get to know in a short time.

His main fault also seems a matter of character (or race?); his judgment is hesitant and his reactions are slow. It is probable that some experience would add to his independence and self-assurance and would also give him the ease of a man of the world, which he lacks at present.

In general, however, he gives a fairly favourable impression. Judging by a short acquaintance, I should think that after some experience and an effective lesson in prudence and discretion, he would have chances of doing successful work.[33]

Surprisingly, Tobias Skog was his real name. His personnel file revealed he had a cover name of Peter Larson but it was not used. Born in Møsjen in March 1917, he joined the army after leaving trade school and helped defend Bodø airfield during the German invasion of Norway in May 1940. An accomplished sportsman and cross-country runner, he fled to Sweden and, after working in the Norwegian Legation, travelled through the Soviet Union, Turkey, Palestine, Iran, India, South Africa and Trinidad before reaching Glasgow in November 1941.

Recruited into the Kompani Linge, a specialist Norwegian resistance group, he was given the rank of second lieutenant and trained by SOE. After his assessment at Stodham Park (STS 3), Liss, Hampshire, his conducting officer described him as 'very highly strung and rather apt to fly off the handle. He is likewise very lazy'. His report from Inverie House (STS 24), the paramilitary training school in Knoydart, Inverness-shire, described him as anti-British, unstable and unreliable. Perhaps this was why Beaulieu allocated Fifi as his agent provocateur? There was no report in his file related to his ninety-six-hour scheme, only a note that he had been sent to Beaulieu on 3 December 1942 in place of Sergeant Haukelid.[34]

Despite Fifi's report, the head of the Norwegian Section appointed him second in command of a five-man team, code-named Operation Seagull, to be landed near Bodø to blow up underground tunnels in the iron ore, copper and zinc mines in Sulitjelma.

On 17 February 1943, the Norwegian submarine KNM *Uredd*, carrying Skog, five other Norwegian agents and thirty-four crew, hit a German minefield southwest of Fugløyvær; all were reported drowned.[35]

REPORT ON TINGULSTAD

I met Gunnar Tingulstad in the lounge of the Angel Hotel, Cardiff, on Jan. 1st at 6.45 p.m. As in previous cases, I introduced myself and explained I had been asked to meet him and see whether I could be of any assistance. Tingulstad seemed surprised at this unexpected encounter, but generally became quite communicative.

He told me that his job was to organise a clandestine newspaper in Cardiff. He had arrived on Tuesday and was staying until Sunday morning, at a small boarding house in Newport Road (he would not give the exact address). He had been instructed to contact a Mr. Beeles [?] in Cardiff and he had been quite successful, since he was, I understand, given introductions to some printing establishments and had been able to find suitable premises for the H.Q. of his paper. He had also got the addresses of two Norwegians, Captain Larsson and Captain Gebrielssen, whom he had called on, but without finding them particularly useful for his scheme. He had planned a 'de-centralised' system for the organisation of his paper, which would ensure complete security for the main H.Q. and the printing press; in case one of the distributors was caught, his branch would lead to some 'phoney H.Q.' and the real centre would not be traceable. The distribution seemed one of the most difficult problems, since it meant recruiting a fair number of people. Tingulstad had been round a good deal. He intended finding some reliable place for depositing secret correspondence, possibly in a shop. One of the side-lines he was interested in was a general check-up on the population of Cardiff; Tingulstad intended getting some statistics or other official information about the number of inhabitants, and grouping according to classes, professions, etc. Tingulstad also gave me his cover story; he was pretending to be spending his leave with friends in Cardiff.

After some drinks in the lounge I suggested dinner, which seemed to embarrass Tingulstad slightly; he finally explained he had not any money left. I did not ask any questions right away, but later learnt that he has received £7 in advance of expenses, but had spent £3 of it before leaving London, so that he had had to borrow some money from a cousin of his in Cardiff. His cousin is married to a Dr Sheppard, an Englishman, and had been in England 20 years. Tingulstad had visited them in Cardiff before and saw them several times in the course of his exercise. He spent New Year's Eve with them and another Norwegian; he said he had not told them the real purpose of his visit to Cardiff and repeatedly asked me not to mention any of these peccadillos in London, since he was quite aware of their being against the rules.

We had quite an intelligent conversation over dinner. Tingulstad speaks very good English and is an interesting talker. He has a good background (natural intelligence; education; manners; etc.) and is extremely keen on his work. He seems to have acquired a good deal of knowledge by observation, intelligent reading, study of various subjects with a bearing on his work (politics, psychology, criminology, etc.) and above all, by self-criticism. He is capable of very sound logical reflection and has a sober and discerning mind. He seems to have made some interesting contacts since he arrived in England among Norwegian as well as English people; he knows Captain Dent (Sunday Chronicle) and seems to have discussed many Services matters with different Norwegian officers and fellow-students. In fact, I got the impression that there is perhaps a bit too much shop-talking and comparing of notes going on among the Norwegian students, since Tingulstad quoted several examples of 'what had happened to other chaps on exercise'.

Questioned about himself and biographical particulars, Tingulstad stated that he came from Oslo and that he had been in Insurance before the war. He said he was communicating with his parents in Oslo through a friend in Sweden. He left Norway nearly two years ago and came to England via Sweden, Finland, Russia, Persia, India, S. Africa and America, travelling with a group of other Norwegians. He had been working with some Insurance firm in London for about nine months before he took up his present job. When asked how he got into the Services, he said he had first been contacted by a Norwegian and, after several interviews with Norwegian and British officers, had been sent on a training course in Scotland, with other Norwegian students. He was cautious about giving any details about his training or mentioning any names of persons or places, but he spoke of his instructors with greatest respect and admiration.

We further discussed some general topics, Tingulstad giving me an interesting picture of the Norwegian Government and Forces, telling me about political matters, about Norwegian co-operation in the Service, about the Norwegian Merchant Navy, the Officers' Training School, the Army Film and Press Unit, etc. Tingulstad seemed rather well informed in Norwegian and other Allied

Government matters. He has original ideas and independent opinions and is not afraid to criticise.

We arranged to lunch together on the following day, for which occasion Tingulstad was going to borrow some more money from his cousin. I was looking at a shop window, about 12.15 p.m. when Tingulstad suddenly turned up; we wandered down to the Hotel where he left me saying he did not think we should be seen going in together. He came into the Park lounge about 15 min. later, saying that it had been stupid of him to recognise me previously in the street, since when we met he was just coming from the Police Station. Apparently there had been a check-up on foreigners at his hotel that morning, and he had been taken to the Police Station because his leave papers were made out by the British, and not the Norwegian authorities. His cover story, however, seemed to have worked, as well as his slightly vague explanation about his papers, and so he was released almost immediately.

After lunch we had some general conversation, and I got the impression that Tingulstad was worried about something or had something on his mind. I was, however, very surprised when he suddenly said he was very worried about the mistake he had made last night. He then proceeded to analyse the situation with astonishingly perspicacious and fair reasoning; he had perfectly understood 'what it was all about' and was positively depressed about his faux pas. I let him talk, to be able to decide what attitude to take. He said that from the start he had had some intuition that there was something wrong with a woman turning up when he was expecting to be contacted by a man; after my introduction, however, he had decided there was no reason to back out, since, even if he was committing an error, and I was very favourably impressed by the amount of imagination, as well as clear reasoning, he had put into it. He had decided that all he knew of me was my name; that my credentials were absolutely insufficient to justify his confidence, that he had all reasons to believe I had not known more than his name and his face when we started talking, and he even decided that this method of approach was very fair, since an enemy agent would most likely be equipped with much more information. Tingulstad had compared our meeting to several real cases he had known in Norway and found an alarming similarity, which finally convinced him that my story was very obvious bluff and that the real purpose of our meeting must be a security test, as well as a general check-up on his exercise. He added that he had often wondered how we knew whether students' reports were correct or not, and that he thought this an excellent system. He said he could 'kick himself' for not having seen through the whole scheme immediately and wondered whether slow thinking was perhaps a general fault with most Norwegian agents.

I was very impressed by his eagerness to see his own mistakes and his courage in admitting them. The manner in which he conducted his critical analysis of the case was a really good effort (particularly as it was based on independent thought, imagination, and deduction.) He said I had given him no particular reason for suspicion – which may have been flattery – but if one thought it over properly it was all the more obvious.

After he had explained the above, I decided that with the shock of this sudden discovery of his mistake still fresh in his mind, this was a favourable moment for a straightforward technical discussion of the case. I may not have been right in admitting the truth about our meeting and I am aware of the fact that an agent provocatrice should keep to teaching people 'indirect and anonymous' lessons. In this case, however, I felt that an immediate, serious and honest discussion could do more good than harm and that, in fact, this was a rare opportunity for outlining impressively the dangers of insufficient security. Tingulstad will get the opportunity of talking over his work with more competent critics and advisors than myself, but I am convinced that he is not likely to make the same kind of mistake again. I expect his report to be honest and, as regards the technical side of his exercise, rather satisfactory.

I might add that Tingulstad has an appreciable sense of cricket; he said he was most grateful for an opportunity of 'talking over the score after he had lost (?) the match', – and actually thanked me![36]

Unusually, Gunnar Tingulstad and Tobias Skog were not their cover names. This seems in itself to have been a breach of security. They were their real names. In Tingulstad's personnel file his age was given as twenty-six, not twenty-nine. Escaping to England in July 1942, he worked in the Norwegian Propaganda Department. He was selected to be infiltrated back as an agent, and after his paramilitary training he was sent to Beaulieu in December. Described as being too fond of drink and women, he got into trouble on a number of occasions before his ninety-six-hour scheme, including being arrested in Knightsbridge after a night of drinking. Sergeant Monsen, his security officer, reported to Peter Lee that Tingulstad was 'a good man, he is well educated and intelligent and I consider him to have been very unfortunate to be arrested on such a charge ... if he were put on his honour to cut down his drinking to a minimum he could stick to his word'.[37]

There was nothing in his file relating to the incident with Fifi in Cardiff but the head of the Norwegian Section must have decided that his lack of security would have been a serious issue. Instead he was seconded to the Norwegian Liaison Service and was killed on active service in Italy on 14 November 1944.[38]

The day after Fifi submitted her report on the two Norwegians, Miller followed protocol and sent a copy to Major Hilton, one of the Training Section officers, known by the symbol M/T.A1.

I enclose Fifi's reports on the last two students, from which you will see that she has again had successes.

I have ascertained from her that in each case her method of approach was as follows:-

Having identified the student, she went up to him and said 'Are you by any chance Mr. X', giving the name under which he was operating, and upon his affirmative reply she then said 'Oh! I think I can be of assistance to you in your work; perhaps you are looking for somebody.' She assures me that this was the method she used in both cases, and I gather that she did not herself suggest that she was an instructress or connected with the Organisation until the student obviously had assumed that she was.

She is a little exercised as to whether or not, in the case of the Cardiff student, she ought, when he had discovered his error, to have discussed the matter with him, but she tells me that he was obviously very conscientious and extremely upset at his mistake and only too anxious to learn. In these peculiar circumstances, I rather feel that she did more good than harm.

I am a little exercised as to our being able to use her for any great length of time, as no doubt students returning from their exercises will quickly spread among the other students the alarming experiences they have had at Fifi's hands. She herself raised this point with me, and has made some very useful comments on the students' discussions among each other in her report on the Cardiff exercise.

If there is anything else that you would like to know on this matter please give me a ring.[39]

On the same day, Fifi was sent her monthly salary and her £19 expenses for the previous exercise. One imagines she had managed to find ways to celebrate the New Year while she was in Wolverhampton and Cardiff.

A few days later, her services were required for another scheme, this time in the north of England, where the temperature must have been much colder.

Will you please proceed to Newcastle on Sunday, 10th January? Convenient train is the 10.50 from King's Cross, arriving in theory at 17.20. Accommodation has been booked for you at the Turk's Head, which is in Grays Street, the main street, in your name of Collard. The room has actually been booked by a Miss Warren, who, I presume, is a member of the R.S.L.O.'s staff. In case you need it the R.S.L.O.'s number is NEWCASTLE 26302, but you will, of course, only make use of it in an emergency.

The student in this case is operating under the name of John Carter, and his description is as follows:-
Apparent age: 29
Height: 5'10".
Face: Long and oval.
Hair: Black, unparted.
Eyebrows: Bushy, black and long lashes.
Other characteristics: Blue shaven cheeks, uneven front teeth, large feet.

He will be in the large bar on the right of the main door of the Turk's Head between the hours of 12.30 and 13.30 on 11.1.43.

He will be carrying a 'Penguin' novel. He will expect to contact someone, who is in fact non-existent.

The exercise upon which he will be engaged is the same as before.

Will you please let me have your report at my address in the usual manner as soon as you conveniently can after your return, together with the usual amount and a receipt for this month's salary?

Wishing you the best of luck,
Yours sincerely,[40]

There was inevitably an amusing story about an overseas student explaining why he was unable to rendezvous with his contact while on his scheme because no one was holding a penguin.

Things did not go according to plan in Newcastle. Although she made contact with Carter, his response was not as she expected. Her report did not admit that her feminine charms had failed her on this occasion but one expects that she had some disappointment at not having the opportunity to share drinks and meals with the agent. When she arrived back in London on 12 January, she sent a handwritten note to Cyril.

I am sorry to have to send you the enclosed pathetic little page instead of a decent report. I am dying to know what happened to Carter [?], or in what way I made a mistake myself. I hate bringing back disappointment.

As far as the receipt of my salary, please let me know whether the enclosed will do; if not I shall write out a proper one with a stamp and all that,

Yours sincerely,

Christine.

REPORT ON NEWCASTLE EXERCISE.

I contacted John Carter in the Turk's Head bar on Jan. 11th, 1943, about 12.45 p.m. He was, unfortunately, not in the large general bar (on the left of the entrance) but had gone into the tap room which is, of course, for men only.

I went up to him and asked him whether he was Mr. Carter, which seemed to startle him. From various symptoms, such as stammering, fidgeting, etc. I gathered that he was feeling somewhat nervous. I briefly explained that I had been asked to meet him and that I should like to speak to him. Meanwhile my presence in the men's bar appeared to create a mild sensation: I had not even had time to introduce myself to Carter, when I was requested to leave the bar. I therefore suggested to Carter that we should go into the other bar, to which he somewhat bluntly replied he thought he would rather stay. (He was obviously very anxious to contact his non-existent friend.) I insisted that I had to talk to him and said I would wait for him in the other bar, where I took a table with a good view of the tap-room door. After waiting about 15 mins, I looked into the tap room again (defying general comments and hilarity) but Carter still seemed to have no intention of joining me. I therefore sent him a message through the waitress, asking him again to come to my table. As he completely ignored this message, I decoded that he was determined to wait for his contact until 13.30, according to instructions, and would then come through the other bar (where I was) to see what I had to say. It was getting on to 13.30 when I thought of going up to him once more in order to explain that the man Carter was waiting for had not been able to come and had asked me to meet Carter instead; I found, however, that I would not be able to enter the tap room again without causing something like a scandal and therefore had to give up the attempt.

Although I watched the door as closely as possible in the crowd, I did not see Carter leave. At 14.10 I was informed by the giggling waitress that 'the gentleman had left'. He must have sneaked out via the cloakroom.

The negative results of this exercise are most regrettable. It would, however, be very interesting to find out what reasons Carter had for avoiding me so deliberately. Judging by his extremely uneasy and nervous manner, one might think it was simply shyness and lack of savoir faire. Our conversation was too short and his manner of speech too mumbling for me to decide whether he is English or whether his knowledge of the English language is imperfect: it may be that he did not understand my explanations at all. A third potential reason is, of course, suspicion; in that case, however, I consider it a serious mistake to have appeared so obviously alarmed or deliberately impolite. The student who takes a risk and makes a blunder is more promising than the man who keeps clear of everything on principle: if this incident had happened in the field, Carter might have lost a chance of getting some information. Fourthly, there is perhaps a slight possibility of Carter having been warned by other students that this kind of security test was likely to occur; it might be interesting to find out what contacts Carter has had with other, more experienced students. In any case, the impression one would get of Carter's behaviour is that he lacks either boldness, common sense or manners.

The true identity of 'John Carter' is unknown but one imagines that he got good marks for his security. On Jonathan Cole's blog about Fifi, he stated, 'student gossip quickly spread, warning them about "the alarming experience they have had at Fifi's hands", or bragging that they "made a conquest" of her. Fifi started to attend "post-mortems" for the schemes, partly to get feedback on her contribution, but no doubt also to make a lasting impression. Students who bolstered their boasts by claiming that Fifi had a mole on her inner thigh got a nasty shock when she suddenly appeared, challenging them to find it again!'[41]

In her interview with Juliette Pattinson after the war, Prue Willoughby admitted that,

> I was in charge of a very nice girl who was a prostitute. We told this girl, Christine, to go to the pub and try to break this chap down and try to get him into bed. After the week was up, he came back to Baker Street and there was a committee of people to interview him about what had happened during this week and he found to his horror that there was this girl amongst the people. Christine could also detect whether they talked in their sleep and note in which language.[42]

Why would Willoughby call someone she worked with a prostitute? Could it have been used in the formal sense to describe a woman who provided sexual favours in return for money, or could it have been used in an informal sense to describe a woman who had a great number of different men friends who often disappeared for several days and wrote reports about meeting them in hotels and restaurants? Might Willoughby's Christine have really been Fifi? There was no mention in her file of her being told to go to a pub; a bar in a hotel, yes, but to break a man down? She was sent to test the security of male agents but there was no mention of breaking them down and certainly no mention of trying to get men into bed. While Fifi might have felt that she would get more response from the men if the rendezvous progressed towards the bedroom, she never mentioned a bedroom in any of the reports in her file. The only unusual activity that she admitted ever having done with a man was hemming silk scarves. While this might this have been a euphemism, in those days it would have been very indiscreet to mention bedroom activities in official documents. Even if part of her brief really was to try to get men into bed and find out what language they spoke when they woke up, it would hardly have been a subject that would be written down. While having relationships with men was not mentioned in any documents in her personnel file or in the history of the Security Section, it does not mean that it did not happen. While it could have been referred to in the numerous redacted pages in her file, it is impossible to confirm or deny it.

Like using honeytraps, the use of prostitutes to obtain information has been little covered in the history of the Second World War. It was not the sort of topic that detailed accounts have been written about, partly to protect the indentities of the women and/or men involved, but also to ensure that the general public were kept unaware of the sorts of measures the government were prepared to take to help them win the war. One imagines there would have been a considerable political storm generated by the religious right and left. While the information obtained in this way might well have been particularly useful for the military, whether there was a special department with responsibility for obtaining, processing and passing on such intelligence has not come to light.

In Russel Miller's *Behind Enemy Lines,* a series of interviews with people involved with the SOE, he included comments made by Claudia Pulver, an Austrian dressmaker who was employed in making, altering and fitting clothes for agents who were about to be infiltrated into enemy-occupied Europe. She stated that as well as agents,

> We also had quite a lot of prostitutes from the brothels of Paris coming in. We made appropriate underwear, very provocative, whatever they needed. They were very important to whoever was in control of them because their clients were a lot of German officers and they got quite a lot of information out of them. They were the ones that came backwards and forwards more often than others, because I think possibly they had to bring their information back personally. We had one who came backwards and forwards ten or twelve times and survived, only to die of a botched abortion after the war, which was quite sad. [...] Then there was a girl who had to have most unusual and very elegant clothes, a riding outfit and an evening dress I remember, because she was being sent into a very elegant position, totally different to the girl who was pushing a bike around with a wireless in the saddlebag.[43]

Willoughby's comment about a prostitute appears to confirm Foot's assertion that a devastating blonde, codenamed Fifi, made it her business to find out whether they talked in their sleep, and if so in what language. Bob Maloubier, one of the French agents, admitted to Juliette Pattinson that some students outwitted the SOE's ploy to ensnare them.

Bob Maloubier recollected his 'blind date' with an attractive woman whom he immediately realized was a plant. When they retired to his bedroom, he confronted her: 'We talked the matter over in my room. Anyway, she said, 'Now what are we going to do?' 'I'm going to kill you' (imitates gun and laughs). I said, 'You're dead.' We talked the matter over. I said, 'OK. You can tell the people that employ you that you came up to my room to extort information out of me and I killed you!'[44]

As Maloubier was flown into France twice, first on 23 August 1943 and second on 7 June 1944, his training at Beaulieu and ninety-six-hour scheme would have been in early summer 1943, the same time as Fifi was working. While it is quite possible that his 'blind date' was with Fifi, it may have been with one of the other agent provocateurs. Maloubier's evidence suggests that the people who employed this attractive woman could only have been the Security Section.

However, Patricia Grant, one of Christine's old friends, told me that she was 'quite shocked at the media coverage of Christine's SOE work. She was portrayed as a glamorous Femme Fatale who exploited her femininity. I can assure you that Christine was more Enid Blyton than Mata Hari! She was however a highly intelligent and perceptive woman, with a theatrical side to her nature which left her totally fearless in her pursuit of what she felt was right. I shall certainly never meet her like again'.[45]

Whatever the truth of the story, Fifi and the other agent provocateurs must have been particularly brave to expose themselves to the possibility of assault by men suspicious of them being prostitutes. Unlike the agents, who all underwent paramilitary training, there was no evidence Christine was taught any self-defence to protect herself from any unwelcome advances.

On 13 January 1943, Miller duly forwarded a copy of Christine's report on the Newcastle scheme to Woolrych.

Dear Colonel,

I enclose Fifi's latest report, from which you will see that the poor girl has had a failure, largely owing to the fact that the student went into the taproom instead of into the bar, to which he was instructed to go. You will recollect that this happened once before.

However, the student in this case seems to have been terrified of her, which I suppose is a satisfactory result.

I have just had the pleasure of a conversation with Captain Forty over the telephone. He informs me that there is a vacancy at your school for the training of girls on a ten-day course, starting on 1st February. We should be exceedingly grateful in this Section if Fifi and my assistant, Mrs. Joyce Skinner (DC/E.G.3), could attend this, as we are very anxious to have them both trained. There would, of course, be no objection to Mrs. Skinner being associated with Fifi, as Mrs. Skinner now operates the latter.

I was informed, however, that there had been a proposal that a Miss Macdonald, who I understand, is attached to one of the Sections, should attend the course at the same time, but Commander Senter has instructed me that there are grave security objections, with which you are very familiar, to Fifi associating with any Section Officer. I have communication with Major Hilton on this subject, and I understand that Commander Senter will also have a word with you.

I trust we shall have the pleasure of meeting you in London again in the near future.

Yours very sincerely,[46]

Who Miss Macdonald was and what Senter's security objections were remains unknown. As there was no woman with that surname in the SOE personnel files, it is possible that she was a Section Officer who had been recommended by the SIS. It is worth noting that Miller recommended his secretary as she had already gone through security vetting before being employed by the SOE and knew enough about Fifi's work from listening to conversations in the Baker Street office, and typing up officers and Fifi's reports.

Joan Prizer, born on 31 August 1913, was a British-American and worked in Postal and Telephone Censorship. She married Wing Commander Stanley Skinner, an RAF pilot who was killed in the raid on Dieppe in August 1942. In November 1942, she was transferred to work in the Security Section. Having signed the Official Secrets Act, she was given the symbol D/CE.3 and became Fifi's case officer.[47]

In the middle of January, Fifi received a letter from Miller thanking her for her Newcastle report and expressing regret that the exercise went wrong. He told her that he would speak to Carter's instructors.

> I do not think you need be in the least concerned at your failure to contact this man, as it at least shows that he is not liable to make contacts outside his operational orders. Still, of course, it would have been more satisfactory of he had been in the proper place, I will try to see that this does not occur again.
>
> With many thanks for your continued valuable work,
>
> Yours sincerely,[48]

A copy of Fifi's report was also sent to Forty. On 20 January, Park sent Miller the pro forma for her next scheme in Nottingham between 25 and 29 January.

> I have asked the R.S.L.O. to book a room for "Fifi" and he will let me know where this will be by telephone as soon as possible, when I will immediately inform you. This room has only been asked for for the night of 25th January, owing to the necessity of 'Fifi' taking a room at the same hotel as the two students for the purpose of provocation. In order to do this, I confirm the arrangement made over the telephone this afternoon, when it was agreed that 'Fifi' should telephone the Regional Officer after arrival, and find out at what hotel the students are staying. The R.S.L.O.'s telephone number is Nottingham 45664, Extn. 89 or 91 and she should ask for Major Finney or Captain Ingram.
>
> Would you please return the forms to me in due course? H. L. P.[49]

The next day, 21 January, Fifi was sent her expenses, advised to catch the ten o'clock train from St Pancras to Nottingham and provided with the contact names and phone number of the Regional Security Liaison officers to ascertain her accommodation. This was the first recorded provocation against women agents. It is also worth noting that, unlike the descriptions she was given of the male agents, details of their clothing was given extra attention. Whether Fifi commented about this to Miller is unknown but he did not subsequently include details on the men's clothing in their descriptions.

The students in this case are two women, under the names of Thompson Beatrice, and Brown Irene. Their descriptions are as follows:-

Thompson Beatrice. Age 31. 5'4". Dark dry hair. Dark eyebrows, brown eyes, sallow complexion, enlarged pores. Inclined to be pimply, and scars of past pimples etc. on forehead in particular. Fullish oval face, sinuous nose, good teeth. Wearing pleated blue skirt (serge), blue woollen jumper, with red band. Small black, felt hat (skull cap effect). Brown sports shoes. Yellowish camel-hair coat.

Brown Irene. Age 31. 5'2". Small build. Straight short cut hair, with auburn tinge. Outdoor complexion. Lined forehead, oval face, thickish lower lip, giving rather a pouting expression. Much movement of face and head. Wearing green and brown striped skirt. Brown pullover. Brown felt hat. Brown shoes. tan coloured overcoat.

The exercise is not as usual. It is suggested that you strike up an acquaintance with the two girls. If possible, before acquaintance is made, shadow them, and discover as much as possible about their activities in Nottingham. It is not thought advisable to approach them through the usual subterfuge. If they try to use you as an innocent cut-out (a mutually trusted intermediary) or agent, allow them to do so, as this would be a good means of penetrating their organisation.

Your return train to London leaves Nottingham 15.27 hours, arriving St. Pancras 18.40 hours, on 29th January.

Will you please let me have your report by registered post, at my address, Mrs. J. Skinner, 36, Crompton Court, S.E.3., as soon as you conveniently can, together with the usual expenses account.

Wishing you the best of luck.

Yours sincerely,[50]

Fifi's report on these two girls was not included in her file. The identity of Irene Bown has yet to come to light but Beatrice Thompson was the cover name of Beatrice 'Trix' Terwindt, a Dutch agent who had been a KLM air hostess before the war. She reached England through Switzerland, France, Spain and Portugal, arriving on 26 August 1942. Recruited by MI9 to work as liaison officer back in Holland with the Pat O'Leary escape line, she received SOE training including the course at Beaulieu.

She must have had good security on her ninety-six-hour scheme as her finishing report, which may well have been based on Fifi's comments, read,

She is very intelligent, capable, resourceful, practical and most discreet. She is hard-working, serious-minded and once she has grasped a point is quick to realise its application. She has had much experience of the world and has mixed freely with all types and classes of people. It would be very difficult indeed to deceive or impose on her.

She has a very pleasant personality, quiet but forceful. At first sight both her appearance and manner are misleading; she seems shy, negative and almost 'mousey' – actually she is quite the reverse. The deceptiveness of her appearance may be most helpful as she might easily go unnoticed. She should prove very clever at persuading others, particularly men, to help her on account of her apparent feminine weakness; she will easily win their confidence and trust.

Her main difficulty is her innate lack of self-confidence, which she always overcomes but not without effort; this will subject her to constant nervous strain which may prove exhausting.

As a leader she would be handicapped initially by her sex and manner, but once she has overcome these difficulties she should be a great success.[51]

'Trix' was parachuted into Holland on 13 February 1943, straight into German hands. As mentioned earlier, the Abwehr had captured and 'turned' a Dutch wireless operator so knew the exact place and time of many agents' arrivals. Taken to a secluded villa in the nearby countryside, she was interrogated for three days and nights. She claimed afterwards that they knew everything about the agents' training courses, where the grandfather clocks were and what tiles there were on the floor. Trix reported that she was surprised at how much more her captors knew about the SOE than she did and was perturbed that the Germans couldn't understand why the British had sent a lone girl who evidently was very poorly briefed about her organisation. Apparently, they didn't realise she was from another covert operations department. After imprisonment in Holland, she was transferred to Ravensbrück, the infamous women's prison, and then to Mauthausen-Gosen concentration camp from where she was liberated by the Americans in May 1945.[52]

Also on 21 January, Miller sent Fifi some interesting news. His plans to give her greater insight into the agents' training had been successful

Dear Fifi,

You will recollect that the last time I had the pleasure of seeing you we discussed the question of you receiving training. I am glad to say that we have been able to fix this up, and you will be going down to one of our Training Schools with Joyce, on the 1st February, for a ten-day course, on which you will get instructions upon the subjects which will be most helpful to your work for us.

At the School in question, for reasons of security, students have to be kept within the grounds of the particular house in which they receive instructions, so I should advise you to take a lot of books, and also a considerable amount of paper, as you will have to take a large number of notes. You will require some warm clothing, and a pair of stout shoes. You will be extremely comfortable, and very well fed, and I can assure you that you will find the instruction very interesting.

Yours sincerely,[53]

Before she went to Beaulieu, because of the top-secret nature of the work she would be doing there, on 31 January, she signed the Official Secrets Act. One imagines that she and Skinner underwent exactly the same training as the students so they would have had far greater insight into their training programme and the conditions they lived in. It also gave them the opportunity to discuss the 96-hour schemes.

While staying in Hartford House, (STS 32A), one of the requisitioned properties on the Beaulieu estate, Captain Forty wrote to Miller informing him that

> As I told you on the 'phone the other day, I have discussed the question of schemes fairly thoroughly with Miss Collard, and we decided that there were a few points which might be changed in her part of the scheme.
>
> First of all, she pointed out, quite rightly, that as an agent provocatrice she should be given considerably more information on the type of man she is to contact. As it is, she may spend several hours summing the student up, finding out his nationality and deciding what method of approach to adopt, which in a short scheme is an unnecessary waste of time. I have therefore agreed that we shall add a potted biography of the student, together with a short character sketch, to the description already given on the pro forma [N.B. there was no suggestion the Training Section would include a description of the men's clothes]. The whole of this should, of course, be communicated to Miss Collard. I think there is a good case for telling her from the start the nationality of the student, unless of course, you have security reasons for not doing so. (Whatever you do, she will find out anyhow.)
>
> The second point we discussed was the method of approach which she should adopt on these schemes. It became quite clear that there were really three types of test to which the student could be submitted.
>
> a. A test of general discretion, in which we are concerned about his reactions to a casual acquaintance who appears to have no knowledge whatsoever about him.
> b. A test of his resistance to provocation. In this, he is confronted with someone who shows some knowledge of what he is doing and approaches him with some apparent authority.
> c. Again a test of resistance to provocation, but this time made considerably harder for the student by the introduction of names of instructors, etc. This third form of test might well be considered unfair by certain of the Country Sections, but I think you will agree that it corresponds very closely to a case such as the one where an agent in the field is arrested before a contact and an agent provocateur is sent, fully primed with all the information extracted from him, to take his place.
>
> I consider that for the time being we should limit ourselves to tests of type a. and b., keeping type c. for the really first-class students, on whom we would only use it after previous consultation with the Country Section. The main point of interest about the two tests we are likely to use is that type a. will take far longer to carry out successfully than type b. Miss Collard has got to get herself 'picked

up' by the man, and this will depend very much on his emotional reaction to her. With some people it might take a day; with others, a matter of weeks.

The proposal I would put forward is, therefore, that except in cases where we choose to give Miss Collard a definite directive, she should use her own discretion as to which method of approach to use, always remembering that there is no reason why she should not change over from method a. to method b. after it has been shown that the student is not likely to be indiscreet with a casual stranger.

I have left it that Miss Collard will act with accordance with these suggestions unless she is instructed to the contrary by you.

In the course of conversation, another point arose which has a certain bearing on the scheme. It appears that Miss Collard has been working with papers showing that she is an alien. It would seem that she would be in a far less difficult position, particularly in restricted areas – harbour areas etc. – where she may have to work. If she could have the normal N.R.I.C. [National Registration Identity Card] of a person of British nationality. As long as there is no security objection to this, perhaps you would take it up. I also understand, though this has no bearing whatsoever on the schemes, that her own papers have been removed from her and she has not yet received them back. She was rather worried about this but thought that perhaps she should not ask about it. Probably there is some excellent explanation, but I thought I ought to let you know.

I think it would be most useful if, after the next few schemes, either I or another instructor from here could meet Miss Collard and see how these suggestions have worked out in practice. She is extremely keen, and her experience on these schemes can be put to very good use if we can have the opportunity of discussing them with her. This has been amply proved by her stay down here.

I hope to be in London next week, and I will look in then to talk things over with you. Incidentally, we are sending in an ordinary official report on both Miss Collard and Mrs. Skinner, which you will see within a day or two.

Yours ever, G. Forty.[54]

Forty's suggestion about Fifi's French identity prompted Roche to write to Major J. D. O'Reilly querying what the position was regarding her exemption restrictions and asking whether she was free to go anywhere in the British Isles. If she was not, he wanted to know what further arrangements would have to be made. O'Reilly's reply read,

CHRISTINE COLLARD,

The above, not being deemed an ally, has to conform with all the regulations laid down under the Aliens Order.

No application was made to me to obtain special exemptions for her and I was specifically asked merely to obtain documents. She is not free to go anywhere in this country without authority.

To obtain exception her Aliens Registration Card should be collected and sent to Major Younger of M.I.5 with a request that she be granted 'Category 2 Exemption'; this covers the whole field.[55]

The following day, Miller replied to Forty telling him how extremely obliged he was for detailing the issues and pointing out that he was in complete agreement with all his suggestions. To keep Roche in the picture, a copy was sent to him.

Dear Forty,

...While I think that the real test is that described by you under (c), I feel that if the country sections get to know in any particular case that this had been used we might find ourselves overwhelmed by their reaction; we had enough trouble, as you know, over test (b), which with the assistance of the Colonel we managed to insist upon as being the minimum of information which the enemy agent in the field would be reasonably expected to have.

Nevertheless, I consider that in very special cases such as that of an agent of the first importance, e.g. a large district organiser or propaganda chief, test (c) ought to be applied.

I therefore agree that except in cases where you give definitive directives, Miss Collard should be left to choose between method (a) or (b) but that she should not use (c) unless special directive is given so to by you.

I fully agree that in each case Miss Collard should be advised of the nationality of the student and should have a potted biography together with a short character sketch. I see no security objections for herself, and I have been rather concerned in the past by the fact that we have been concealing from so intelligent a woman matter which her curiosity would probably compel her to find out for herself.

With regard to her papers, I have long felt that her cover as an alien is unsatisfactory, but I am taking this up with Commander Senter as there may be some impelling over [1943 typo for 'other'] reason for which we are unable to change it.

A meeting is, in my view, most desirable between yourself or another of your instructors and Miss Collard, after her next few exercises, and [I] should be pleased to arrange this at your convenience.

Mrs. Skinner is very anxious after her training with you, which she very much enjoyed, to try her hand at this work in provincial towns. If you agree, I should be very grateful if, when a suitable subject for her is sent on an exercise, you would advise me so that I can give her a test. As you yourself have had the advantage of seeing Mrs. Skinner, you will be able to choose the student.

I shall be going on leave for a much overdue seven days next week, but shall be back Tuesday week.

Yours very sincerely,[56]

On the same day, Miller forwarded Forty's concern about Fifi's identity card not allowing her access to restricted areas to Roche, and, referring to Forty's suggestions, had Skinner type up a note commenting that, 'You will remember we had trouble over this in Liverpool, and shall no doubt have it again in other restricted areas. Do you not think that this poor creature could be allowed at least to operate under her own nationality?'[57]

What was the trouble in Liverpool? Her report from Beaulieu shed some light on it.

> Very intelligent, quick and well-informed. She has very considerable imagination and made a number of most useful suggestions.
>
> She is very enthusiastic about the work on which she is being employed, for which she has considerable aptitude. She is not, however, quite so good at other types of subversive work such as surveillance.

She appeared to have had some difficulties as Major Wedgwood, acting for the commandant at Beaulieu, reported that Captain Towns had written to him on 4 May telling him that Fifi had been picked up for the second time in Liverpool when she was on an exercise. Towns had spoken with Chief Superintendent Tomas of the Liverpool City Police Special Branch about it and it had been arranged that she should not be disturbed and suggested that 'on future occasions FIFI should tell any Police Officer who approaches her that Superintendent Thomas knows all about her. This would prevent trouble in the future'.[58]

Reading between the lines, Fifi may well have been stopped and questioned by the police in a restricted area. If she had wandered into the docklands, either on her own, with one of the students or with someone else, it is possible the police thought she could have been a prostitute or maybe she had been acting suspiciously. Roche's reply, two days later, did not seem overly concerned about the Liverpool incident but was quite positive about Forty's ideas.

> I was not, in fact, told about the complication that had risen in Liverpool or that she had given my name until D/CE.G.3 [Skinner] mentioned that matter to me last week and I made enquiries. I agree with what Forty says about her mode of approach.
>
> As regards her papers, the original reasons for her having foreign cover were:-
>
> (a) She does not look English;
>
> (b) She will be heard speaking French or German
>
> (c) People are more likely to be curious as to why a girl of that age is not apparently engaged on National Service if she travels on English papers.
>
> I think these reasons still operate, but I am arranging to have a talk with her and will cover this point.
>
> Progress was made on in other respects though. D/CE.4 [O'Reilly] reported to D.CE on 16th February that it was now deemed practicable to eradicate the entry in the A.R.C. belonging to Miss COLLARD. Chief Inspector Robinson suggested the issue of a new one and I enclose A.R.C. 1093520 which is endorsed 'issued in lieu of A.R.C. 1069020 reported lost'. The entries in the new card link up with the other documents
>
> A Category 2 exemption endorsement has been obtained from M.I.5.

Miss COLLARD should be asked to sign the new A.R.C, and told that she is now free as air to travel etc.

I return herewith Miss Collard's Ration Book, Identity Card and I.B. 23.[59]

When Miller came back from leave, he was updated with the recent developments regarding Fifi's course and Forty's correspondence with Roche. On 24 February, he wrote to Roche,

...through sheer luck it appears that I have avoided this rocket which has found its home in Major Forty. I would much like the opportunity of discussing this matter with you, at a time convenient to yourself, both as regards the particular questions raised by M/T. [Woolrych] and as regards the wider question of how to deal with this somewhat forceful young man.

As to the first point, I must say that I still hold the view that some, though it may be limited, biographical particulars should be given to the A.P. in each case, because it is almost certain that in the field the enemy would have some knowledge of the personality and history of the victim.[60]

A week later, Park sent instructions for Fifi's next exercise. However, the names and description were redacted.

I set out below the details of a standard 96-hour scheme taking place in Birmingham and Wolverhampton between 14th and 19th March 1943, for which provocation is required.

The name and descriptions of the two students for whom provocation is required are as follows:

[Details redacted.]

I have notified the R.S.L.O., Birmingham that Fifi will be operating on this scheme, and perhaps you would let me know as soon as possible where you would like me to ask him to book rooms for 'Fifi' at the two towns, and on which dates.[61]

Notes in Fifi's file suggested they were the Criterion Hotel, Wolverhampton on 15 and 16 March and the Midland Hotel, New Street, Birmingham from 17 to 19 March. There were also instructions that she should telephone Bayswater on 16 March to find out where the agents were staying in case she wanted to change her hotel. Her report on the Wolverhampton exercise included a number of redactions.

[Redacted[was supposed to be in the bar of the Victoria Hotel, Wolverhampton from 6.30 p.m. to 7.45 p.m on Monday March 15th.

As I had been advised not to use the word 'scheme' in any conversation with [redacted] I gathered that I was requested to try 'Test 1' on [redacted] i.e. to approach him as a complete stranger. I therefore planned to turn up to the rendezvous rather late, when [redacted] would have given up hope of being contacted by the man he was expecting, and would most likely be more inclined to engage in a conversation with a stranger. I arrived at the Victoria Bar at 7.10

p.m. but [redacted] was not there. Of the three or four men in the bar at that moment one might have been considered to answer the description I had been given of [redacted] but he looked at least 35, and his manner seemed 'local'. When I asked him whether he was [redacted] he said 'No.' He was still in the bar when I left about 8.10 p.m. and I was convinced by that time that he could not be [redacted].

On the following day, March 16th, I telephoned Bayswater in order to find out [redacted]'s address and work out some other way of approaching him. His address was given as 43, Vicarage Rod, Wolverhampton, but when I went round there – in the evening – I found that Number 43 did not exist in Vicarage Road. I was told by a woman to whom I chatted in the street that there was a Vicarage Street 'somewhere out of town', but I did not succeed in finding out exactly where it was. I later learned from Capt. Dykes (alias Juniper) that there is another Vicarage Road in Penn (?) near Wolverhampton, but that 43 Vicarage Rod, Penn, was not [redacted]'s address, but that of the woman who was also on the Wolverhampton exercise. Capt. Sykes had been informed that [redacted] was staying at the Peacock.

I left Wolverhampton on Wednesday morning, March 17th.

Une reussite dans le genre navet. (A success in the turnip style).

C.C.[62]

The report on her visit to Birmingham was more successful as her man fell for her entrapment and spilled the beans. What proved interesting was that her experiences at Beaulieu and discussions with Forty had given her a much greater insight into the Training Section and much greater confidence; her report reads as if she was one of the instructors.

REPORT ON PARKER (BIRMINGHAM EXERCISE).

Shortly after my arrival at the Midland Hotel, Birmingham, (March 17th) I was rung up by Captain Dykes (alias Juniper). We lunched together, after which Capt. Dykes took me round to the Police Station to introduce me to Mr. Sanders of the Birmingham Police.

I much appreciated the opportunity of 'comparing notes' with Captain Dykes and of discussing various practical aspects of the schemes. Capt. Dykes, is, I gather, exceedingly well acquainted with Birmingham and other towns in the Midlands and might be very helpful with advice and suggestions on local matters (rendezvous, etc.) for future exercises.

In the case of this exercise, a more fortunate choice of meeting place for Parker and myself might have produced better results. I was informed that ladies are not admitted to the Midland Bar unaccompanied, which completely upset my chance of tackling Parker as a pick-up, according to original instructions. My work on this exercise was therefore unsatisfactory.

I saw Parker go into the bar at 6.30 p.m. and followed about ten minutes later. Since in the circumstances I had to start with 'Test 2' I approached him in the usual manner; I asked him whether he was Mr. Parker, then introduced myself (which he seems not to have noticed, since he later asked me what my name was) and explained in the vaguest possible manner that I had been asked to meet him. I added that I had known he would be in the Midland Bar at that time because 'I had heard he was to meet someone there, but I had been told the person could not come'. I almost thought I had overdone the vagueness when Parker asked who exactly had sent me (very carefully avoiding the word 'instructions'); however, when I just said: 'Oh the people you saw ...' and glanced round, whispering I did not want to mention names. Parker seemed quite satisfied and did not waste any more time on elaborating the introduction.

I then proceeded to question him on (i) the exercise, (ii) his biography, (iii) his training. Although I tried to approach all subjects from the angle of someone ignorant, or superficially informed, of Service matters (avoiding technical terms, asking silly questions, making irrelevant comments, etc.) Parker never showed any signs of suspicion at all, with the possible exception of refusing (rather apologetically) to mention the name of the training school. Throughout the conversation he does not seem to have been aware that he was being questioned methodically and maliciously, although I tried to make it as obvious as possible to mention the name of the training school.

The Exercise.

I started the conversation by asking Parker whether I could be of any assistance to him in Birmingham, and whether he would be interested in any introductions I might be able to arrange. I added that, of course, I did not know what the purpose of his stay in Birmingham was but that he must tell me all about it, so that I could see whether I could do anything for him. Parker did not immediately give me a prompt summary of his instructions in technical terms, but went into a lengthy and somewhat confused description of the different problems and of the purpose of his Birmingham job. From which I gathered that he was supposed to lay the foundations of a subversive organisation in Birmingham, find and 'vet' potential recruits, explore the possibilities of sabotage (particularly railway), and study general political tendencies in Birmingham.

He further told me that his cover story was that he had come to Birmingham as a representative of the Canadian Film Board to get material for a film on the bombing of Britain.

He told me that he had met a printer Mr Black (?) who had supplied him with some quite valuable information, but he felt 'rather on thin ice' with Mr. B. since he had been instructed to use a supplementary cover story to Mr. B. which seemed to confuse him, he intended to see Mr B. again on March 18.

He had also interviewed a number of people on his own (mostly intellectuals I gather) and found a number of apparently reliable, promising potential recruits. I did not get the impression that his investigation expeditions in and around Birmingham had been very successful, particularly the G.W.R. (Great Western Railway) seemed to be rather unapproachable to him.

Parker seems to have an observant and comprehensive mind, for people rather than for machines and other practical things perhaps. I should describe his outlook as gentle and ponderous. He is definitely intelligent, his intelligence apparently being of the academic type; analytical rather than practically critical. He lacks the cynical and perhaps utilitarian spirit of the tough business man or the man of the world; he, very aptly, described himself as 'not sufficiently aggressive'. He seems what I would call 'bookishly naïve' in some of his ideas, and has very little self-confidence.

He told me that he was very glad to have had the practical experience of this exercise, particularly because it had made him realise certain difficulties of this kind of which he had not thought of before.

The difficulty of approaching people. Parker said that interviewing strangers seemed a great effort to him and made him very nervous and embarrassed. Moreover, he said he found it practically impossible to get information out of people without letting them guess what it was at the back of his mind.

The difficulty of interweaving his cover story and his real activities. He seemed worried by the fact that when he introduced himself to a stranger as a Canadian film representative, he could never find a suitable transition to bring the conversation round to the matters that really interested him. Lack of subtlety and savoir-faire?

The self-consciousness and mental discomfort arising from a 'subversive' kind of life.

Loneliness. Porker thinks that in the field he would probably not only miss the distraction of ordinary human society, but also feel an occasional urge to unburden his mind.

I was favourably impressed by the fact that Parker was at least discreet in his manner of talking; he went to endless trouble to avoid the vocabulary of the trade and showed no signs of boastful professionalism. He seems immune to flattery, probably because of his utter simplicity.

[Several paragraphs redacted]

Training.

In general, Parker spoke of his training with greatest enthusiasm. He said that the first two months of his training had been far the happiest of his life. He was full of praise and admiration for the organisation and 'set-up' of the training, as well as for most of his instructors and the selection of subjects.

Since his transfer to the last training school he has been at (he would not name any of them as I have pointed out before) his enthusiasm seems to have cooled off slightly. He said that he was now losing interest or getting impatient, because the last course had given him a new and fascinating material to work on. He tried to explain, however, that he and his fellow students had now reached a point where the reality of the work in the field suddenly appeared very close, and, at times, frightening. Many new questions had arisen, and he felt these questions were left unanswered. He was wondering whether the attitude of the instructors was slightly theoretical or whether the instructors were 'getting tired of going over the same course so many times'. What all students felt they needed, he said, was an ordinary tough chap who had done it all himself and whom they could ask questions about innumerable details of life in the field. Parker doubted that a practical expert of that kind would make a good instructor, because, he said, the art of teaching and of executing a thing were often opposed, but he suggested that it would help to develop the students' self-confidence and relieve them of their anguish about many unknown things, if they could occasionally consult someone who had experience of work in the field.

The conclusion of the account of my impressions of Parker, I should say that although he is a clear, articulate (if somewhat slow) thinker, he does not strike me as possessing just the right kind of intelligence for this work; he seems to have neither an outstandingly rapid and lucid brain, nor any kind of intuitive genius. He is, however, most methodical and conscientious, and it would, therefore, perhaps be more prudent to see whether more experience would make him more confident, more independent, practical and alert. If he succeeds in improving upon there (and probably various other) points, I think he might make a very thorough and reliable assistant organiser, although I am not inclined to think that he would ever be a strong, active, independent leader on an important job.

Summing up my meeting with Parker, I am disappointed to find that once again the obvious and primitive trap of 'Test 2' has worked. I am at times inclined to think the use of so malicious a ruse most distasteful. I have to insist on the absolute fairness of this method. Compared to what is most likely to happen in the field, it is even very mild and innocent. It would be a pity to have to give up this method, because it does give the students a good chance of using their brains (or just their low cunning) and of 'ne pas se laisser faire'. In view of the slightly too frequent success of 'Test 2', however, I should like to suggest that students be particularly warned of this type of enemy C.E. [counter-espionage?] If the occasional occurrence of similar methods was mentioned to the students and the danger of it pointed out, they would stand a very good chance of defending themselves properly. Besides, a lesson thus learnt first in theory and then applied in practice might prove very effective in helping the students to outwit all the Fifis they are likely to meet in their future carrier [sic.][63]

The real identity of Parker has yet to come to light. As there are dozens of Parkers with personnel files, one might be him but it could also have been his cover name. While his honest insight into his training and schemes would have been useful for the Training Section, one imagines that his willingness to trust a complete stranger and divulge so much would have made the head of the Country Section question his suitability for the field.

On 22 March, Park sent Miller a note informing him that

Fifi's services are required for an exercise which is to take place in Liverpool and Manchester from 24th to 28th March.

Her prey will be in the Bar Lounge of the State Café, Dale Street, Liverpool, at 18.30. hours on 28th March. His name is QUINAUX, and his description is as follows:-

Age 28; Height 5'9"; black hair; dark brown eyes; square head; freckled face; dimpled chin; hair usually untidy; speaks quite good English (broken).

He will be awaiting an imaginary tall fat man.

A room is being booked at Liverpool, probably at the Adelphi Hotel, for the nights of 25th and 26th March. I will confirm the hotel later. HLP.[64]

There is a personnel file for 28-year-old Paul Goffin, who was also known as Paul Quinaux,[65] but there was no report on him in Fifi's file.

At the end of March, O'Reilly contacted Warden telling him that the

Ministry of Labour headquarters was going to instruct the local authority to place Fifi's card in the dormant section. 'They have retained her calling up notice. Should FIFI ever be worried please let me know. JOR'.[66]

Fifi's successes and the increasing number of students prompted the Security Section to take on another agent provocateur. Thirty-six-year-old Edinburgh-born Winifred Davidson, *née* Watt, was taken on in early February 1942 and, like Fifi, she had been put on the blacklist to ensure she was not called up for other employment without reference to Roche. Details of her earlier life are missing from her personnel file but a note mentioned that her husband was in a Japanese prisoner of war camp. How she came to the attention of SOE is unknown, but Fifi must have had to spend some time with her discussing the best tactics to adopt to achieve the best results.[67]

Mrs Skinner's personnel file included no reports on any agents she might have provoked. There was no indication that they were redacted, but a note dated 1 April 1943 stated that she had been signed off as 'unsuited for particular work for which she was engaged'. One wonders therefore what had prompted the Security Section to take such action.[68] Skinner was recorded as working in the Special Security Section until 1943, when her position was taken by Margaret Sample, who worked there until 1944, during which time she took part in three interviews. Christine Chilver was not listed as being on their staff.[69]

Fifi and Davidson's first joint scheme was during April. Park provided details, but they were only found in Fifi's file.

96 Hour Scheme

1. A 96 Hour Scheme is taking place at Sheffield between 18th – 23rd April. There are two students, Cicely HUMBLE and Charles Edmund MARTIN, and they are due to arrive at Sheffield at 15.33 hours on 18.4.43. Provocation is asked for Mrs. HUMBLE who will be in the Royal Victoria Station Hotel from 12.30 to 14.00 hours on 19.4.43, first in the cocktail bar, then lunch in the main dining room, then coffee in the lounge. Mrs. HUMBLE is described as follows.

'Age 35 – 40. Height 5'6", slim build, shield-shaped face, blue, wide-set eyes, straight nose, thin lips, short upper lip, slim, long hands.'

2. There is another exercise at Nottingham, also from 18th – 22nd April. There are two men engaged – John Henry HUDSON and Richard PERKINS. Provocation is requested in the case of John Henry Hudson who will be in the cocktail bar of the Victoria Station Hotel, Nottingham, from 12.00 to 13.30 hours on 19.4.43. he is a civilian and is described as a refrigeration engineer. His personal description is as follows:-

'Age 30 – 35, Height 5'7", stocky build, round face, fair hair, pointed nose, small scar at tip, one front tooth broken off at tip.'

Both men [*sic*] arrive at Nottingham at 16.28 hours on 18.4.43.[70]

Underneath was a note asking if they could be informed of the names of the two 'A.P.s', whether they wanted rooms booking and what dates. A subsequent note referred to rooms being booked for Miss Collard at Sheffield and Miss Davison [*sic*] at Nottingham for 18 to 22 April inclusive.

Davidson was instructed to contact Richard Perkins instead of Hudson in the Green Bar. Perkins was described as 'Age 40, Height 5'5", curly dark hair, high forehead, deep lines from nose to corner of mouth'. Fifi was told to go to Victoria Station Hotel in Nottingham and the Royal Victoria Station Hotel in Sheffield.

On 17 April, the following request was sent to 'Miss Collard'.

Will you please proceed to SHEFFIELD on Sunday 18th April to take part in an exercise? There is a train from St. Pancras at 12 o'clock arriving in Sheffield at 4.33 p.m. Accommodation has been booked for you at the Royal Victoria Station Hotel.

The R.S.L.O.'s telephone number is LEEDS 30785 (Major Hordern or Captain Marryat), but please do not make use of this except in emergency.

The student you have to contact in this case is a woman, operating under the name of Mrs. Cicely HUMBLE. Her description is:

'Age 35 – 40. Height 5'6", slim build, shield-shaped face, blue, wide-set eyes, straight nose, thin lips, short upper lip, slim, long hands'.

She will be in the Royal Victoria Station Hotel from 12.30 to 14.00 hrs. on Monday 18.4.43 – first in the cocktail bar, then lunch in the main dining-room, then coffee in the lounge.

There is another student engaged in this exercise under the name of Charles Edmund Martin, but you are only required to contact Mrs. HUMBLE. The exercise upon which they are engaged is the same as before.

Although the above-mentioned contact at the Royal Victoria Station Hotel has been laid on for you, I suggest that you might try to contact Mrs. HUMBLE on the train to Sheffield. Both the students will be travelling from London on the same train as yourself.

I enclose £10 advance of your expenses, for which please sign and return to me the enclosed receipt.

You will return to London on 23.4.43 and I should be grateful if you would report to me at 39 Porchester Gate the following morning at 10.30 a.m. bringing with you an account of your expenses and written report of the exercise. In connection with the account of your expenses, will you please attach any receipts for money you have spent (i.e. Hotel bills, etc.) and also the <u>exact</u> change from the £10 and not the nearest round sum.[71]

The identity of Cicely Humble is uncertain. There was an SOE personnel file for a Daphne Doris Humble, *née* Jenkins, but she would only have been nineteen in April 1943 so it is unlikely that it was her. However, it could have been forty-year-old Cécile Lefort. Born Cecile Mackenzie, she was brought up in France, married a Frenchman and escaped to England in 1940, where she joined the Women's Auxiliary Air Force. Like Say, she was recruited to work in SOE's F Section on January 1943. When many SOE agents in France were arrested over the following months, there was a desperate need for replacements. Cécile had a villa on the Brittany coast, which had been used as a safe house for agents returning by boat to England, but sending her back to work with the escape line was deemed too dangerous as she would undoubtedly be recognised. Instead she was trained as a courier to assist Francis Cammaerts's Jockey network in south-eastern France. Although her training would have included a course at Beaulieu, the only report in her personnel file was from Wanborough Manor (STS 5), dated 10 March 1943. Given the timing, it could well have been her who Fifi provoked.

Cécile was flown out of Tempsford by Lysander on 16/17 June 1943, but after only three months in the field she was said to have been betrayed, and she was arrested on 15 September. Interrogated in Lyons and Paris, she was then transferred to Ravensbrück, where it is believed she was executed in 1945, before the Allies arrived.[72]

Fifi's report on Cicely was not included in her personnel file and the identity of Charles Edmund Martin is unknown. The identities of John Henry Hudson and Richard Perkins have yet to come to light. Davidson's reports on her exercises were not included in her file.

On 17 April, Park wrote to Warden providing details of the next scheme.

An exercise is taking place between 26th – 30th April in Liverpool and Manchester. Provocation is asked for in respect of a student named Eric RUSSELL. Description as follows:- 'Age 30, dark curly hair, blue eyes, height 5'10", round face, good teeth, fresh complexion, small scar under chin on left side, sturdy build'. He will be in the Adelphi Hotel Lounge, Liverpool, near the main entrance between 1900 and 2000 hours on 28.4.43.

A note underneath read, 'Will you please let me know which member of your team is selected for the job and whether a room at the hotel is required.'[73] D/CE.2 arranged accommodation for Fifi for the nights of 27 to 30 April and on 24 April Fifi was sent the details and her expenses.

Fifi's first exercise in London was at the end of May 1943 when she was asked to try a different method of approaching the student.

Miss Collard.
    A special 'Silent' scheme is taking place in London from 23rd to 27th May for the benefit of a French officer who knows no English.
    His name is 2nd Lieutenant Jean DELANDE. He will be arriving in London on the evening of 22nd May as a Fighting French Officer on leave and as identity papers he will be carrying D.R. 104. He will probably be in civilian clothes. He will be engaged on an exercise similar to that of students on 96-hour schemes.
    His description is:
    Height: 6 ft., olive complexion, long face, pointed chin, thick dark eyebrows and dark wavy hair. Aged 22 years.
    He will be at the Giraffe house at the Zoo from 2.30 p.m. on Sunday 23rd. If you fail to contact him there, he will be at Oddenino's (restaurant) at a table in the arcade from 12 to 1 p.m. on Monday 24th. If you succeed in picking him up among the animals at the Zoo on Sunday, do not attend rendezvous at Oddenino's.
    Except that the student speaks only French, the exercise is the same as before.[74]

While Lieutenant Jean Delande sounded like his real name, there was no personnel file with that surname. No one of that name was recorded in Pierre Tillet's list of infiltrations into and exfiltrations from France, so Delande must have been a cover name. Fifi's attempt to make contact with him did not go according to plan. On 29 May, Warden wrote to Woolrych at Beaulieu.

> I enclose report from FIFI on the Silent scheme in London. Her failure to report at the Giraffe House rendezvous on Sunday 23rd is partly my fault. When briefing her, it occurred to me that she might not be able to get into the Zoo on a Sunday without a member's ticket and I unfortunately mentioned this possibility to her. She apparently tried to telephone to the Zoo on Sunday morning to find out about this and as there was no reply, decided it was not worth going up there. I think that, having failed to confirm whether or not she could get in, she should most certainly have gone there and found out definitely.[75]

For whatever reason, the report was not in her file. However, as she had been given expenses for the scheme, she returned £9 15s 10d. When Venner (D/FIN) queried them, Warden explained that the 1d 'Special Agent No.1' claimed was for a newspaper. 'I asked her about this and she said she only charged for a newspaper when she found it necessary to have some ostensible occupation when waiting in a café or elsewhere to watch someone. This seems fairly reasonable, so I have let it pass.'[76]

A second attempt at a 'silent scheme' was planned for 6 and 7 June, for which she was provided with the name and particulars of the student.

> 2nd Lieutenant GREL. Age 29, 6 ft tall, well built, very dark, Latin type, thin face, deep set eyes, good features.
> This student will be acting as a Free French Officer on leave and will probably be in civilian clothes.
> GREL will be at the Giraffe House at the Zoo at 14.30, and at the Restaurant at the Zoo at 1515 on Sunday 6th June. On Monday, 7th June, he will be on the terrace at Oddenino's (or if wet in lounge, near main entrance), at 12.30. HLP. £5 expenses.[77]

This attempt did not work either. Warden explained to Woolrych and Major H. H. Hale, another Training Section officer, that

> She and GREL seem to have spent a very unhappy afternoon together at the Zoo! FIFI mentioned to me when handing in her report that the presence of an F.S.P. on these silent schemes makes it more difficult for her to contact the student – chiefly, I think, because it puts her off her stroke, as she does not like an audience![78]

There was no report on Grel, whose identity is unknown. Whether Davidson was given a 'silent scheme' has not come to light.

On 17 June, Fifi was sent ten £1 notes for her next exercise. This time she was sent to Bristol, where she was booked into a room at the Grand Hotel for 24 and 25 June.[79] On her return, she submitted the following.

REPORT ON BERESFORD

I met Beresford in the American Bar of the Bristol Grand Hotel on 26.6.43 at 6.30 p.m. He was sitting at the bar, absorbed in his paper and did not take any notice of me. I sat down next to him, ordered a drink, and, seeing that he was not amenable to casual conversation, I addressed him directly.

Beresford seemed slightly startled; it took him a minute or two to decide to look up from his paper. I introduced myself and, finding Beresford obviously suspicious and very much on his guard, I decided to make my story as convincing as possible, I said I had been asked by 'Major James' to meet Beresford, to see whether he wanted assistance of any kind in Bristol.

Beresford thought quickly and then suddenly said 'Thank you very much', he was having a grand holiday in Bristol. He explained that he was writing a 'silly book' about bombed cities and that he had come to Bristol for a few days to get a scoop. I said I was a journalist and might help him by putting him in touch with the local press and with some people who could give him interesting stories. Beresford did not seem too keen to accept my offer. He was, however, able to discuss his book intelligently and seemed fairly well up on technical details about the printing and publication of a book.

I enquired casually whether he had been able to find accommodation in Bristol, and he said 'Yes', without giving his address or any particulars.

Towards the end of our rather pally chat, Beresford mentioned Major James again and, giving me a description, said he had been at school with him. I explained that I had just met him recently in London and that, on hearing I was going to Bristol on a reporting tour, Major James had asked me to look out for Beresford, in his likely haunts. I appreciated Beresford's intelligent handling of a false situation; he thought quickly and said the right things to fit into the pattern of our respective cover stories.

I mentioned that I had looked into Crocker's bar on the previous evening because I had been told he might occasionally hang out there, but that I had not seen him. He replied, after some reflection, that he had not been there; which was an unnecessary lie.

Beresford took leave after about half an hour, pretending to be busy and thus forestalling an invitation to dinner.

Throughout the interview, his manner was easy and natural, except for a certain nervousness which sometimes became apparent in slight fidgeting and in a kind of arrogance rising from shyness.

After a very short interview, my impressions of this student are not very clear. He certainly seems very alert and a good thinker. I believe him to be enterprising and independent, perhaps with touch of self-willed, fancy individualism; however, he seems serious, alert, and conscious of responsibility, so that I am inclined to think he could well be entrusted with a job of some importance, that is, if the results of this scheme are technically satisfactory. I wonder, however, whether he would not produce the best results in work, if given fairly large scope and considerable independence. Keeping in mind that my judgement in this case is summary and based merely on intuition, I do not feel sure that I should like to depend on Beresford, in team-work. But he might make a good freelance, if allowed to act on his own, 'sans façons' [informal].

With the 'independent type', responsibility is usually more effective than any authoritative influence.[80]

There was no-one with the surname Beresford in the SOE files but there was a thirty-two-year-old Euan Beresford Butler, also known as Captain Beresford, who was Fifi's target. After education at Eton, he worked for *The Times* and the *Daily Mail* before joining SOE.[81]

On 15 May 1943, Michael Thornley, the head of the German Section, contacted Woolrych at Beaulieu requesting that Butler be provided with a special course.[82]

> I hope that 4703 [Butler's code number] will be taking up an appointment as Chief Representative of the German Section in Stockholm. I am anxious that he should do a full three week's course at Group B. It is hoped that he will be operating under the cover of A.M.A. [Assistant Military Attaché], but this has not been settled. Should be given the fullest possible instruction in methods used by the Swedish Police, Gestapo, concealment of codes in letters, secret inks, current explosives, devices etc.[83]

Using the cover name of Major Beresford, he started the course on 2 June and stayed in Hartford House (STS 32a). When he finished his scheme in Bristol, he was asked to write up a detailed account of his four days. He stated that his cover was a bank official on holiday and was gathering information for a book entitled *Two Years After: The Blitzed Cities Carry On!*, which he hoped to sell to the Ministry of Information. He mentioned meeting Contact A on 26 June on the Cathedral Green at 11.30. He described her as a working woman who went dancing every lunchtime. 'I enlisted as my chief informant pro tem and gave her certain definite tasks. These she had not yet been able to carry out when I met her a second time,' adding later that she was 'intelligent and reliable under a deceptive mildness of manner. Should have been more useful as informant in view of her position'. The official report on the scheme stated that he was given two contacts.

> The first contact was a Miss Robinson, who reports well on him. His original approach was plausible and his manner during the two meetings was convincing. He talked to her for a considerable time before asking for her help, leading the conversation skilfully in order to find out what type of person she was. He took the usual security precautions when entering and leaving her house, arranged danger signals with her, a 'dead' boites-aux-lettres, discussed the question of pay with her and gave her a stern warning about withdrawing from the organisation.[84]

Miss Robinson does not appear to have been Christine. Presumably she was another of the Security Section officers. He admitted having lunched on 25 June at the Grand Hotel, having previously visited the American bar, but added, 'No contact.' He was instructed to go to the Grand Hotel the following day at 1830 hours and 'was contacted there by agent provocatrice. Not followed.'[85] In the security report, under the heading 'Agent Provocatrice', it stated,

Fifi had no difficulty in picking out Beresford in the American Bar of the Grand Hotel, Bristol. She tried to get into conversation with him but had little success. She, accordingly, had to try 'Approach No. 2' and told him a Major James had asked her to assist him (here she used the name Beresford) whilst he was in Bristol. She reports that he was momentarily taken aback, but finally pretended that the assistance to which she referred was in connection with the book he was writing on bombed cities. He pretended to know Major James and claimed to have been at school with him.

According to his report Beresford claims to have realised immediately that this person was an agent provocatrice or a police spy. However it seems strange that he should have assisted her by pretending to know a fictitious person.

Fifi reports that she was unable to obtain any information from him.[86]

Interestingly, the report stated that his second contact was a male agent provocateur from the R.S.L.O. but that Beresford failed to keep the rendezvous. During his police interrogation, this agent provocateur was present but Beresford did not know who he was. It was noted that 'this student was extremely indiscreet in his conversation with him, admitting that his real work would not be done in this country and that he had recently been trained in "one of the schools in the New Forest"'.[87] Woolrych's final report mentioned his exercise and clearly used some of Fifi's observations.

He is very intelligent and well informed: he has a very active and original mind, but his imagination is occasionally a little wild. He has immense initiative and was full of new ideas. He worked extremely hard and with great enthusiasm, but was inclined sometimes to be inaccurate and forgetful of facts. He has great powers of leadership and should inspire confidence. He has considerable practical ability as a planner but in the exercise which he carried out he did not reach such a high standard. He has very great, perhaps excessive self-confidence; when, however, he is up against a difficult situation he is inclined to show signs of nervousness.

He is impulsive and in moments of stress is inclined to be rather rash. For these reasons he is more easily trapped into mistakes and indiscretions than his intelligence would lead one to expect. He displays true emotions too clearly. He has a charming personality and should make friends everywhere.

He has a strong sense of humour, and is a good talker and knows it; he can also listen. His most serious failings are occasional lapses of discretions which are certainly not intentional; he is, however, inclined to say more than is absolutely necessary. For all these reasons, it is advisable that in his work he himself should remain as much as possible in the background.[88]

Thornley must have decided that the urgent need for Beresford in Stockholm overrode his security shortcomings and, after a crash course in demolitions at Arisaig House (STS 21) in Scotland and a nine-day course in explosives at Frogmore Park (STS 18), Watton-at-Stone, Hertfordshire, Beresford was flown out to Sweden on 7 August. He survived the war.

As soon as Fifi returned from Bristol, she was given another exercise, this time in Birmingham. Unusually, the name of the student and their description was not included in her file, but clues were found in her report.

REPORT on 96 Hour Exercise at Birmingham from 27th June to 2 July 1943.

I entered the lounge of the Grand Hotel, Birmingham, at 12.35 p.m. on 29th June, 1943, waited until 1.00 p.m., then looked into the dining room and grill, and finally returned to the bar-lounge, without having spotted RUSSELL. He turned up about 1.15 p.m., wandered around, and then ordered coffee.

His slightly embarrassed manner, somewhat continental dress, and generally 'foreign' appearance led me to suppose that the man I was observing was obviously RUSSELL; his appearance, however, did not strike me as answering the description very exactly, and he was carrying a copy of Liddell Hart's 'The Way to Win Wars' instead of a timetable. I therefore hesitated to approach him immediately. After about 15 minutes of silent observation, I heard him ask someone for a light; his accent being distinctly foreign, I decided to contact him. The only means of doing so was to have him called into the hall by a page-boy.

So we eventually met in the hall, and I introduced myself, apologising casually for not having recognised him immediately. As we left the Grand Hotel, I explained that I was the secretary of Captain Johnson who had intended to meet RUSSELL himself, but had, unfortunately, been summoned to Liverpool unexpectedly. He had asked me to contact RUSSELL and enquire whether I could help him in any way, as guide, interpreter, etc. I suggested going round to my hotel to talk it over and said I was at RUSSELL's disposal until 'Captain Johnson' himself arrived at Birmingham.

RUSSELL did not show any immediate reaction to my introduction, and made clever use of small talk and compliments in order to play for time. He was most cautious and non-committal, and seemed unwilling even to come to my hotel for a drink. We went to another hotel, in Temple Street, where RUSSELL proceeded to grill me. He did not attempt to conceal the fact that he was anxious to find out all about me, and that he had reasons to suspect me. He shot direct questions, asking for a description of 'Captain Johnson', enquiring about my work, the address of my office in London, etc. and scrutinising me with a cunning smile. He finally said he was sure that I had forgotten part of 'Captain Johnson's' message – obviously alluding to a password, – and that I might be of great help to him, if I only mentioned the 'crucial matter'.

His cover story was that he was a journalist, on the staff of 'France' and that he was spending a holiday in Birmingham, helping in the Wings for Victory campaign by selling painted silk scarves. The story did not strike me as a particularly convincing one, particularly as RUSSELL seemed unable to refrain from occasional giggles while telling his story. Further, he did not make any effort to consolidate it by adding realistic details. It was not at all clear why he should have chosen to spend holiday at Birmingham, particularly as he said that he disliked the place, that he did not know anybody there, and that he found it almost impossible to find accommodation.

After our preliminary conversation, RUSSELL seemed to have made up his mind that he could not trust me and that he could not talk. his good resolutions were, however, apparently limited to that negative conclusion, he made no particular effort to play his part in every detail, or to keep his conversation strictly within the limits of his cover story nor did he have any hesitation about taking me to the Queen's House Hotel where he was staying. He asked me to do some sewing (!) for him, and I spent about an hour and a half hemming silk scarves.

We talked about general matters; the war, propaganda; etc. I asked occasional questions about RUSSELL's private life and his past. He said he had come to England in April 1940, and was still waiting for his call-up (!). He further told me that he was Canadian, but had been brought up in France. He said his pre-war occupation was journalism, and he had started by doing clerical work in a newspaper office at the age of 17, after which he had gradually worked his way up and become a reporter on a provincial paper. This seemed a slight contradiction, since he had previously declared that he had always lived in Paris. He did not put the story across with much conviction, and his apparent lack of interest in, or knowledge of, letter would seem rather unusual for a journalist, particularly a French one.

During the conversation RUSSELL made several more attempts to sound me, asking questions at random, trying to 'recruit' me – ('What would you do if England was occupied by the Germans tomorrow?') – and searching for some sort of link or recognition sign. His basic idea was sound scepticism and a definite suspicion, but I did not get the impression that he was treating our mysterious encounter as a serious matter. His 'interrogation methods' were not very elaborate and his whole attitude somewhat inconsequent; on one occasion, for instance, he came out suddenly with a blunt question 'What is the name of your son?' which I took to be a password, and which he, subsequently, found impossible to explain away.

At about 4.30 p.m. we left the Queen's House Hotel and returned to town, where we had tea at the same hotel in Temple Street. RUSSELL had got fairly familiar and seemed to treat me as a sort of colleague, apparently considering me quite trustworthy, as long as he did not divulge the full story of his real activities. He told me about his methods of exploring Birmingham, gave some details about his daily routine and programme, and asked me to assist him in buying a pair of sun glasses (obviously for disguise purposes). I got the impression that he did not attach much importance to details because he was too lazy to 'keep it up'. During the conversation there were frequent giggles and chuckles for no apparent reason, and on one occasion he remarked that the 'little game' we were playing was intensely amusing.

On the whole, however, my impression of RUSSELL was favourable. He seems active, and independent, and is certainly keen and very sure of himself. He possesses a certain charm of manner and a very Latin feeling for the manifold advantages of good talk and brilliant flattery as useful weapons in the battle of gab. I hope that his somewhat light, inconsequent attitude was due merely to a lack of imagination in 'playing the game' and that in the field he would work with more serious concentration. As far as the whole of the exercise is concerned, I am unable to judge RUSSELL's effort, but if he has succeeded in combining good technical results with his free-and-easy manner, I should give him full marks.[89]

Russell's identity is unknown. If it was his real name, there were seven personnel files for men with Russell as a surname. Her report shows how much more professional Fifi was becoming as an agent provocateur. She was taking her work very seriously; having had experience of the agents' training programme, she asked for permission to attend the 'post mortem' debriefing sessions the students had with the Training Section after their scheme, not at Beaulieu but in a flat in London. Park contacted Forty, informing him that Fifi had made the following suggestions:

(1) That she should be permitted to attend the Post-Mortems on these 96 hour exercises in order to hear what criticisms the student may have to make about her approach to them. If the Post-Mortems are held, as I hope they will be, at 14 Malvern Court, there is no security objection to her attendance, D.CE has approved this suggestion. I have mentioned it to Major Wedgwood (at Beaulieu), who could see no objection.

(2) Fifi is not satisfied about the arrangements made for her to pick up students. Her complaint is that the student's mind is focussed on identifying the individual whom he has been told will be meeting him at the rendezvous. He therefore has no interest in Fifi, and does his best to repel her advances. Fifi has therefore to plunge into what she calls her second test and address him outright by his name. In order to get over this difficulty, Fifi has suggested that the civilian contact should be asked to stand the student lunch, that Fifi will be at the place appointed for the lunch, that the contact who will previously have been informed about her or introduced to her, will introduce her to the student as a friend or relation of his; the contact will then, after a short time, make an excuse for departing, leaving the student with Fifi.

This suggestion is sufficiently good to justify trying it out at least once. I have mentioned it to Major Wedgwood who thinks it is worth while trying. I have also mentioned it to Lane of Bristol, who is perfectly prepared to put it into operation if the next exercise in which Fifi is engaged is sent to his area.

(3) If the suggestion in paragraph (2) is put into effect, the suggestion which I am about to set out does not rise. Fifi complains that the descriptions of the students given to her are not always sufficiently full for her to be able to identify the students at once (see her report on the scheme which has just taken place at Birmingham).[90]

The flat where the suggested post mortem was to take place was at 14 Malvern Court, Onslow Square, Chelsea. This was where Miller was staying when he was in London, but there was no mention in Fifi's personnel file that she attended them. That is not to say she did not; Prue Willoughby confirmed that at one such session on 18 July, Miller contacted her about her next exercise, this time including, possibly as a result of her suggestion, a far easier method for her to identify the relevant student. Maintaining a professional relationship, he addressed her as Miss Collard.

With reference to the exercise taking place at Hounslow at. resent, in which some of our Czech students are engaged, will you please suggest a suitable rendezvous at Hounslow, at which you could be introduced to one of the students, and let me know as soon as possible, where this will be.

The student selected for your attention is No. 2 on your list. He is a professional Army officer, and he lives at 50 Wallington Avenue, Hounslow.

As soon as a rendezvous has been decided upon, steps will be taken to effect the introduction, but I will communicate with you further upon this, before settling the final details.

I have now got photographs of all the men engaged on the exercise, and can let you have the ones you require, as soon as the rendezvous has been fixed up.

Yours sincerely.

Flight Lieutenant.[91]

The outcome of this exercise is unknown, as her report was not included in her file; neither were the photographs of this or subsequent students. No doubt they were returned to their files. As there were four Czechs, whether Davidson accompanied her is unknown.

Her next exercises were in Manchester, Salford and Preston between 2 and 7 August.

MANCHESTER
Room booked at the Midland Hotel, Manchester for nights of 2nd, 3rd, and 4th August.
Rendezvous at the Grand Hotel bar between 1900 and 2000 hours on 3rd August.
There you will contact:-
Philip BROWN
Description: 5'7"; 35-38; fair wavy hair; wrinkled forehead; knob on right; hollow features; thick bushy eyebrows; flat nose; may have a moustache; middle finger on right hand deformed.

SALFORD
Rendezvous at the Salisbury Hotel, Salford on 4th August, in the lounge. To reach this, you go through the main entrance in Trafford Road, and on the left hand side, a doorway leads to the lounge and concert room.
There you will contact:-
John William MILLER.
Description: 5'10"; about 30; convex nose; depressed base; ears stick out, large lobes; thick lips; deep dent under lower. Clean shaven, prominent chin.

PRESTON
Room booked at the Park Hotel, Preston, for the night of 5th August. Rendezvous at Bull and Royal Hotel at the Long Bar on the ground floor. Walk under the arch off Church Street, in which the Bull and Royal stands, and turn through door on left which will take you into the Long Bar on the ground floor.
There you will contact:- [redacted].[92]

Neither Brown nor Miller had personnel files so these must have been their cover names. Davidson's personnel file, unlike Fifi's, included no written reports on the students she had met over the five months to August. Unusually, there was no indication that they had been redacted, but a note written by Senter on 11 October 1943 read, 'Please note on record that 10211 [Davidson's reference number] was employed by this organisation between March and October 1943. The file on this subject is in the D/CE Safe.' The reason why her file was in the Security Section safe was not revealed until September 1944, when a memo advised that

> 10211's employment consisted in acting as an agent provocatrice to students taking part in 96 hour schemes from Group B. Her employment was terminated because the students whom she had met on the exercises succeeded in continuing their acquaintance with her in London after the exercise was over. In spite of orders to discourage this conduct, subject appeared to make no strenuous efforts to see that they did not occur. She was given as a reason for her dismissal that there was not sufficient work for two A.P.s and that as she was the junior of the two and did not speak foreign languages, it was therefore necessary for her to go.
> The file on 10211 is marked 'Category B' and is with D/CE.Q.[93]

So with only one agent provocateur, at the end of July, Roche sent Park a memo relating to obtaining Fifi's cover as a journalist. He was asked to contact Lionel Hale, the head of the Press Propaganda Department. Given the symbol D/Q, it had been a D Section department and played an integral role in producing 'black' (false) propaganda, spreading rumours and 'secret journalism'.[94]

Cover for A.P.s

Please see D/Q on this, who would like to meet Fifi and Mrs. Lamb, and consider whether he can help them over journalistic cover.

I discussed this at some length with Fifi some months ago, but I do not think she ever did anything about it.

Further, would you please give each of them a note in writing, carrying on it an acknowledgment for them to sign, making it clear that they must in no circumstances pretend to be employed by any Government department and, in particular, must not pretend to have any connection with the Ministry of Information. This is most important, as I put that request to the Director General of the Ministry of Information, who turned it flat, and I should be put in a position of very great embarrassment if it was reported to him that either of them pretended to be employed by the Ministry.

Finally, I was surprised to learn that my name and telephone number have been given in case either of them gets into difficulties which cannot be resolved with the aid of the R.S.L.O. This should be altered and some appropriate substitute (for example, an alias for yourself) substituted, due care being taken to see that both D/CE.Recs [Records Section] and the telephone exchange have full particulars of the alias chosen.[95]

As there was no personnel file for a woman surnamed Lamb, it is possible she was an employee of Hulton Press Ltd, 40–43 Shoe Lane, W.1.

It is worth noting that Fifi's next instructions to go to Birmingham and Coventry did not include details of the train she should catch. Maybe she was considered experienced enough in using the railways to be able to make her own decisions about transport arrangements. One imagines that she had acquired an up-to-date timetable to make her job easier.

BIRMINGHAM

Rooms have been booked for you at the Midland Hotel, Birmingham on the 9th August. On arrival at your hotel you will immediately get in touch with Captain Dykes, telephone Calthorpe 1174 and you will act entirely under his direction. You will probably be instructed by him to make contact with student whose name and description Captain Dykes will give you at a rendezvous either on the evening of August 9th or at midday on August 10th.

COVENTRY.

After completion of the Birmingham exercise you will go to Coventry where you will meet a student answering the following name and description:
[paragraph redacted]
This student will be in the bar of the Queens Hotel at 7.30 p.m. on the 10th. Again you should act under the direction of Captain Dykes but should he fail to give you instructions you should go ahead to Coventry in the usual way.[96]

Her visit to the Midlands did not go according to plan. In her report, she stated that

Both exercises failed on account of the students' failing to carry out instruction for rendezvous.

On Aug. 9th, Major Dykes and I kept the Grand Hotel, Birmingham, covered from 6.30 p.m. to 7.30 p.m., but there was no sign of the student (Pearl Whimsy). We did notice a woman answering the student's description enter the Grand Hotel, but she left after spending a few minutes in the cloakroom and did not even enter the bar.

On Aug. 10th, Major Dykes accompanied me to Coventry, where we watched the Queen's for more than half an hour, without success. As the bar was closed (sold out), Major Dykes instructed the bar-maid to send the student to the White Lion, in case he turned up; we waited for him there, but he did not arrive.

Considering that none of the four students on this exercise seemed at all willing to play, it might be interesting to investigate the reason of their shyness. There seems to be reasons to believe that students were warned of agent provocateurs; if this was the case, the students should be made to understand that it is foolish to avoid any potential danger in as obvious a way, instead of dealing boldly and skilfully with difficult or delicate situations. If the students did really suspect provocation (or any other difficulty of the kind) and missed their rendezvous because they were afraid, it is plain that they are not fit for work in the field.[97]

Pearl Whimsy was twenty-nine-year-old Pearl Witherington's cover name. She was born in Paris to British parents and after her father died she worked at the British Embassy. Following the German invasion, she escaped to the unoccupied zone in 1940 and worked with one of MI9's escape lines. She eventually escaped with her family through Spain and Portugal, arriving in England in July 1941. Recruited by the SOE, she was trained as a courier. Her personnel file includes reports on her ninety-six-hour scheme in Birmingham. Following a police search of her room, she was taken into the police station for questioning and the chief constable's report was not very positive. Her report claimed that the contact at the Grand Hotel was not there when she went at 18.30, but this was not what Fifi reported, nor the contact she was supposed to meet. George Bluck was presumably a cover name.

PROVOCATION
Student: Pearl Whimsey
Contact: George Bluck

I discussed with Fifi during the afternoon of 9th August our plans for provoking Pearl WHIMSEY, who had been given a bogus rendezvous at the lounge of the Grand Hotel, Birmingham, from 18.30 hours that evening.

To test out new methods of provocation by means of introduction, I formulated the following plan:

As it was a female student it was not easy to get into communication as a member of the public as she would be bound to assume that anyone approaching her was the person who was supposed to keep the rendezvous, therefore a more direct method would seem advisable and more certain. I decided to go straight up to her and say that it was no use her waiting as the person she was expecting could not come. I then intended to invite her for a drink in the American Bar. By pre-arrangement Fifi would be in the hall, between the lounge and the bar. I should call her and ask her to come along for a drink as well. Conversation between Fifi and myself would indicate that Fifi was a journalist, in Birmingham in connection with her work, and I should also hint that her war experiences, i.e. exit from France, were interesting. Having indicated that Fifi was a person who could be of use, but having given no reason to the student that she was anything to do with the organisation, I intended leaving at some moment, when the student could not very well depart without appearing rude, or hurried, is when she had a full glass. The above was the plan.

I went to the lounge of the Grand Hotel at about 18.40 hours, but there was no one there, or in any of the bars who could possibly answer to the description of WIMSEY. I contacted Fifi outside three times during the next three quarters of an hour so that our plan could work should WIMSEY be late. I did see one person come into the hall of the hotel about 7.10, look at her watch, walk straight down some steps in the direction of the Ladies Retiring Room, from which she emerged after lapse of some three or four minutes, but she went straight out again. I think this was WIMSEY from the description given, and Fifi also thought the same.

Bluck told me he was meeting someone at 4 o'clock outside his works. I parked my car some distance away to watch. WIMSEY arrived about three minutes early, looked at her watch as she came round the corner, and doubled back out of view. A couple of minutes later she again came into view, walking slowly down towards the works entrance, and hung about in a rather forlorn manner until Bluck drove up at about one minute past 4 o'clock. She went straight up to him and went inside.[98]

Pearl's argument that her contact was not there at 18.30 led Beaulieu to insist on students waiting for an hour at their rendezvous. Woolrych's final report described her as being 'of average intelligence and fairly practical, but rather slow in picking up new ideas. She has, however, a good memory and does not forget what she has once learnt. She worked hard and seems keen on her job'.[99] Briefed for a mission to help Maurice Southgate's network in the Tarbes, Chateauroux and Bergerac area, she was flown out of Tempsford on 22 September. After Southgate's arrest, she took charge of a group of about 1,500 French members of the Maquis and led them in attacks on the German army during the D-Day landings.[100]

Clearly Fifi felt confident enough in her assessment of the exercises to pass judgments on students. Whether by this time she was sitting in on the debriefing sessions was not mentioned in her file, nor whether her opinions about the agents' suitability for work in the field were acted upon. One imagines that if she did make such comments, they would have been taken into consideration in Woolrych's final report. However, the ultimate decision as to whether the students were sent into the field was taken by the head of the Country Section.

In August 1943, Senter took over as head of the Security Section with responsibility for all SOE paramilitary and training schools across the country. Assisting him were one lieutenant, three majors, three captains, secretarial staff and security personnel. There was no evidence that there was anything but business as usual.[101]

Fifi's next exercise was in Bristol, but she was given no instructions as to the accommodation or the student's cover name. Presumably, this was because she was using the new technique of being introduced by the student's contact and then being left alone with him or her. What follows is Christine's longest report, four pages long.

REPORT ON THE 96 HOUR EXERCISE at BRISTOL
between August 16th – 20th, made by FIFI.

On Monday, August 16th, I had an interview with Major Lane and Mr. Morris (MORTON's contact) and we discussed the new method of arranging a meeting between the student and the agent provocateur. Mr. MORRIS was to invite MORTON to lunch on the following day, and we decided that I would turn up 'unexpectedly' and join them. According to the story which we worked out, Mr. Morris and I had met in London in 1940; Mr. Morris had collaborated with me and some journalist friends of mine, on an article about economics; shortly after that, I left for France; we subsequently lost sight of each other and were surprised to meet again, by chance in Bristol.

I am inclined to think that a story of this kind has to be prepared very carefully and in great detail. Our preliminary talk was, however, necessarily somewhat sketchy, since time was limited, and moreover, Mr. Morris did not seem to feel too sure about coping with such detail of elaborate bluffing tricks. The Bristol experiment has shown that if the 'introduction method' is to be a success, it is important that (a) the story should be worked out with care and precision, and (b) the people taking part in any bluff scene should have a certain 'talent for improvising', and (c) they should, if possible, know each other sufficiently for easy, natural team-work.

The choice of an intermediary is, perhaps, somewhat difficult; I am not sure that it would be possible to use contacts for this job, in all cases, since it seems to demand more than general keenness and interest, and it certainly means a good deal of preliminary work and extra trouble.

On Tuesday, August 17th, about 1.00 p.m. I looked into the Grand Hotel bar, where I found Mr. Morris in company of Morton. Our preliminary conversation was somewhat improvised, and Mr. Morris seemed to feel the lack of 'background to the story' as much as I did. However, we both talked fast, and the situation developed fairly smoothly. We all lunched together, and MORTON, although secretly observant and critical, played the game very nicely and was talkative and sociable. In the course of the conversation I had explained the purpose of my stay at Bristol and dropped a hint about being free for the day, so that when MORTON mentioned a road-side inn which he had discovered the day before, it seemed quite natural for Mr. Morris to suggest that we should both have tea there in the afternoon. The arrangement was, perhaps, made a trifle too quickly; feeling that I might have agreed a little less promptly, I began to wonder whether MORTON had caught the 'nuance'. I had to give him good marks, when later on he told me that he had noticed this detail and that it had made him think ...

Mr. Harris left us after lunch, and MORTON and I had coffee and a drink in the lounge. MORTON proved an indefatigable talker. Having discovered that I knew the United States – (a coincidence which, by the way, made MORTON more suspicious that anything else about our meeting!) – he told me the inside story of the entire Riga gossip chronicle ... We had several most amusing hours talking about food and telling dirty stories – apparently MORTON's pet hobbies. I gathered from the conversation that MORTON had spent ten or fifteen years travelling in Scandinavia, Finland, Russia, the Baltic States, Germany and the Low Countries, and that he speaks Dutch, Flemish, German, Danish, Swedish and a little Estonian.

Between 3 and 4 p.m., we left the Grand and took a bus to Westbury Hill, where we spent the afternoon at the Mulberry Tree Inn. I risked occasional, rather careful questions about MORTON's activities, but he was somewhat brief in replying; according to his cover story, he was (rather mysteriously) connected to the Dutch Forces in England; he had come over to this country at the beginning of the war and was, at present, working for some timber import firm in London; he had come to Bristol 'to settle some private affairs' and to have a general look around, with a view to settling down there, later on, in case his firm should decide to transfer him to Bristol. I gathered that he has lived in

London for a considerable time, and that he has a lot of connections and is of independent means, all of which fitted the part of a business man very nicely. As far as his stay in Bristol was concerned, he gave me the impression of a leisurely bon vivant, rather than that of a man on a business trip; he seemed to take things easy and to have nothing to do.

We sat in the inn garden for several hours and then went for a walk up to Blaise Castle, MORTON still chatting away, talking about politics (rather common sense, business-like views on International affairs) chuckling about innumerable naughty anecdotes, describing gastronomic marvels in a mixture of all languages, sketching little 'etudes comparatives' of different countries and nations, analysing the charms and drawbacks of bachelor's life, and of course, talking about women with considerable gusto. One has to describe a bewildering, fanciful case of MORTON's non-stop talk, in order to point out the curious quality of his mind. All his voluble frivolity and fantastic nonsense seem to hide a lot of sound common sense and intelligence. He has a keen sense of observations, and his business experience has taught him a great deal about people; good salesmen are good psychologists. Having knocked around for many years and met an unusual variety of human types, he has developed a certain intuition and insight which enable him to sum up people rapidly and in a subtle way; his talk, for instance, is just a way of listening. His conclusions and diagnoses are often cynical, but always intelligent and full of humorous understanding. Apparently frivolous and superficial, he is really the sober, solid Dutchman, very hardboiled and commercial minded. He does not seem to indulge in abstract thinking at all; he talks in metaphors, prefers examples to deductions; and probably thinks in images and in figures; an essentially practical mind.

He has, of course, all the self-confidence one would expect of a man of his age and experience; he is, perhaps, inclined to be obstinate in doing things his way and not very keen on giving up his habits, particularly when they mean comfort. (He had, for example, decided to stay at the Grand Hotel in Bristol, although he knew it was against the rules; he considered that he was less conspicuous in the Grand, and that, anyway, the Grand was a better setting for his cover story and his personality, than a mediocre little boarding house or hotel would have been). He knows the value of money, and seems to have a sound sense of responsibility and the necessary prudence. I am unable to form any judgment as to his technical efficiency, enterprise or general capability. A detail which seems worth mentioning is his habit of mixing languages, which might necessitate some concentration practice in one given language, for some time before he goes over.

After spending the afternoon at Westbury Hill, we returned to town and dined at the Grand, upon which we had coffee and some drinks and MORE TALK. I was slightly disappointed about having failed to find out anything worth knowing, after 6 hours of concentrated diplomacy, and decided that MORTON must be suspicious. I therefore made a direct attack, and remarked casually that I was sure he realised that I had been sent to see how he was getting on and whether he was having any difficulties. He gave a radiant smile, and replied that he had seen through the whole arrangement from the start, because 'Mr. Morris's moustache twitched'; I pressed him for more criticism, concerning my own acting, but he was presumably too tactful to say anything to me personally. I was, on the other hand, surprised to find that, once his suspicion had been aroused by that one detail, he spent the whole day observing me, interpreting everything I said or did, and finding some suspect meaning in the most negligible coincidence. All this came out in perfectly easy chatter, after which he told me about his mysterious rendezvous on the previous night, and explained how it had been laid on, after he had already received his general instructions. He asked me whether I knew Captain Angels, and when I said I did, he seemed quite happy to be able to talk things over at last, and discussed his instructions and the progress of his Bristol job with me.

He was, however, still rather reticent about details of his training, the names of the Training Schools he had been to, his real name and particulars of his private life. It was only when I declared the exercise definitely over and our conversation 'off the record' that he got more communicative on these points.

He had a difficult moment after he had spilled the beans, apparently without worrying about it at all. I asked him what justification he thought he had for making all these confidences and mentioning names, without even attempting to sound me as to my trust-worthiness. He explained that, theoretically, he thought himself justified in accepting me because Mr. Morris, who was definitely a friend, had introduced me to him and had left us together without giving MORTON a special warning about me. I maintained that MORTON had heard that Mr. Morris has last seen me three years ago, and that he had meanwhile been in enemy occupied territory, which should have been sufficient reason to distrust me, without any specific warning. To that, MORTON replied that he could agree only in theory, for in reality his suspicions had told him I was connected with the scheme, which meant I belonged to the Organisation and was, consequently quite trustworthy.

In brief, MORTON spilled the beans quite calmly, when I tried Test Two, because he considered that the exercise was over as from that moment. I must admit it is difficult to be severe about an indiscretion committed in similar circumstances; most of the students I have met have been unable to stick to the abstract, theoretical rules of the game, when their common sense dictated a different, much simpler reaction. A student who will not play is, obviously, difficult to test; on the other hand, I do not feel sure that complex, 'artificial' logics should be encouraged where straightforward practical thinking seems a much healthier policy.

I met MORTON again on Wednesday, August 18th, when he told me more about his job in Bristol, he said he really did not consider schemes very difficult ('One could really do the whole work in half a day') but he did find the exercise gave him varied and useful experience. He mentioned having been for occasional walks round the railway station, factories, bridges, etc. but he did not seem to have made a great effort to get into places and to study the items of interest very thoroughly; his attitude seemed, on the whole, rather happy-go-lucky. Which, I hope, is just another of his cunning tricks; it would be a pity if a man of MORTON's experience and general intelligence turned out to be slack or inefficient.[102]

If Morton was his real name, he could have been either the Campbell, Paul or Robert Morton who all have personnel files.

No sooner had Fifi returned to London than she was sent instructions for exercises at Reading and Cheltenham between 22 and 27 August. This time, she was to revert to the earlier method.

> Reading. 1st Rendezvous at the Saloon Bar of the Ship Hotel, 4 Dukes Street, Reading, between 1900 and 2000 hours, 23rd August 1943.
>
> Student: [redacted]
>
> Description: [redacted]
>
> A room is being booked for you for the night of 24th August in Cheltenham. Should you not be told before you leave where this will be, contact Major Lane, Bristol 23346.[103]
>
> Cheltenham. The rendezvous at Cheltenham is the lounge of the Lansdowne Hotel, Lansdowne Rod, Cheltenham, between 1900 and 2000 hours on 24 August.
>
> Student: [redacted]
>
> Description: [redacted]
>
> A room is being booked for you for the night of 24th August in Cheltenham. Should you not be told before you leave where this will be, contact Major Lane, Bristol 23346.[104]

While Fifi was in Reading and Cheltenham, there had been developments in arranging a more convincing cover for her as a journalist. Hale sent Park the following memo.

> I attach a copy of 'Housewife' in which I have been browsing with a view to Fifi joining the staff.
>
> One of the drawbacks is that most of the articles (at any rate in this particular copy) appear to be signed; and therefore Fifi cannot claim them as her own. There are one or two, however, which are unsigned: e.g. 'NEITHER TO CHANGE, NOR FALTER, NOR REPENT', which I am sure any good girl would be glad to claim as her own work.
>
> Would you like to get in touch with Fifi and ask her to study this copy of 'Housewife', together with any copies she can get hold of on the bookstalls, and tell us whether she thought it was humanly possible that she could in actual fact produce printable articles?
>
> I do not think it is absolutely necessary that articles of hers should really be printed, but it would to a certain extent help if they were.
>
> I also attach a copy of 'Farmer's Weekly', but I do not think it is up Fifi's street. [A note underneath stated that he would be seeing Halton next week][105]

The following day, Miller sent the following letter to 9 Nevern Court.

> Miss Collard,
>
> Mr Hale whom you met last week, has sent the attached copy of 'Housewife', which he has been browsing with a view to you joining the staff.
>
> He points out that one of the drawbacks is that most of the articles (at any

rate in this particular copy) appear to be signed, and therefore you could not claim them as your own. There are one or two, however, which are unsigned: e.g. 'neither to change, nor falter, nor repent', which it would seem possible to claim as one's own work.

Would you, on Lionel Hale's recommendation, study this copy of 'Housewife', together with any other copies you can get hold of on the bookstalls, and let me know in due course whether you think it possible that you could in actual fact produce articles such as these, which could be printed.

Hale does not think it absolutely necessary that articles of yours should really be printed, but it would to a certain extent help if they were.

I also attach copies of 'Farmer's Weekly', which Hale has sent me, but he does not consider these really up your street!

Yours sincerely,

Flight Lieutenant.[106]

Fifi's report on her visit to Reading and Cheltenham is missing from her file, but she was able to discuss it, presumably with Miller, as on 26 August there was an unsigned report which reads

Conversation with FIFI.

As Fifi herself has stated in the last paragraph of her Cheltenham report, she is rather worried about the present value of 96 hour exercises for students. From her own point of view she has felt that the last few exercises she has been on have proved pretty unsuccessful, and she has become uneasy at the recurring traits of discontent, boredom and knowledge of what is going to happen to them on 96 hour exercises, noticeable in the different students of different nationalities.

Fifi has obviously been giving these schemes a great deal of thought recently; and her view is that for several reasons, and except for the very young and inexperienced students, 96 hour schemes as they now stand have ceased to be of much value for the students. Her reasons are roughly as follows:-

1. Atmosphere of unreality.

Fifi contends that unless a student has a most fervid imagination (a quality probably not very desirable in students) it is almost impossible for him to believe himself in enemy occupied territory and every policeman, and even every contact of any kind, a potential enemy. There is nothing on these exercises to help him feel anything but safe, and judging by the recent attitude of some students whom she considers most promising and intelligent, they regard the whole scheme as a farce. They find they have a very great deal of time on their hands in an unknown town and several have commented that the whole exercise could be put into a few hours. As most of them seem to be expecting Police interrogation, even that in no way frightens them; and Fifi feels that with nothing to jolt them into using their brains quickly, and no tight corners arising from which to extricate themselves, the point of the exercises is rather lost.

2. Leakages.

The fact that most of these students do know what to expect in 96 hour exercises is evident, and Fifi says it is by no means confined to French students. In this connection [redacted] statements to Fifi, embodied in her Cheltenham report, are interesting, and probably account for other suspected leakages recently.

3. Fifi's provocation.

Fifi has brought up the question of provocation as it now stands, in the last page of her Cheltenham report on [redacted]. Mainly, she feels that the present method is an unfair test of the student; all the cunning and carefully thought out A.P. tricks that might occur in the field, over a period of weeks, have to be packed into three days. During all recent exercises, Fifi has had to show the student that she knows his name early on; with the result that the student is either so pleased to find someone with whom he can discuss 'shop' as belonging to the same organisation, so he feels quite safe in doing so; or he adopts a rather giggle attitude and plays up just to please her, letting her know that he is doing so. This latter method leads Fifi to believe that she may therefore get a rather false impression of the student. These criticisms apply more especially to the older, experienced students, of whom she has had several lately; they know most of the tricks of the trade and are not for a moment taken in by her. Hence the giggly attitude is adopted, which is now occurring with alarming frequency.

Fifi feels that even if pre-knowledge of 96 hours schemes by students does not exist, they have now become too stereotyped to be of much value. At present they contain no element of surprise to test the student's powers, and she feels that a new system containing a series of 'jolts' to the student would be of far more value.

General Comments.

Fifi also elaborated a little on various points of view that had been put to her by students whose intelligence she respects recently; and who have felt they could safely talk shop with her. There is a feeling that their instructors are getting stale, and that they are tending to be slightly more produced instead of treated each on their own merits and capabilities. They tend to regard their instructors as not really caring what happens to them either in the Field or while waiting to go into the Field, and this 'not wanted' feeling is felt more especially by those who have no family or friends in this country.

Fifi has noticed the difference in the enthusiasm for the job in hand shown by those who have ties in this country, and those who are quite independent; it is invariably the former who have the stability and zeal necessary.

During their training, the students feel that there are millions of questions they would like to ask about actual conditions in the field; recently one or two have commented to Fifi that they suspect their instructors are not quite up to date on technical details in the field; and since they have no occasion to talk to, or see, people who have actually returned from the field, there is no-one they can overwhelm with a volley of questions about conditions in the field, such as 'What kind of control [police check] exists in such and such a place, what happens if you walk into a food office, what sort of food restrictions do they have' etc. etc. on these points there seems to be a slight lack of confidence among the students, and she believes that many of them are certain they will never come back; in fact, recently one student told her he was quite sure they never did. Fifi had therefore wondered whether it would not be possible for the

Christine Chilver in her glamorous
ball gown looking like a 1940s film
star. (Courtesy of Paul Tonge)

Christine relaxing in a garden. (Courtesy of Paul Tonge)

Portrait of Christine. (Courtesy of Paul Tonge)

The 'Keep mum – she's not so dumb' campaign was issued in 1942 to caution against careless talk. It was intended to remind soldiers of all ranks that when in the company of a beautiful woman, beauty may conceal brains, and that women could act as spies as well. (Courtesy of the National Archives)

Flying Officer Cyril Miller, security officer at 'Bayswater' (MI5's interrogation centre), who oversaw Fifi's work. (Courtesy of the National Archives)

SPECIAL TRAINING SCHOOLS,
ROOM 98,
HORSE GUARDS,
WHITEHALL, S.W.1.

DECLARATION

I declare that I will never disclose to anyone any information which I have acquired or may at any future time acquire as the result of my connection with this Department, unless such disclosure is necessary for my work for the Department.

In particular I declare that except under the conditions aforementioned, I will in no circumstances give away any information concerning :—

1. The name, alias description, identity, location or duties of any past, present or future member of this Department.

2. The name, alias description, identity, location or duties of any member of the staff, or any persons working with this Department, either as a member of the forces or as a civilian.

3. The nature, methods, objects or subjects of instruction of this Department.

4. The location or name of any establishment of this Department.

5. The past, present or future location, movement or employment, either potential or factual, of myself, any other member of or any person working with this Department.

I declare moreover that I understand that I am personally responsible for any disclosure of such information I may make and that disciplinary proceedings under the Official Secrets Acts 1911 and 1920, the Treachery Act 1940, or the Defence (General) Regulations 1939 may be taken against me if I at any time or in any way contravene the terms of this declaration.

Signature *Christine Collard*

Witness_____

Date *January 31st, 1943*

FIFI

The Official Secrets Act signed by Christine on 31 January 1943. (Courtesy of the National Archives)

Rosemary 'Pat' Say, who was interned in France with Christine, but escaped back to England and worked in SOE's F Section. (Courtesy of the National Archives)

Gunnar Tingulstad, provoked by Fifi in Cardiff on 1 January 1943. (Courtesy of the National Archives)

Tobias Skog, alias Peter Larson, provoked by Fifi in Wolverhampton in December 1942. (Courtesy of the National Archives)

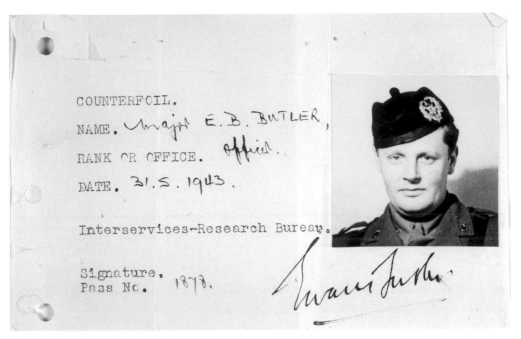

COUNTERFOIL.

NAME. *Major* E.B. BUTLER,

RANK OR OFFICE. *Official*.

DATE. 31.5.1943.

Interservices-Research Bureau.

Signature.
Pass No. 1878.

Euan Butler, alias Captain Beresford, provoked by Fifi in Bristol in June 1943. (Courtesy of the National Archives)

Cecile 'Pearl' Witherington, code-named Pearl Wimsey, whom Fifi attempted to provoke at Birmingham in August 1943. (Courtesy of the National Archives)

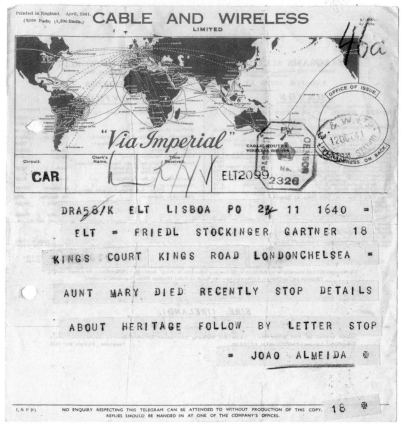

German telegram to Friedl Gartner, deception agent Gelatine, informing her that her cover address in Lisbon was blown. (Courtesy of the National Archives)

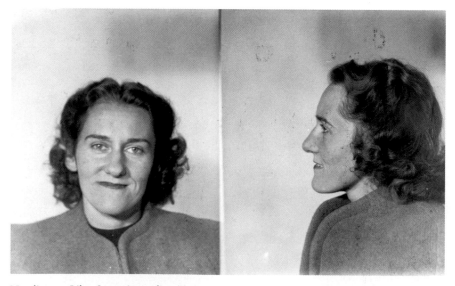

Natalie, or Lily, Sergueiew, alias Treasure, double-crossed the German secret service by sending them misleading messages created by MI5. (Courtesy of the National Archives)

Lily's identity card. (Courtesy of the National Archives)

Lily with Emil Kliemann in Lisbon, March 1944. Kliemann was Lily's case officer for the Abwehr, German military intelligence. MI5 had sent her to reassure him that she was still his agent. (Courtesy of the National Archives)

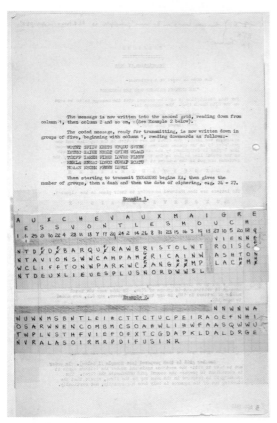

Left: Examples of the code Lily used to encrypt her messages to the Germans. (Courtesy of the National Archives)

Below: One of Elvira Chaudoir's letters with the secret ink exposed. (Courtesy of the National Archives)

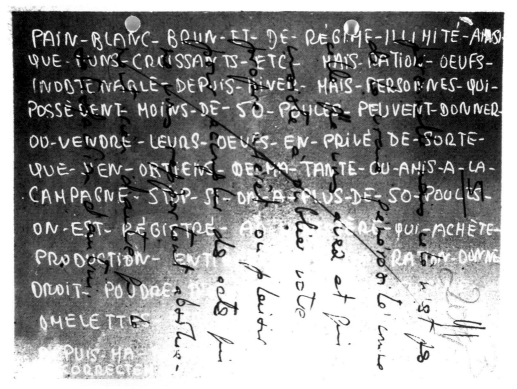

students to have some contact with agents who had returned from the field, to restore their confidence.

At the risk of sounding sentimental, Fifi also commented on the lack of comfort these students have on periods of leave, waiting to go off, etc. who have no family or friends in this country. The obvious answer seems to be to go out and get blind drunk; but again this attitude of 'unwanted, not cared for' by their employers or anybody else crops up. She has gathered that they spent their free time usually in some hotel with lots of other students, and just talk shop; and pick up girls who from our point of view may be extremely undesirable. Fifi has wondered whether it might be possible for these men to stay at any rate for part of their free time, with families who were both security mined and would give them a good home for a short time; and who would be willing to have them.

Finally, Fifi believes that the independent students often suffer greatly from mental loneliness before going into the Field; they feel that there is no-one whom they can discuss with and settle up little matters that they would like to have settled before they go off; these worries, and occasional complexes about some condition in the field, about which they do not know, and cannot find out; or some feature about which they dare not speak, finds some of them in a rather unhappy state of mind.[107]

Whether the SOE took up Christine's suggestion that returning agents should be sent to Beaulieu to talk to the students about what living behind enemy lines was really like and answer any questions they might have is unknown. There are reports that some returned women agents visited Beaulieu, which gave the women students a chance to ask the sort of questions their male instructors would have had no knowledge of.

My research has not found evidence that agents were provided with accommodation with families before their departure. Maybe the issue of security was too great. Instead they were 'looked after' at requisitioned country houses where there was good food, an open bar and attractive, young FANY [First Aid Nursing Yeomanry] officers at hand to 'entertain' them. When they were fully briefed for their mission, FANY drivers would take them in blacked-out cars from London or the training school to Gaynes Hall, about half-an-hour's drive from RAF Tempsford or RAF Harrington, from where many agents were flown out from. The girls would play cards with them, help with jigsaws and crossword puzzles, dine with them, dance and, if needed, take them out for drives, meals or cinema visits to help while away the waiting hours.

It is not known whether this report prompted Colonel Maurice Buckmaster, the head of the French Section, and Vera Atkins, his secretary, who took a personal interest in all the women agents sent into France, to be at the airfield for their departure and to give them a little present like a gold pen, a cigarette lighter or a silver brooch to remind them of SOE.

Fifi's next instructions were to visit Cardiff and Nottingham.

CARDIFF
A room has been booked for you at the Angel Hotel, Cardiff for the nights of 6th and 7th September.

Student: [redacted]

Rendezvous: The Lounge, Ground floor of the Angel between 12.30 and 1.,30 p.m. on Tuesday, 7th September.

R.S.L.O's telephone number Cardiff 8540, Major Grant or Captain Callaghan.

Nottingham.

A room has been booked for you at the Victoria Station Hotel, Nottingham, for the nights of 8th and 9th September.

Student: [redacted]

Method of introduction: On arrival in Nottingham = R.S.L.O. [Major Gerald Glover or Captain In [...] telephone 45664 if you ring before 7.p.m. If [...] Major Glover at Nottingham 45826 or [...] 65252, and they will tell you [...] following day.

They intend to ask the contact, Mr. Colin Campbell to have the student to lunch on Thursday, and to get you to join them there. In case of need, the contact's description is:

Aged about 48; married; medium build; inclined to be stout; fair complexion; about 5'10" tall; wears spectacles; Bank Manager.

[Rest of page redacted][108]

On Denis Ingram's recommendation, Miller sent Fifi's report on this exercise to Major Glover in Nottingham with a request that, as it was the only copy, he should return it. However, for whatever reason, it was missing from her file.[109]

On 3 September, Woolrych sent a memo to Park, who had been promoted to Flight Lieutenant. A copy was forwarded to Lieutenant Colonel Young.

A.P. INTERVENTION

There are several interesting points and important matters of principle involved in Fifi's reports on the 96 hour schemes which took place in Reading and Cheltenham between 23rd and 17th August 1943.

Let us take them singly:-

A. One would dearly like to have a microphone record of her opening gambit with students and the first 10 minutes of their conversation. That would settle the point finally as to whether her approach is 'realistic' or 'fair' to the student.

It is evident that many students, [redacted] amongst them, resist her blandishments and only open out when they get the impression from Fifi that the exercise is over and that they can now talk. in the case of these two students it was conveyed to them by Fifi remarking that they had probably realised that she had really been sent to meet them, and to find out whether they were really going on all right at Reading, and Cheltenham, respectively. Thereupon the students smiled broadly, stated that they realised that the whole thing had been a test, and then proceeded to 'spill the beans'.

The question to determine is whether this really represents adequate security or not. On the one hand every form of exercise in this country must, to a certain extent, be a convention, and the student may justifiably feel that the exercise has been called off by such a remark as this. On the other hand, an A.P. in the field might be shockingly unfair, and use just such a ruse to make her quarry talk. What do you think?

B. At the last Panel A. meeting, it was suggested that the new technique of initial meeting between the A.P. and students should be put into force and that the A.P. should pose as a friend of the R.S.L.O. or whoever is meeting the student, and should be invited to join any drink or meal which the R.S.L.O. is standing to the student. It is important that the A.P. should blow in as a casual visitor. Otherwise the student might hold that the R.S.L.O. had intended to introduce the A.P. and was, therefore, more or less vouching for her bona fides.

I hope that you will be able to lay on this form of approach will all the R.S.L.O.'s as I think you will agree that the present system of meeting is highly artificial and undoubtedly presents undue difficulties to the A.P. in making her approach. On the other hand, the A.P. undoubtedly scores a point when the student says 'Oh, I was expecting to meet a man of such and such a description'. In the field such an opening, even if the A.P. failed to get anything else out of the quarry, would be highly suspicious and possibly damming.

C. [redacted] views on the training and the exercise are very interesting. She says that 'he has the same difficulty as most of the students; he misses a certain realism, as well as practical details, in the general instruction, and is, as regard the 96 hour scheme, unable to work himself into the state of mind of reality'.

It is difficult to see what further realism can be imported into the course here. He could, of course, indent for a firing squad and shoot one student per day with the remark to the others, 'Well, now perhaps you see...' but it would probably not be a popular feature. There can, of course, be no 'realism' where there is no danger. Most students of the non-intellectual type much prefer exercises to lectures. One cannot help thinking that [redacted] was trying to prepare the ground for an unfavourable report, which, in point of fact, he did not get.

D. It is quite obvious that [redacted] knew a great deal too much about the 96 hour scheme before he went, and that his first flat opposite the South Kensington Hotel represented a very poor security effort. Some attempt should surely be made to stop too much contact between students at various stages in their training?

E. Fifi asks 'Does the provocation test really give a true example of potential dangers in the field?' That is a question which she alone can answer. One cannot, as she remarks, reconstitute the real conditions of work in the field where there is no 'enemy' and, therefore, no real danger. All that one can do is to present a 'parallel' situation.

In our view the work of A.P's is fully worthwhile if they test the students thoroughly to see whether they are prepared to 'talk or not'. Nearly every kind of ruse is legitimate provided that they do not disclose information about Beaulieu or mention such a term as 'exercise', which might give the student the idea that they were a kind of umpire. The side-lights gained in students' characters alone are often extremely valuable and very penetratingly reported. I should hate to be deprived of Fifi's reports, which are as entertaining as they are accurate.

F. It is probable that both the A.P's feel that they are not earning their keep if they do not produce a 'kill'. There may even be, for all one knows, mild rivalry between them. From our point of view it cannot be said too emphatically that there is no question of either success or failure. A demonstration that the student is A.P.-proof is just as valuable, if not more than that he is vulnerable or weak.

I think it would be quite a good idea if Fifi came down here, when she is free, to have a talk with the Instructors regarding these exercise. Do you think you can arrange that? We can always put her up for a night or so at the Cottage [The Rings].

Yours ever,[110]

Miller's reply to Woolrych read,

A.P. INTERVENTION

I was very sorry indeed not to have a longer discussion with you on your letter regarding the above subject.

On thinking over the points you raise, I am quite sure that the best solution would be for Fifi to go to Group B. and discuss all her difficulties, with you and the other instructors. Fifi is, in fact, fully employed until the end of next week. If her services are not urgently required during the week beginning 20th September, I will arrange for her to visit you.

Have you considered the possibility of arranging a course for four or five of Colonel MacIver's officers? You may remember that this has been discussed at a Panel A. meeting. Colonel MacIver has asked for a month's notice of any course which you are able to arrange. Will you please let me have your views on this?

Yours sincerely,
Flight Lieutenant[111]

There were no further visits until November 1944. Although no documentation has come to light to confirm it, Training Section appeared to have decided to stop using agent provocateurs. Possible explanations could be that students and instructors had learned of their employment and had prepared for provocation or that some of the women had resorted to sleeping with the men to elicit information or had developed relationships with agents after their course.

By the middle of September, Hale had arranged with the Hulton Press to provide Fifi with cover as one of their staff and sent the following memo to Park.

FIFI

I saw Edward Hulton today and he agreed to give Fifi a nominal job on 'Housewife'. I explained to him that this was for the purpose of providing cover for her movements round the country on certain training exercises.

I told him that I thought it would be better if Fifi could actually produce some articles for 'Housewife', but that I did not expect him to print any such articles irrespective of their merit. Have you asked Fifi whether she thinks she could turn out an article or two, for which I suggest either some garbled version of her experiences in France, or some such story as 'English women in wartime as a Frenchwoman sees them'?

I left it with Edward Hulton that I would arrange a meeting between himself and Fifi. We might have a word on this.[112]

At the bottom of the letter Park had written a note. 'Prue. Please let me know when she returns from Group B.' Fifi must have gone to discuss her difficulties with Woolrych and the instructors. A week later, Hale informed Senter that he had talked to Fifi at Malvern Court and told her that

(1) The proprietor of 'Housewife' was prepared to give her a press card, and to allow her to describe herself on her visiting card as a correspondent of 'Housewife'. And

(2) That I thought it would greatly help her cover if she actually contributed something to 'Housewife'.

I therefore sketched out for Fifi four articles which I thought she could write which might be printable in 'Housewife'. She has certain natural qualms about her ability to write them; but I think I have persuaded her that all she has to do is to set down her views on paper so that I can lick them into shape. I have told her that I would like these articles as soon as possible, since I do not want her enthusiasm for journalism to die down. Would you, therefore, in any dealings you may have with her, consider that it would be a good idea to harry her for these articles. JLL[113]

However, there were other things on her mind. On 17 September, she had received a request from the Foreign Office informing her that Mr. Secretary Eden had asked her to call in connection with her mother. As Fifi was acting undercover as Christine Collard, she asked Park for help. He contacted Senter.

I attach herewith the letter from the Foreign Office which Fifi received on 17.9.43 and handed to me yesterday.

The background necessary for a proper understanding of her mother's situation is as follows:

Mrs. CHILVER is, as you know, a Latvian, but married to an Englishman, who joined his father-in-law's business in Riga, which after his death, was in 1939, pretty flourishing. In that year Fifi left Riga, and in 1940 the Russians occupied the Baltic States, seizing everything and paying no damages. The family business and property was included in this seizure; and so Mrs. Chilver and her other daughter took all they could, and fled to Sweden as refugees. There, as British subjects, and so existing on British Consular aid, they have been ever since. Though they have wanted to come to England, the possibilities have been more or less non-existent, having no friends over here to help them, or cash on which to do it. For the last three years, therefore, the two have lived on a very small Consular subsidy, most of which goes in paying rent for their flat; and the sister, who is very deaf, has a poorly paid job in the Press Reading Room of the British Legation in Stockholm; she speaks perfect Swedish.

The attitude of the Consular Service to these two is, as far as Fifi can gather, at present this:- They do not want to go on paying for them to live at their expense in Sweden if there is any alternative, since they believe that the Chilvers will never be able to pay any part of the expense back. Meanwhile, they have learnt of Fifi's existence and address in London from this sister, and so are doubtless after what she is doing and whether it would not be possible for her to support the mother if she was sent to England. The sister they would like to stay in Stockholm since she earns money and does a useful job. The mother, however, is ill; how ill Fifi has only recently discovered, and it appears she has a very bad heart, cataract in both eyes and anaemia. The Consulate however, had her medically examined by a specialist recently, who said, amongst other things, that an air trip would most certainly kill her. In spite of his report, however, the Consulate are still agitating to get her over here; and if they were to stop paying the subsidy, Mrs. CHILVER would have to apply for a Labour Permit out there in the hope of making a living, which would also probably kill her as she is quite certainly unfit for any kind of work.

Given the choice, Fifi's own view is that the two ought to stay where they are till the end of the war. Her mother is able to receive free expert medical treatment in Sweden; the two are very good friends and would be miserable if separated; and Fifi feels that besides being awkward from a job point of view, it would certainly be impossible to keep three people on £25 a month, should they come here; and if they did they would most certainly want to live with her.

While Fifi is most reluctant to trouble you with her private affairs, the following are the points on which she would very much appreciate your help and advice:-
(1) What is she to say to the F.O. [Foreign Office] with regard to her job? She presumes she will have to leave the Collard part of it out, but she has no CHILVER identity card. She also feels it would be unwise to dally with any journalist story. They are, however, bound to enquire minutely into her financial situation and will want to know why she does not pay income tax etc. (Her family in Sweden have no idea what she is doing, nor how much she earns, though they have been questioned about this by the Consulate out there). They will also presumably want to know why she appears to be exempt from the Services. Can you guide her on these points?
(2) For the last year or so, Fifi, from her very slender Bank balance, has been sending direct from her bank to her mother £25 at such intervals as it can be afforded. She believes that the Consulate are not aware of this, since her mother specially requested that it should not be sent via them but direct to her private address – the reason probably being that should the Consulate get to know, they would immediately cut down their subsidy. Fifi thinks that this £25, irregular though it is, may make all the difference in saving them from acute hardship; as it is, she believes their poverty to be such that they have been unable to buy a single personal garment since they have been there. Fifi is going to find out from her Bank how often they are sending this money, and will let us know; she is able to go on sending it at present, but since she is unable to save at present, before long it will come to an end. Shall she therefore tell the F.O. about this payment or not? While wishing to be perfectly honest, she does not want to think of her family even poorer than at present, by giving this information.
(3) There is this additional background which Fifi thinks the F.O. are acquainted with, but she will repeat it. Having liquidated all her Riga property, her mother has drawn up a complete inventory of their possessions there. The claim has been acknowledged by the Board of Trade here, who have a very complete

dossier on it. Fifi has already been to see them about it, though they are unable to do anything about it until the end of the war and until they know whether the international post-war arrangements between G.B. and Russia will include repayment by Russia of her debts in this respect. The property, according to the B. of T., should realise £50,000; but they are unwilling to take the risk of starting to pay out now; they say, however, that the claim, legally is perfectly valid and in order. This acknowledgement by the Board of Trade must presumably give the Chilver family a bit more standing than they might otherwise have.[114]

The matter was forwarded to the top of SOE. Victor Cannon-Brookes, one of Gubbin's deputies who was working at the Ministry of Economic Warfare in Berkeley Square, was informed of Fifi's predicament. Understanding the politics of the situation, he wrote to A. O. Hutcheon at the Foreign Office.

Miss Chilver is employed by us on special work in connection with the training of our people and I think, if you agree, it would be wiser to conduct our negotiations through me rather than with Miss Chilver direct.

Earning £4 a week. £50,000 claim from USSR.

Hoped that the Consulate would continue to support Mrs. Chilver and her daughter without calling on Miss Chilver for any contribution.[115]

The £50,000 claim was compensation for the loss of her family's property in Riga. Cannon-Brookes's intervention appeared to have resolved the matter and taken the pressure off Fifi enough for her to work on the articles. However, with little experience of being an author, her manuscript was rejected. On 13 October, Hale sent a memo to Senter.

I am sorry to give you trouble, but I thought it was universal knowledge that newspaper and magazine editors, on receipt of MSS typed on both sides of the paper, threw it straight into the waste-paper basket. It would be a pity to spoil Fifi's chances by a gaffe of this sort. Do you think, therefore, this article could be retyped [a] on one side only of the paper, and [b] with somewhat wider margins?

As the coloured maid of Mrs. Dorothy Parker said when giving notice because she had a rooted objection to finding an alligator in the bath – 'I would have mentioned this before only I never thought the matter would come up'.[116]

With all the refugees, foreign soldiers, airmen and sailors in London, it had become a much more cosmopolitan city. Their attempts to develop amorous relationships must not have been lost on Fifi as they provided her with the stimulus to write an article for the 'Housewife', giving women advice on how to better understand what she called 'continental men'.

CONTINENTALS, COMPLIMENTS, CORSAGES AND KISSES ON THE WRIST

'He is really novel' she said 'only, you know, he's – well, just a bit Continental ...'

One often hears that remark nowadays; it's a flashlight on a question which is puzzling many English girls.

England today is Europe's 'Hotel Cosmopolite', and to the English-woman falls the role of hostess. Compared with all the other jobs English girls have tackled since the war, this one certainly isn't 'tough'. In fact, sometimes it seems rather delicate ...

There are quite a few practical problems to start with; 'Where do I get a recipe for a Russian sakuska?' – 'How do I make my hat look French?' – 'What is Norwegian for Good Evening?' There are already a good handful of question marks for the smart girl and skilful hostess.

But there is more to it than experimenting in foreign cooking, or glamorising the dull but ineluctable Make-Do and Mend. Or even learning to mix a good cocktail of 'Skal', 'Sante', and maybe 'Prosit'; you've got to get the knack of people, and we mean Continental people. It is not always easy to find a way of seeing eye to eye with them; there is something about them which makes them seem 'different', strange, puzzling, a little eccentric, – in fact, 'just a bit Continental'.

Now, between you and me, that 'something' lies in their ideas of women. Continentals differ from Englishmen in their way of living, in their customs and manners, in their behaviour towards the other sex, – greatly because they differ in their ideas on women. (Of course, you'll never tell them you found out!)

The average Englishman looks upon a woman primarily as a human individual, whom – if necessary – he specifies as a pal, a colleague, or just a unit. It is only occasionally that he recognises Eve in her disguise as a secretary, driver, Chief Warden, or whatever it may be. But even after she has successfully walked him down the garden path which leads to a Happy End, he will still refer to her as his 'partner', – as if marriage was a business merger or a tennis match!

To a Continental, a woman is, first and foremost, a woman; frail and dangerous, illogical and wise, strange, incalculable, and slightly 'out of this world'. In England it has often been said that Continentals are 'sex-conscious', – remark which is true in a way, but not quite fair, because it leaves out all the earnest thought and delicate poetry which the average Continental dedicates to Woman. The amount of lyrical imagination and scientific study he has spent on the 'feminine enigma' is, indeed, a fine homage to you and me, my little dears, and a great thing to live up to.

Which gives you the main clue to dealing with Continentals. The golden rule is just: remember you are a woman. It sounds simple enough, but in this business-like, utility-minded age, it needs saying again and again: in spite of slacks and battle-bowlers, in spite of factory-shifts and barracks-drill, remember you are a woman. Particularly when you are with a man from the other side of the Channel. He isn't forgetting it.

So make a routine of little things. Keeping your smile fresh and the seams of your stockings straight, for instance. Sitting down with poise. Avoiding lipstick on your teeth and specks of dust on your shoulders. Walking, really walking, instead of striding along with swinging arms. And, by the way, never call a man 'old thing'. The picture of the perfect woman is easily spoilt by a careless, slap-dash little inelegance of that sort; and our Continental friend will notice it straight way. (He's got an uncanny way of seeing almost without looking – perhaps less frequent a talent with men than looking without seeing ...)

Anyway we've got the portrait of the perfect woman, outlines in three strokes of the brush; glamour, grace and gentleness. It won't be long before a Continental comes along and stops and looks and frames it all in a poem. Why, yes, – a poem of good cocktails and 'esprit' ... shaded lights and the right tune ... silly, thrilling little presents ... crazy ramblings in old street ... and the perfume you have always wanted ... and compliments, of course!

Compliments are an art, like eating, talking, drinking, reading, making love, or just doing nothing. Once upon a time there was, no doubt, a Continental of good sense and elegance, who had devoted his life to the study of those indispensible superfluities that make living an art, – and he invented compliments. Unlike many foreign inventions, they are not popular in England, whereas France holds this century's record in compliments, the French 'genre' being not only pretty and witty, but also convincing.

A Frenchman will start with a few lines of a suitable quotation from music or poetry, dedicated to you; then, making it more personal; he will probably resort to comparison and tell you that 'your eyes are like a summer afternoon' or that you have 'a mouth like an orchid'. After that, he may warm up and start being really personal.

Anyway, a French compliment will always be imaginative and subtle, since the object of intelligent flattery is to tell a woman that one is thinking hard about her. For this reason a Frenchman will never state the obvious – 'You have golden hair', or exclaim 'Wizard!' as if you were an aeroplane. And he will avoid platitudinous superlatives such as 'The prettiest girl in the world' as much as hearty under-statements such as 'Not so dusty'. But don't let him get too sophisticated. Not all compliments are roses without thorns, so if he remarks that your way of walking reminds him of Somebody's Minuet in G. flat, – think before thanking!

Another form of compliment is appreciation; a well-bred Continental generally remembers what you wore yesterday or a week ago, and he will never fail to notice a new dress or a different hat. Latins and Slavs are experts on feminine elegance (which is perhaps the reason why many Frenchmen dress badly themselves) and they make excellent technical advisers for a shopping tour. Commenting on your hand-bag or your new hair-style is part of their etiquette; when you get out your lipstick and powder, they will watch the process with the interest of a connoisseur, one eye half-closed, occasionally suggesting: 'A little more on the left cheek...'

One often wonders why so many Englishmen seem embarrassed by the sight of a flap-jack; they look away as if trying not to notice something the dog brought in. It's probably polite, but a little too much of that kind of politeness can make the most promising evening just a long drink of cold water.

Your Saturday night will never be a flop if you have a Continental escort and a good sense of humour, for, whatever you think of the foreign style – and you may not fall for it straight away – you will always find it fun. Besides, a real woman cannot help being thrilled by gallantries.

Gallanterie, the technique of masculine charm, is another great art, as old

– and as full of surprises – as a good bottle of wine. Like any other art, it is made up of certain conventions and of personal inventiveness or genius. The fixed conventions are merely general rules of politeness; the rest is what he really means.

Take handkissing, for instance. An ordinary handkiss is the Continental way of saying 'How do you do' to a woman, but if that very same handkiss lands on your palm, just where your glove buttons up, it means to say a lot more. A kiss on your wrist may get dangerous. Hungarians and Yugoslavs should not, as a rule, be allowed to kiss higher than the elbow, if you wish to avoid duels and suchlike. With Latins, a kiss on the shoulder is noncommittal, whereas fingertip kissing may be allowed only at the end of a perfect Continental evening.

A Continental evening – how many lovable ghosts cling to that word! Cannes or Kitzbuhel, way back in 1935 ... That thrilling green hat from Vienna ... A handkissing Count with a tongue-twisting name ... Salada d'homard at a funny little restaurant in Soho ... And flowers.

Flowers are getting a bit rare, these days, so when you do receive some, the gesture is particularly flattering. Flowers are very important and a man of the world chooses them most carefully; selecting the right shade of face powder for the lady's complexion isn't half so tricky as finding flowers to suit her personality.

It is a pity that the symbolic sense of a bouquet should have been lost in modern times. Originally, one flower was considered just a token or souvenir, three meant a special compliment, two almost a proposal, and a dozen – nothing at all.

But even in our days, there are still many customs attached to flowers. A Frenchman, if he has some 'chic' and a good memory, will send you some on the day of your Saint. A cordage of flowers arriving just in time for your evening date is, perhaps, a bit of a pre-war luxury, but if you receive a big bunch of Lilies of the Valley, and it happens to be the First of May, don't get alarmed and mistake it for a wedding bouquet or something; it is only a traditional spring greeting from a French friend. Paris on May-Day each year is a mass of little white flowers; everybody wears them and sends some to all his friends.

No portrait of a Continental is complete without a mention of the Menu and the Wine-card; in the science of gastronomy our friend will outshine any man in the world. Watching him plan a meal or hearing him talk about wine is sheer poetry. At least, it used to be ... And while we are on the subject of Dinner for Two, just a word of warning; if he lets you do all the choosing and then just orders exactly the same, it means that Monsieur has plans. He will most likely suggest walking home afterwards, – a jolting taxi is so unromantic! – and you might spend quite some time saying Good Night ... If you don't agree, however, you'd better be firm about it; there is not a man in the world who will not take 'No' for 'Perhaps', if it comes from a woman. Except possibly a Pole, who tends to take it to mean 'Yes'.[117]

In the middle of October, Hale informed Senter that he'd taken Fifi to see Edward Hulton, the publisher, who was pleased with the article and said he would ask *Housewife* to publish it. He arranged a press card for her and gave her permission to add *Housewife* on her visiting card. 'While I am away I suggest D/Q.10 [one of Hale's staff] might have any further dealings with Hulton. I think it would be well if you keep Fifi up to the mark about articles; even if they are not published, it shows willing if she submits them.'[118]

Other submissions were reported as sent to Hulton Press throughout November and December, but copies were not found in her file. An examination of the late-1943 and early-1944 copies of the *Housewife* at the British Library revealed none by Christine Collard, but there were a few articles without any author attribution. Whether she had been given time off to write articles or Woolrych wanted her to have a rest from the exercises is unknown as there is a significant gap in her file until March 1944. If pages had been redacted, there was no official stamp confirming it.

Given her connections with Miller, it is possible that she was helping him in the Bayswater Interrogation Centre, known as BSS. This had been set up on 15 January 1943 to interrogate agents before they left and test the adequacy of their cover stories. However, this work had to be discontinued to focus on interrogating agents once they returned.

Following the Abwehr successfully penetrating the Belgian and Dutch Resistance and arresting large numbers of agents in late 1942 and early 1943, some wireless operators had been 'turned' and were sending German-inspired messages to London. There were also cases of Germans posing as escaping refugees, being sent down the escape lines in an attempt to destroy them. Consequently, MI5 had to consider all escape lines as penetrated and the Security Section was ordered to interrogate all returning agents at Bayswater, especially those who had escaped German captivity.

Fifi's knowledge of German would have been particularly helpful in checking their individual security, their bona fides and that of their networks. Returned agents had to write a report on their activities, which might generate queries from their interrogators. The intelligence gathered was then passed on not only to the Country Sections but also to the supply and camouflage sections of the countries concerned. Later, the BSS Section investigated all allegations of enemy penetration and double agents, kept up to date with the activities of overseas circuits and advised Country Section heads on penetration and double agents, as well as liaising with MI5 and Section V, SIS's Counter-Espionage Section. By the end of June 1945, they had interrogated 454 agents.[119]

It is very likely that Fifi got to know one of her lifelong friends while visiting Bayswater. Jean Alexander, known as Alex, studied journalism at King's College, London, worked as a private secretary, joined the WAAF in 1939 and worked in the Air Ministry. She was in a relationship with another SOE officer, Squadron Leader Felgate. In October 1943, when she was twenty-seven, she was recruited by Boyle, transferred to the Security Section and promoted to Squadron Officer with the symbol D/CE.LI, later changed to BSS/L. As an intelligence officer, she edited reports and provided questionnaires for interrogations, eventually becoming head of Bayswater's Intelligence Sub-Section.[120]

She and Fifi clearly had a lot in common; a note in her personnel file described her as 'well above the average in intelligence, practical, thorough and sensible. In character she is trustworthy, reliable, unassuming but self-confident. She was obviously keen, took a great interest in the instruction and worked very hard. She is tactful, discreet, has a sense of humour and is a good mixer. She seems admirably qualified for the work she is to do and she has a very good understanding of the principles involved and good grasp of detail.'[121] She spoke French fluently, knew a little German and Italian, had travelled in France, Italy and Egypt and her hobbies were writing and literature. Maybe she had helped Fifi with her *Housewife* articles.

As well as the Security Section using women for provocation purposes, Woolrych employed some of his female staff at Beaulieu. Noreen Riols was a seventeen-year-old in 1941, studying at the French Lycée in London when she was called up. Her French attracted her to the attention of Buckmaster, who got her work in F Section, organising parachute drops into France and training students to deliver secret messages. To avoid her mother being concerned, she told her that she was working in the Ministry of Agriculture and Fisheries.

In February 1944, she was transferred to Beaulieu, where officially she was a 'secretary' but unofficially she worked as an agent provocateur with two other women, Jean and Dorothy. Jean was a South African who had followed her fiancé to Britain, but he had enlisted in the army and was fighting in the Western Desert. Dorothy was described as 'a very pleasant woman, very easy to live with, but was also something of a mystery. However, we didn't ask questions. It had become a way of life.'[122]

Riols admitted that they were used as decoys and that, for obvious reasons, they never met or had contact with the students before they met them on their schemes. Jean went to Southampton and Riols went to Bournemouth.

> Like the other occupants of the block of flats at Orchard Court, the inhabitants of both these large coastal towns hadn't the remotest idea, I don't think they even suspected, what was going on under their very noses.
>
> A student would be let loose in Bournemouth and told that a young girl wearing a headscarf and a dirty mac and carrying a shopping bag would probably be walking along the sea front opposite the pier pavilion at a given time. He was told to detect her and, once he had found her, to follow her and discover where she was going and whom she might be meeting, without her suspecting anything. This also worked in reverse when they were taught how to detect if someone was shadowing them and then to shake them off without any suspicions being aroused.[123]

Riols's autobiography details numerous experiences she had in this work, including what she described as

> the 'James Bond' exercise ... [which] took place in hotels, without anyone suspecting the drama being enacted before their very eyes.
>
> There were two very pleasant hotels in Bournemouth, the Royal Bath and the Lincoln. I preferred to operate at the Royal Bath, because adjoining the dining room was a large terrace overlooking the sea which, on a warm moonlit

evening, lent itself to a very romantic scenario, making my task much easier. The Lincoln unfortunately didn't possess such a commodity. Very often, on a student's last night of the course before being returned to his section in London, where his fate would be decided, his conducting officer would invite him out for dinner to celebrate. The conducting officers sat in on many of the classes and watched the students closely, studying their different reactions to situations, their relationship with other students, whether they were level-headed, practical, gossips, volatile or knew how to 'hold their drink' or 'keep their cool'. Every student wasn't favoured with an invitation to dinner so I can only think that the officers chose those they suspected might talk.

Beforehand a little one-act play was worked out between the officer and myself. When he and the future agent were in the hotel lounge having a drink before dinner I would stroll in, and the officer would exclaim in surprise, 'Noreen, how lovely to see you. What are you doing in Bournemouth? Come and have a drink. Meet my friend.' Or he might say to the agent when they linked up, 'An extraordinary thing happened this afternoon. I bumped into a girl I hadn't seen since the beginning of the war. I was at school with her brother.' My little brother was still at school at the time, so that was stretching it a bit far. But the bod wasn't to know that. 'She's staying in Bournemouth for a few days, and I've asked her to join us for a drink. You don't mind do you?'

If the future agent were a Brit he usually minded very much. He'd been looking forward to a boozy evening with the boys, and here was this wretched woman coming to put a damper on things. But the foreigners were often very pleased, since they didn't have that many opportunities to meet English girls. When the second glass of sherry arrived the officer, as planned, would ask me to join them for dinner, and after a few blushing protestations, I would gracefully accept his invitation. But when it was time to put down our glasses and stroll across to the dining room, there would be a telephone call for the officer. He would return, apologising profusely: something had happened which had to be dealt with immediately. 'But you two go ahead and start dinner. I'll join you as soon as I can.' Of course, he never did, or only when the meal was over. Then it was up to me. This is where the Royal Bath's superior facilities came into play. If it was a warm, moonlit night, and I could edge my victim onto the terrace overlooking the sea, there was more of a chance that he would relax, possibly become sentimental ... and talk.[124]

Another permutation of the honeytrap was for the officer to return from the phone call, drop a room key and money on the table, tell the diners to enjoy themselves and he would see them the following day. In Clare Mulley's article in the *Telegraph* about Britain's forgotten female spies, she stated that this story has often been parodied in Bond films, with the beautiful women who set out to entrap their male target quickly finding themselves seduced. 'But women like Chilver and Riols were made of sterner stuff.'[125]

Riols did not mention this permutation, but detailed the reactions of some of the students exposed to the trap. One young Danish student, who she described as 'a gorgeous blond Adonis', did not need much persuasion to follow her out onto the terrace.

I think he was rather attracted to me. At the time I weighed twelve kilos less, didn't have white hair and didn't need glasses to read the small print! Once propped against the balustrade, gazing at the sea, he became sentimental. They often did. It was to be expected. On a glorious moonlit evening, with the silver-tinted sea lapping gently against the shore below, the scene was set for it. He asked me whether we could spend the following Sunday together, and I accepted his invitation knowing full well that there was not the slightest chance of my being able to keep my promise. But his invitation gave me my lead, my chance to probe further, enquire about his next move, his activities, his final destination ... and his intentions. In the end he talked, he told me what he was doing and where he was going.[126]

When Woolrych, interviewed those who had 'talked', she would walk into the room and they would be asked if they recognised her. Most took it well, she reported, shrugging their shoulders and realising that they had been fools and had made a stupid mistake. They recognised that they had jeopardised their chances of being sent on a mission for which they had undergone many months of arduous training. The young Danish student who fell for her trap called her a bitch when he saw her with Woolrych.

No woman likes to be called a bitch. I didn't. And I was upset. But it was then that I discovered Woolybag's compassionate side beneath his stern exterior. 'It's no good you upsetting yourself,' he said kindly to me afterwards. 'If he can't resist talking to a pretty face over here, he most certainly won't once he's over there. And it won't be only his life he'll be risking, but the lives of many others as well.' I knew he was right, but I couldn't help feeling sorry for the poor young man. He had survived six months strenuous training, eight or nine months if he were destined to be a radio operator, learning escape tactics, how to rid himself of handcuffs, react under torture and during interrogation, handle explosives, make bombs, live off the land, shoot at a moving target. And Beaulieu was far from being a holiday camp. This young Dane had survived all that yet, because of one stupid slip on a moonlit evening, he might not be allowed to carry out his mission, that mission he had worked so hard to achieve.[127]

Riols admitted that her life with SOE was based on deception, on telling lies and acting on others' lies. She lied to the students, to her mother, her friends: everyone she met outside the organisation. Because she had signed the Official Secrets act, 'it was inevitable. I was unable to tell them the truth, reveal what I was doing.'[128] Simpson described Fifi as one of the expert liars in the world. That attribute must have partly been what attracted her to the Security Section where she was to perfect it throughout the war.

When the National Archives opened previously classified SOE files in 2000, Riols reported being often asked by the media if she knew Fifi. When she told them she didn't, some reporters must have read Foot's book, as they told her that she was a very attractive woman who was used by SOE to find out whether prospective agents talked in their sleep. She told them, 'What nonsense. That's just a figment of someone's over active imagination. There was no such person as Fifi.'[129] She wondered afterwards whether 'Fifi' might have been Dorothy, who was older than her and Jean, and never accompanied them on their trips to Bournemouth and Southampton.

> She often disappeared to London for a few days. 'Dorothy', I remember asking her when she returned from one of her jaunts, 'Do you stay in your flat when you go up to London?'
>
> 'No', she replied, 'Usually in hotels.'
>
> 'Whatever for', I pursued in my ignorance. Or was it ignorance? Probably just pig-headedness, not knowing when enough is enough.
>
> She smiled enigmatically and replied vaguely, 'Oh, I do a bit of sleep walking.' And left it at that. I didn't understand. But something prompted me not to pursue the matter further.
>
> But, intrigued by the media's persistent questioning, I began to wonder what Dorothy had been doing on her 'sleep-walking' jaunts to London. She was certainly not the kind of woman anyone could ever mistake for a 'tart': rather the opposite. But she knew a great many agents: their photographs in silver frames, with touching dedications to her, jostled for place on her dressing table. And I couldn't help wondering whether Fifi had existed after all, and wasn't merely the product of someone's fertile imagination.[130]

The BBC-documentary researchers never managed to track Dorothy down. Noreen thought she had emigrated to South Africa, but thought it just as well they never located her as it would have caused friction if the wives of the agents had been watching the programme with them.

Riols thought that Woolrych's secretary, Dorothy Wicken, was also engaged as an agent provocateur, but there was no evidence in her personnel file to confirm that she was engaged in such work.[131]

On 2 March 1944, Tom Wells, the head of Bayswater, symbol BSS/A, contacted Park, telling him that

> we had the pleasure of having Fifi here yesterday afternoon, and I understand from her that her visit here enabled her to complete what she wanted to do. I accordingly, at her request, return the papers forthwith. TAW[132]

The next document begins with a redacted paragraph which may have detailed the task or tasks she was involved with. Who the author was and the exact date is unknown, but it appears that, having been employed for almost two years, Fifi had the confidence to query the possibility of being given a pay increase.

> I find it very difficult to estimate what Fifi's work is worth because she undoubtedly plays a very valuable part in the 96-Hour Schemes, and I doubt very much whether we should find anyone else who would do the job so well. At the same time, I feel that the salary which she is getting is sufficiently generous that she could not earn so much elsewhere, I therefore, do not recommend any increase.
>
> There is another consideration which we must bear in mind. That is, that

sooner or later we shall stop running schemes for Continental students and Fifi's job will then have finished. We shall, presumably, accept some responsibility for assisting her to find another job. [A note in the margin read 'Doubt it'.] The higher her salary is at that time the more difficult this task will be.

I have written somewhat fully in the hope that you will have a word with me and let me know what line to take next time Fifi raises the question, as raise it undoubtedly she will.[133]

Park wrote a note underneath thanking the sender and adding that he thought that she was being quite adequately paid and should be told that there was no prospect of an increase. 'You can tell her I am no longer concerned but hope to see her sometime personally.'[134]

Fifi must have had concerns about her health, and spoke to the Security Section about it; in the middle of August, Senter wrote to Dr Isaac Jones, 4 Queen Anne Street, W.1.

I understand that Capt. Betts has asked for you to see Miss Christine Collard and that you have given her an appointment for 4 p.m. on Monday next, 24th August.

Miss Collard has worked for us as an 'agent' in this country for the past two years and has done some excellent work in various lovely and unlovely provincial towns, in reporting on students during their training exercises. The work has involved, especially with travelling conditions, a fair amount of strain and the first question that arises is whether she is in need of some rest. The second question is that I believe she had some health complication over a year ago and I do not know whether that has been satisfactorily cleared up.

[Paragraph redacted.]

You are, of course, at liberty to show this letter to Miss Collard if you desire to do so and it may be useful to you to know that I personally engaged her originally and she knows me my name; we have met on several occasions since she started this work.[135]

The details of her medical condition have not come to light, but the suggestion is that she was exhausted and needed rest. However, as there were no reports on students' schemes since the previous September, one wonders what exactly she had been doing. The doctor agreed that she needed rest, so Senter gave her one month's sick leave on full pay, with the matter to be looked at again at the end of the month in view of the doctor's report.[136]

With the Allies' success in forcing a German retreat from France, they invaded Belgium to help push them out of the Low Countries. Consequently, there was a reduced demand for SOE agents to be sent into the field. Not wanting to lose Fifi's skills and knowledge of the Security Section, plans were put in place to find her alternative employment.

While she was on sick leave during October, she had an interview with Boyle, in which she asked to be sent to France. Worried that she might be recognised, he refused. However, he discussed the possibility of her working for MI5 with Max Knight. Forty-three-year-old Knight, a former naval officer, was reported to have been recruited by both SIS and MI5. Desmond Morton, the head of SIS, engaged him as his 'agent runner' and Sir George Makgill, Vernon Kell's agent runner for MI5, requested his services. At their behest, he joined the British Fascist Party, rising to become its Director of Intelligence, and successfully infiltrated six fascists into the British Communist Party. He had no qualms about using women as agents, and in 1932 he infiltrated twenty-two-year-old Olga Gray into the Friends of the Soviet Union, who became secretary and reported lover of Harry Pollitt, the secretary general of the Communist Party of Great Britain. She found evidence showing that they were trying to pass blueprints of secret naval plans of anti-submarine bombs and detonators to officials in the Russian Embassy. In what became known as the Woolwich Arsenal case, the conspirators were caught and jailed in 1938.[137]

In 1938, Knight was given his own department of counter-subversion, known as B5(b), and the symbol M. He handpicked a team, known as 'Knight's Black Agents', and used honeytraps to break into Soviet and Nazi spy rings, details of which can be read in the following chapter. Fifi's skills and experience in tempting unsuspecting individuals to disclose information by offering them help, sympathy and, according to some sources, sexual favours, must have aroused his interest in recruiting her.[138]

A letter in Fifi's file, dated 4 November and thought to have been written by Boyle, stated,

> I interviewed FIFI last week and had a talk about her with Max Knight on the 1st November.
>
> We both take the view that she is a woman of quite outstanding capacity and that if we were 'Head of the Secret Service' we should see to it that she got some long-term training to equip her as a high grade agent. She pressed several times to be allowed to go to France as an agent but I took the view that she was too well-known there for the risk to be taken. You may remember she was responsible for rescuing Flight Lieutenant Simpson and escorting him home.
>
> She has had her sick leave, in agreement with D/FIN, on full pay, but I think the agreed period must have come to an end.
>
> I feel that (a) she will be of great value eventually, probably in connection with Germany and (b) that the plans of the authorities thus concerned are too chaotic to encourage much hope that she should be placed now.
>
> I think it would be a pity if we lost her and her financial position is that our Russian allies have expropriated her family property in Riga and she is dependent on what we pay her.
>
> Partly with a view to giving her an extra accomplishment that may be useful to the state and partly to keep her available, I suggest for your consideration that she might be trained as a W/T operator. If you agree with the above, perhaps D/CE.G could see D/FIN and D/SIGS on your behalf.
>
> Note: I think D/CE.G ought to attend to her papers now; she is English but for the purpose of the work she did for us, she was given imitation French identity.[139]

By the middle of November, Miller had got the tentative agreement from

Boyle and the Finance Section for her to receive additional training, but it would entail changing her identity back from the Frenchwoman Christine Collard to the Englishwoman Christine Chilver and making arrangements with Forty at the Training Section.

> I should be grateful if you would arrange for Miss Christine COLLARD to attend a W/T course at the W/T Training School. She will be available in about three weeks' time.
>
> She should be regarded as a D/CE Section student. Special arrangements are made for her pay and I would be grateful if any questions arising on that subject could be referred to me. She is not a F.A.N.Y. and I do not think it would be practicable for her to join the F.A.N.Y. for the purpose of this course.
>
> I should be pleased to supply further information which you may require about this lady.[140]

It was agreed that she should attend the three-month wireless telegraphy course at Grendon Hall (STS 53a), Grendon Underwood, near Aylesbury, Buckinghamshire, on the same rate of pay, £25 a month.

Having finished her sick leave, to occupy her before the course started, she was given instructions to go on two more exercises in Chester and Manchester. On her return she submitted handwritten reports, which show how much her character analysis had developed over two years.

> Report on Jack Benny (Chester, 28 November, 1944)
>
> Benny swallowed the story of a 'helpful journalist' in one gulp. When I approached him and asked whether he was Mr. Benny, his reaction suggested rather a kind of eager friendliness than surprise or suspicion. My non-committal questions about 'how he was getting on' and such like met with no critical reticence or wary standing; after hardly a few moments' shyness, Benny let himself be drawn out and with proving confidence, settled down to telling his tale.
>
> We first discussed his Exercise, Benny giving me a neat outline of his brief, Contact, Innocent letter and Playfair letter (both with explanations of what he had put down and how), Boites aux postes (dead letter boxes), Billets, Target (North Wales Cheshire Power Station.) He also told me what the original arrangements and conventions for our R.V. (rendezvous) had been and gave me the description of the man he had been expected to meet; his only reaction to the unexpected turn the R.V. had taken seemed to be mild surprise and innocent wonder. In order to justify our meeting, I promised to introduce him on the following day to some local engineer who would be able to give him information about, or an introduction to, the N.W.Ch. Power Station. – I was, at this point, beginning to think Benny somewhat unalert and incompetent and was, therefore, very surprised when he showed unexpected security-mindedness on some smaller items in his story; he was, for instance, unwilling to reveal the name of his Contact (Although he had given me various other bits of information about the man); and my question concerning the whereabouts of Benny's lodgings met with an amiable 'Never mind that'. – From his apparent

contradiction a picture of the student's mind began to shape. I questioned him further during dinner and after that we talked until 11 p.m.

[Several paragraphs redacted.]

The opinion I had formed of Benny by the end of our interview is, on the whole, favourable and permits me to attach relatively little importance to his blunder in this test. – In character he seems sound and rigorous, toughened by good discipline and hard work, – an independent, enterprising sort with clear aims and straightforward ways, as well as considerable self-assurance. ('Happiness is a matter of will-power' – May he never grow old!) Altogether rather what magazines, I believe, describe as 'The American Boy type'. – His mind seems active, clear, sober and safely on the practical side, a mind to deal with facts and with things rather than with fancies and abstractions. His method of thinking, as far as I was able to acquaint myself with it, appeared to consist mainly by cheerful simplification and of resolute, constructive tackling of the useful; ideas, people, situations are analysed as far as they come to pieces properly, like motorcars; the problematic and the irrational are bulldozed away instinctively. A very good and sound kind of mind, on the whole, and definitely showing possibilities in this type of work, – Somewhat unguarded, however, against subtle difficulties and concealed dangers. Which might well be the explanation of Benny's reaction to the A.P. test; he was, probably, only concerned with carrying out his instructions, briskly and intelligently and 'making a success of' his scheme as a whole; by reason of his mentality, he could hardly have been expected to dawdle over finicky complexities, to imagine danger, suspiciously, where it was not directly obvious, or to spend much dubitative speculation on uncertainties. Unless I am much mistaken in this analysis, certain points to be emphasised in Benny's final briefing would appear obvious. –

Report on Denis Pritchard (Manchester, 29 November, 1944)

Pritchard was a stunning contrast to Benny. If Benny had immediately reacted with friendliness and gullibility, Pritchard's attitude was, from the start, all suspicion and alertness. My introduction, explanations and sympathetic questions were met with utmost reserve, slightly antagonistic wariness, feigned suspicion – (unfortunately accompanied by giggles) and last but not least, a number of questions, noncommittal and intelligent: who had sent me; how did I recognise him as the Pritchard I was looking out for; etc. After quietly letting me finish my tale, the student took the earliest possible opportunity of bringing out his cover story; he said he was an actor, in search of a job in Manchester, and pointed out that he was a British subject but had lived in the States for a number of years, as well as in France and Spain. The problem created by the misfit of our respective cover stories the student did not try to solve, beyond assuring me repeatedly that the whole matter must be based on a misunderstanding, which he did not appear very keen to investigate. Nevertheless, he let himself be led into a discussion of actors and audiences, which ended with an invitation to dinner and several hours of conversation, all non-business and most of it woolly, took us wandering from Surrealism to Faustus. The student finally appearing to sink into a very under-graduate hand-holding mood, I terminated the [redacted].

Our random nibbling at a variety of heterogeneous subjects was not of any particular help in getting a clear impression of the student's mind and personality. I did make out that Pritchard has a thinking, observant, imaginative mind and considerable sensitivity; he is a good listener and has the habit of watching people and wondering about them. I got the impression that his cover story was mostly fictitious; his general knowledge of the theatre appeared, on a number of points, surprisingly scanty, although he probably has some experience in amateur acting. What his actual milieu or his intellectual level is, I was unable to find out; a good, though motley background of reading; a lot of intelligent, original ideas produced by muddled thinking; a curious mixture of understanding and immaturity; and a number of other such apparent contradictions made it difficult to draw any conclusions about Pritchard's mind since these things pointed neither to a practical working person, nor to an intellectual with a trained mind. – As a person, certainly an individualist; possibly neither very manageable nor easy to place in a job, but somehow promising for this kind of work; the type of man one would expect surprises of in the field. Beyond this rather unsatisfactory guess I am unable to give any opinion on Pritchard's character, technical abilities, or suitability for the job. Which, in a way, is a credit to him, since it proves his case in sticking to his cover story, as well as suggesting the (very advantageous) undefinable, 'camouflage' quality of his personality.[141]

The identities of Jack Benny and Denis Pritchard remain unknown. Documents in her file show that she was sent on another excursion from 13 to 15 December, but there were no details included. How she spent her third Christmas in England is unknown. One imagines that she had built up a circle of friends within the Security Section, but quite possibly she had got to know others in SOE or locals she had met during her free time. There was no indication that she was in a relationship with anyone. Understandably, her reports and correspondence only dealt with her professional life.

One imagines that when Fifi was informed that she had been accepted onto the wireless telegraphy course, she would have been very pleased. However, when she learnt that it started on New Year's Eve, she had the confidence to discuss with Miller and/or Willoughby the possibility of delaying it. Celebrating with friends must have been a much more attractive option that starting a course with people you've never met.

On 18 December, D/CE.P, possibly Prue Willoughby, wrote to Major Alan Burnes, symbol MT/3, at the Training Section and sent a copy to Sigs.O (Grendon Hall).

Further to D/CE.G's telephone conversation with you on Saturday morning regarding the course for Miss COLLARD, I have seen the lady who states that she will be unable to commence the course starting Sunday, 31 December, but she will be ready by the following Sunday, the 7th January, and I should be grateful if you would arrange accordingly .

I asked her whether she had any previous knowledge of wireless work, Morse code, etc., and she informed me that she had some time ago done a certain amount of wireless transmission and was also familiar with the Morse alphabet but added that she was somewhat rusty.

D/CE.G has previously been in touch with Sigs.O who knows the purpose of the intended course and will accordingly be able to advise you regarding her syllabus.[142]

The excuse Burnes used to explain the delay was that 'she was required in connection with a number of schemes that unexpectedly arose during September'.[143] Whether she really had done any wireless transmission work before was not indicated in her file. Maybe, as a skilled liar, she mentioned it to increase the chances of her being accepted on the course. Two days after Christmas, Burnes was sent another request.

> I should be grateful if you would let me have details regarding the course which Miss COLLARD is to attend commencing on Sunday, the 7th January in order that I may advise her as soon as possible the numerous details which she will be required to know, such as the addresses to be given to her friends and relatives.[144]

Christine was provided with the address and told to take no other effects than her own personal garments, to catch the train leaving Marylebone for Calvert at 11.20 a.m. on 31 December and that she would be met on arrival at Calvert station.

Until June 1943, Grendon Hall had been used by MI6 as a transmitting and listening station, but SOE took it over as a fourth receiving station to handle agents' traffic. It was also being used by the OSS to train wireless operators who were to be sent into Germany.

In the middle of January 1945, Knight contacted Senter telling him that he wanted to meet Christine at 'the House' for a chat. This was one of SIS's safe houses in Camberley, near Reading. Senter told him to contact her at Thame Park (STS 52), Thame, near Oxford. This was an unexpected mistake as Thame Park was where SOE's wireless operators were sent on a nine-month training course, but the Security Section had arranged an alternative three months' tuition for her at Grendon Hall. Consequently, Knight's invitation went unanswered.

When Senter realised the mistake, he visited her to discuss Knight's wish to meet her in person and in early February, contacted him to explain.

> [Redacted] She says it is not very easy to speak on the telephone from there with privacy.
>
> She probably could get away about lunch time on a Saturday, and make her way to Reading. It is difficult to be sure of getting into Aylesbury, apparently, but she could travel from a small station called Calvert.
>
> She is very anxious to accept your invitation, but also anxious (and I think rightly) not to appear to claim special privileges while she is a student there.[145]

As well as receiving Knight's invitation to meet, she would have been pleased to receive her February salary from Miller, which had been increased to £30 a month with 10s in expenses for the December exercises, which had been returned from her old address. His final paragraph read, 'I hope you are not finding things too wearisome and that they're not working you too hard.'[146]

Her reply, her only correspondence from Grendon Hall, was a letter to the Finance Section thanking them for forwarding her salary and the 10*s* note owed her for her December expenses. She reported having forgotten about it, adding, 'Punching a key is, perhaps, not an occupation designed to sharpen one's mental faculties.'[147]

In the meantime, Boyle contacted D/CE.P (Willoughby), telling her that

> I took the opportunity in passing today, of mentioning to AD/X.1 [Captain A.C. Dawson] that I adhered to the view that FIFI was a candidate for long-term employment, especially in the C.I. [Counter Intelligence] field, and that no doubt the opportunity would arise.
>
> I told him that she was being trained in W/T and that in my view this should not be interrupted unless he was in very urgent need of someone with her qualifications to work, say, in Berne or Stockholm.
>
> I advised that she would be unsuitable and wasted in a short-term 'shock' role. [The rest of the correspondence was redacted.][148]

Although Knight was keen to meet Christine, he was unable to fit her into his weekend schedule. Consequently, Senter arranged with Major Byrne, the officer in charge of Christine at Grendon Hall, to allow her to spend a day and a night in London for a meeting, the excuse needed for her to meet Knight at what he called 'the House', near Reading. This was Llanfoist, a secluded country house near Camberley, about a fifteen-mile drive from Reading station. This was his weekend retreat where he escaped the stresses of London, a safe house for agents and a place where fellow MI5 officers, journalists and friends could be entertained overnight and work discussed.[149]

When she eventually met up with Knight at the end of February, they had a long talk, after which he wrote to Senter.

> I found her in what I can only describe as a rather unsettled state of mind; but I think this must be primarily due to her somewhat difficult situation at the establishment where she now resides. For instance, her officers and colleagues down there seem to sense that she does not 'fit in' with their picture, and this gives rise to a certain amount of comment.
>
> Further, she is always being asked questions which are natural ones, but to which she cannot easily give the answer: such questions as –
>
> (a) What type of set are you going to take with you?
> (b) What weapons are you going to take with you?
> (c) What code are you going to use?
>
> As none of these considerations really affects her at the moment, it is easy to understand that she feels a little diffident about things.
>
> With regard to her future, she tells me that she is definitely prepared to undertake some long-term work (presumably under S.I.S.) either in Germany or in some neutral country.

She adds, however, that she would be willing to undertake some short-term mission – about which I believe you have already spoken to her – in the interim, if such was considered really useful and necessary. I gather that she has already acquainted you with most of this.

I somehow feel that the next most useful thing to do would be for you to ascertain from S.I.S. whether they have indeed any post-war plan in which there is a definite niche for Fifi. I feel that if we do not ascertain this fairly soon, there is a danger of her interest waning, or at the best what is still a very objective attitude becoming a purely subjective one.

I really think that any approach to S.I.S. would be much better carried out by yourself, than by me, as at the moment, my lines of communication appear to be a little thin.

I do not know whether the above is of the slightest use to you; in fact, I have an uneasy feeling that it is rather feeble; but it does represent a précis of some one-and-a-half-hours' conversation.

Yours ever,

Max.[150]

A note in the margin suggested the letter be shown to Weinzierl CSOIL. Maybe Weinzierl was involved in the post-war plans for Germany. Senter's reply a few days later thanked Knight for his letter about his attempts to find Christine further employment.

As regards the first part of the letter, she did discuss these points with me, and frankly, I think she is making rather too much of them, as she has a simple answer, namely: 'I believe I am under consideration for a possible job in Germany, but no details have been fixed, and I therefore don't know the answers to any of these questions.'

As regards her long-term future, I fully appreciated that the uncertainty inherent in the present phase must be unsettling to her in a number of ways, but at the same time, I feel a trifle disappointed that she has not shown more general faith in the future; for example, she talks of the 'impossibility' of obtaining books in German to revive her knowledge of that language. That, I think you will agree, is an unnecessarily defeatist attitude.

As regards her long-term future, I continue to believe that that is a matter that should be taken seriously, as I feel that she could be a very useful long-term asset. I feel rather, and I think she does, that her role ought to be C.I. or C.E. [Counter Intelligence or Counter Espionage] rather than an Intelligence role.

You may not have heard that [Lieutenant Colonel Raymund] Maunsell's future has at last been settled, and he is to be head of the Counter Intelligence Bureau under the Central Commission for Germany, i.e, a long-term appointment. I feel that he is an officer who would appreciate the value of FIFI's services at the proper time, which may not be for some time ahead, and that our problem is to keep her usefully employed in keeping her on the books as long as necessary, especially if her destined role is thought to be along these lines.

It would help me to know from you whether you agree with my distinction between C.I. and I. work for her.

I am most grateful for your letter, and for the trouble you have taken, and if you agree with the Maunsell point which is new, I think I ought to make an effort to see her again soon, and possibly to cast a fly over Maunsell at an early opportunity.

Yours ever.[151]

Having successfully used Olga Gray and Joan Miller, his secretary, to compromise enemy agents, his discussions with Christine and the imminent victory over Hitler's Nazi regime may well have prompted him to write a confidential memo in April 1945 on MI5's successes during the war. Entitled 'On the Employment of Women as Agents', it challenged the common reluctance to recruit women in terms that today might be described as misogynistic.

... there is a very longstanding and ill-founded prejudice against the employment of women as agents, yet it is curious that in the history of espionage and counter-espionage a very high percentage of the greatest coups have been brought off by women. This – if it proves anything – proves that the spymasters of the world are inclined to lay down hard and fast rules, which they subsequently find it impossible to keep to, and it is in their interests to break.

It is frequently alleged that women are less discreet than men; that they are ruled by their emotions and not by their brains: that they rely on intuition rather than on reason; and that Sex will play an unsettling and dangerous role in their work.

My very own experience has been very much to the contrary. During the present war, M.S. has investigated probably hundreds of cases of loose talk; in by far the greater proportion of these cases the offenders were men. In my submission this is due to one principal factor: it is that indiscretions are committed from conceit. Taking him generally, Man is a conceited creature while Woman is a vain creature: conceit and vanity are not the same. A man's conceit will often lead him into indiscretion, in an endeavour to build himself up among his fellow men, or even to impress a woman; women, being vain rather than conceited, find their outlet for this form of self-expression in their personal appearance, dress etc.

It is not entirely true that women are exclusively ruled by their emotions, and it is to be hoped that no officer, when selecting a woman for training as an agent, will choose the type of woman whose make-up is over emotional. On the other hand, the emotional make-up of a properly balanced woman can very often be utilised in investigation; and it is a fact that woman's intuition is a direct result of her rather complex emotions. That a woman's intuition is sometimes amazingly helpful and amazingly correct has been well established; and given the right guiding hand, this ability can at times save the Intelligence Officer an enormous amount of trouble.

On the subject of Sex, in connection with using women as agents, a great deal of nonsense has been talked and written. The first consideration for choosing any agent, man or woman, should be that the individual be a normal, balanced person. This means that, in connection with Sex, they should not be markedly oversexed or under-sexed: if over-sexed, it is clear that this will play an over-riding part in their mental processes, and if under-sexed, they will not be so mentally alert, and their other faculties will suffer accordingly. It is difficult to imagine anything more terrifying than for an officer to become landed with a woman agent who suffers from an overdose of Sex, but as it is to be hoped that no such person would be chosen for the work, there is no need to go further into this point.

It is true, however, that a clever woman who can use her personal attraction wisely has in her armoury a very formidable weapon. Closely allied to Sex in a woman, is the quality of sympathy; and nothing is easier than for a woman to gain a man's confidence by the showing and expression of a little sympathy; this cannot be done by an undersexed woman. However, it is important to stress that I am no believer in what may be described as Mata-Hari methods. I am convinced that more information has been obtained by women agents, by keeping out of the arms of the man, than was ever obtained by sinking too willingly into them; for it is unfortunately the case that if a man is physically but casually interested in a woman, he will very speedily lose his interest in her once his immediate object is attained; whereas, if he can come to rely upon the woman more for her qualities of companionship and sympathy, than merely those of physical satisfaction, the enterprise will last longer.

The aforegoing rather cold-blooded statements must not lead an officer to ignore the possibility of woman agent genuinely falling in love with an opponent; there is always an outside risk of this, but I can state quite definitely that in twenty years' experience, I have never known case of this occurring; and the best way to guard against such an eventuality is to hark back to the original selection of an agent. During the time when the Officer is getting really acquainted with his agent, he should, in the case of a woman, pay particular attention to the types of men that the woman concerned likes and dislikes; and his future direction of her should, to a very large extent, be guided by the knowledge which he has obtained during this initial period.

One of the positive advantages of employing women as agents is that any woman possessed of some secretarial ability offers unique chances for exploitation; for if it is in an organisation against which the agent is to be directed, the ultimate objective should always be to secure for the new agent some secretarial position, either part-time or permanent, with the movement concerned. No official or other single individual ever has the same opportunity for obtaining information covering a wide area as does a clerk or secretary. A woman as placed will have a much wider grasp of the day-to-day doings in a movement, than any of the officials of the movement will ever dream of. I would state categorically that if it were possible for any business magnate or government official to be able to see into the mind of his secretary, he would be astounded at the amount of knowledge concerning the general affairs of the business or department in question which lay in the secretary's brain.[152]

No doubt he was thinking of Joan Miller while writing the last paragraph. Knight, who served as a model for M in Ian Fleming's James Bond adventures, acknowledged that there was always a risk of a woman agent falling in love with her opponent, but he had never known of such a case in his twenty years' experience. Whether Davidson had fallen in love with one of her 'students' is unknown, but she clearly had had some attachment to them as she was willing to see them in London.

His most effective intelligence-gathering method was to arrange a secretarial job for a woman agent in the organisation that was to be targeted. Interestingly, Davidson, Skinner, Wicken and Miller had all been secretaries. 'No official or other single individual ever has the same opportunity for obtaining information covering a wide area as does a clerk or secretary.'[153]

Before Fifi's training at Grendon Hall had finished, she wrote to Senter informing him that

> I have been advised that it could be profitable for me to stay up here a few weeks longer than scheduled, 'to add some extra practice to my course'. The supposition is, in my own quietly malicious opinion, mostly prompted by the fact that the place is rather understaffed and overworked and generally a bit vague – which makes individual, fast and concentrated work almost impossible. Be that as it may, a few weeks more will certainly do me no harm – (although I doubt that anything short of five years in a lab could make me a historical prodigy) – and I have, therefore, accepted the suggestion with biting enthusiasm and have agreed to stay on until about mid-April.
>
> In view of our last conversation, however, I thought it advisable to inform you of this matter hastily, in case you would like me to complete the course without delay, perhaps you would let me know. I would then insist on getting through by the end of this month, as promised. If I do not hear from you, I shall take it that I need not put up my socks with undue zeal and will go on pressing violets and reading Yeats until April 15th.
>
> Yours sincerely,
>
> Christine
>
> P.S. I presume that Max will have given you a resume of the talk I had with him about three weeks ago and I hope we will be able to discuss things further in the not too distant future.[154]

By 23 March, Boyle had agreed that she would be working in Germany following the completion of her course and after certain enquiries had been made, presumably by MI5's own security officers. She finished on 13 April and her final report revealed that, unlike most other students, she did not need to participate in physical training. After nineteen days' Morse and Procedure training, her speed for sending messages increased from zero to sixteen words per minute and for receiving increased from five to seventeen. 'A fairly good Morse style but tends to did dots. Taught V, Y, Z plans. High grade security and ordinary SOE procedure. Broadcast and crack signalling.'

After seventeen hours of technical lectures she was reported as 'very keen and hard-working but lack of any previous knowledge proved to be a distinct disadvantage'. She spent forty-three hours being trained to tune and maintain BMK.II, but learned to tune AMK.III, VP.Tx, MCR.1. and Polish OP.3. (wireless transmitting and receiving sets. MCR was a midget set) and was reported to have been 'keen to learn. Can tune sets accurately and is capable of repairing simple faults in the BMK.II.'

After thirty-nine hours of Code training, she was reported to be able to do them 'quickly and accurately. Taught L.O.T.P. [Literal One Time Pad] and AZD.1. with code 53.' Part of the course included sixteen days on mobile wireless telegraphy training. This was done at Belhaven House (STS 54b), a former school in Dunbar, in Scotland. Like the students who were sent to Beaulieu, she was given schemes that lasted three weeks. Unlike them, however, there was no agent provocateur to test her security, only an observation made by one of the officers. She was reported to have

> worked very well and made good contacts. Good operator so long as she does not try to send too quickly. Her first scheme (using set B.II) was only fair, in that she had considerable difficulty in finding the Home Station. She also made several careless mistakes in procedure. Her second scheme (using set B.II) showed a great improvement. She made contact quickly and worked her skeds [schedules] well. Her third scheme, using high grade security procedure (on set AMK.III) was equally successful. She experienced difficulties with the procedure and made a high percentage of contacts.[155]

As students who graduated from Grendon Hall were often sent to operate behind enemy lines, the course also included weapons training. Christine practiced for sixteen hours using .22 and .33 weapons and her instructor commented, 'Although her grip is rather loose, she is a reasonably good shot. Rather slow on the trigger. STEN: Position rather bad and grip slack. Only fair.'[156]

Captain Chisholm, one of the Royal Signal's training instructors, commented that she was 'a keen, intelligent and hard-working student. Lack of any previous knowledge of the subject handicapped her in the technical training but she made very good progress and should prove to be a reliable operator'.[157]

Arrangements were made for Christine to be provided with replacement documents in her original name and by 19 May she had her Alien's Residents Certificate returned and her false one destroyed. At the end of May, she was officially laid off from the SOE and given new identity papers under the name of Christine Chilver. She was issued with a National Residents Certificate, a Ration Book, clothing documents and N.S.55 and N.S. 2(W) (old documents) and told that 'if she experienced any difficulty with the Ministry of Labour, she was to inform D/CE.P. He was to contact Mr. J. H. Phillips at their headquarters, 15 Portman Square, W.1. and to ask him to allow her "to take up such employment as she herself may desire".'[158]

On 21 June, Major Mott, who had been transferred to Beaulieu to deal with the more-difficult agent-handling problems, added a memo to her file.

> I saw Mr. Phillips at Portman Square this afternoon and explained Fifi's present position to him. He undertook to contact the appropriate Appointment's Officer in his Ministry with a view to arranging an interview for Fifi at which no questions will be asked regarding the nature of her service while with this

Department, and also that every effort would be made to utilise her varied accomplishments to the best advantage in whatever job she, herself, desires; probably a civilian post with one of the Allied Control Commissions. N.G.M.[159]

There were several redacted pages and redacted documents at the end of her file which may have related to her work in Germany, but no further evidence appeared in her file to confirm it. On 5 June, the Berlin Agreement had given the Allies supreme control over Germany with Britain taking responsibility for territory west of the Oder-Neisse line. She applied for a post at the Allied Control Commissions for Germany and Austria, giving Major Mott and Squadron Leader H. E. Park as referees. Squadron Leader Park's reference acknowledged that he had known her for three years and that 'she is trustworthy and reliable and is in every way suitable for employment of a confidential nature'.[160] Maybe Christine worked with the Allied Command Commission under Field Marshall Montgomery, using her German skills interrogating captured enemy personnel. As the last page in her file was redacted, one is uncertain whether she did work in Germany or was employed by MI5. Their files have not been opened to the public and even today they neither confirm nor deny an individual's involvement in their organisation.

5

Christine's Post-War Life (1945–2007)

Research by Anita Singh and Gregory Walton for the *Telegraph* article 'Revealed: identity of Fifi the stunning wartime spy' made no mention of her post-war employment, only revealing that, after retiring from the service, Christine lived an anonymous life in Chelsea, West London. Her mother, despite her poor health, moved to England to live with her and she kept up her friendship with Alex, who had married and become known as Alex Felgate.[1]

Patricia Grant, one of Christine's old friends, stated that after the war Christine used her excellent French skills to work as a translator and, as Alex's husband died shortly after their marriage, she and her mother shared the Chelsea flat with Alex, who worked in her Jewish family's textile business.[2]

When her mother died in 1966, Christine inherited half her mother's share of the confiscated property in Riga; the other half went to her sister in Sweden. Both in need of money, they made enquiries about claiming compensation from the government of the USSR. In S. W. Magnus's article, 'Foreign Compensation and the Taxman', he stated that

> in 1967 the British Government reached an agreement with the USSR for the resolution of certain long-standing disputes relating to various territories, including the Baltic States, ceded to the USSR at various times between 1940 and 1951. In consequence, the Foreign Compensation [Union of Soviet Socialist Republics] Order 1969 (SI 1969/735) was made and certain frozen Baltic assets were passed to the Foreign Compensation Commission for distribution under the Order.
>
> Miss Chilver and her sister both made claims in respect of the Latvian property nationalised in 1940 on behalf of their parents and in their own right. Each established claims to the extent of something over £60,000 and received payment at the rate of 42.57 per cent, or just over £25,000. Of these sums respectively paid to each sister, by far the greatest portion represented the mother's interest, being in each case over $56,000 of the established claims and over £24,000 of the amount paid. These sums were duly paid during the years 1972 and 1973.[3]

Patricia Grant told me that Christine and Alex then embarked on a building conversion project in the Wye Valley, near the Welsh border, which entailed many years' work. They purchased jointly a derelict property in Lower Mesne, St Briavels, and an old cider press which, because of the dogs she kept, became known as 'The Kennels'. Christine laboured for years to restore the gardens which sloped down to the river, building terraces and landscaping them so that 'they looked truly beautiful by the time she finished'.[4]

In 1998, she published a booklet in Latvian and English in an attempt to raise Latvians' awareness about animal sentience. It included oblique references to the war years. 'Animals are magnificent teachers; they try so hard to make us behave in a manner of which we need not be ashamed ... As a child I used to listen to our animals just as I listened to adult conversation.'[5]

In 2001, she opened an animal shelter in Riga, known as 'Dzīvnieku Draugs',[6] and when the staff there was told of her wartime past they were surprised to learn that she had led such an intensely private life. They reported that she was devoted to animal welfare and that that was all she spoke to them about on the few occasions that she visited. She had few friends, they said, and rarely visited public places.

Christine and Alex engaged Janice Cutmore, a local woman, as a cleaner, who became Christine's carer after she had a hip operation. Christine died on 5 November 2007, aged eighty-seven. She had let few people into her life and Alex was the only mourner when she was cremated. Cutmore continued to look after Alex until she died in 2011, and was left part of the estate and Christine's wartime mementoes. She told reporters that 'it was an isolated house and they liked to be away from everybody. All their photographs were in an album, and the only ones on show were of their animals. Christine knew her mind and nothing would change it. But she was fair and when you got to know her she was lovely ... Alex told us a bit about Christine's work after she died. She said Christine would go to a pub all dressed up and see which one of the new recruits would say, 'Guess what I do for a living?'.[7]

Hugo Whatley, the new houseowner, reported that 'their garden was extraordinary. They had so many plants here. It's rundown a little now but you still find the odd wonderful plant they planted. After what they went through in the war, I think this was a way for them to get away'.[8] Those who knew Christine remembered her as 'one of life's real good people', but after the war her remarkable story remained untold. Her outstanding contribution to the SOE in helping to ensure the survival of many of their agents once on operation behind enemy lines deserves to be acknowledged.

6

Maxwell Knight's Female Infiltrators

Knight's post-war account of his counter-subversion department's role provided additional detail about the employment of women agents, but he omitted any reference to Joan Miller. This, one imagines, was to protect her identity. Although Olga Gray's successful infiltration of the Communist Party of Great Britain had increased Knight's reputation within MI5, when her involvement came to light in the trial in March 1938, her cover was blown; she was given £500 by MI5 and made a new life for herself in Canada.[1]

Needing a secretary, Knight appointed nineteen-year–old Joan Miller in September that year to work with his four case officers. They knew him by his cover name of Captain King, or just as 'M'. Their offices were in converted prison cells at His Majesty's Prison at Wormwood Scrubs, one of the least likely Luftwaffe targets. As Kell had been convinced that a German invasion would attack key government buildings in the capital, he had transferred MI5's Security Service from Thames House, Millbank, and Horseferry Road, WC1, to a less obvious location.

With the success of the Woolwich Arsenal case, Knight had increased his team to twelve by the time war broke out and, recognising Joan's potential as an agent provocateur, he spent a lot of time going through the details of the case with her. In her autobiography, *One Girl's War*, Miller admitted how impressed she was with Olga Gray. Gray, only nineteen when she started, managed to keep her wits about her for seven years on a dangerous undertaking and showed great vigilance and perseverance. Miller made no mention of Gray being in a relationship with one of her targets.

Not long after starting at the 'Scrubs', Miller developed a relationship with Knight and became his mistress. Although they were together for three years, she asserted that he was impotent and the relationship unconsummated. Even though he was twice Joan's age, she was captivated by him. She described him as having cultivated some engaging eccentricities, such as smoking long, handmade cigarettes and being 'rather tall and lanky, with a Wellington nose which he referred to as "my limb". Always dressed in stylish shabby tweeds, he made a conspicuous figure about the place'. When she first met him she was conscious of 'the charm this smiling man possessed – charm of a rare and formidable order. His voice, which I found hypnotic, confirmed the impression.'[2] She found that

> the Woolwich Arsenal files were as full of intrigue as any work of fiction specially concocted to satisfy the avid thriller-reader: plots and plans, illicit photographs of naval guns, shifty foreigners, fateful attaché cases deposited in left-luggage compartments, conspicuous brown paper parcels passing from one impassive conspirator to another at Charing Cross Station. And, at the centre of it all, an MI5 agent keeping tabs on everyone round her and keeping her head at the same time.[3]

Over a meal at the Author's Club, Knight explained to her that he was concerned with counter-subversion, blocking the threat to British security from both the extreme left and extreme right. As Russia was not in the war at that time, he considered the Comintern – Communist International – to be a threat, but he had already infiltrated agents into their organisation. He wanted Joan to join the Right Club, an anti-Semitic and anti-communist organisation, and pass herself off as an ardent fascist. He had already infiltrated forty-one-year-old Mrs Amor,[4] who, known as M/Y, was using her maiden name rather than her married name of Marjorie Mackie.

By the time war broke out in September 1939, Knight had learned that the Right Club's policy was an effort to penetrate not only other anti-Semitic and anti-communist organisations, but also the services of Government departments. Its head was Captain Archibald Ramsay, a Scottish Unionist MP, who was friendly with Sir Oswald Mosley, the founder of the British Union of Fascists and leader of the Blackshirts, and William Joyce, his deputy and later the mouthpiece of the Nazi propaganda machine. Ramsay boasted that he had contacts in the Admiralty, the War Office, the Foreign Office, the Army and even in Scotland Yard.

The Club's membership of around 230 individuals was listed in what was known as the Red Book and included various MPs, lords, earls and other influential conservatives who were trying to oppose and expose the activities of organised Jewry. Although outwardly professing not to be connected with other fascist movements, its members were also involved in the British Union, the Imperial Fascist League and the Nordic League. In a speech to the latter, Ramsay made statements that Knight interpreted as pro-German in tone and almost amounting to incitement to riot.[5]

When Amor reported that Ramsay had expressed concerns that he did not have a contact in the Postal Censorship department, Knight arranged for her to be transferred into it. Ramsay and his wife, Maude, welcomed the news with glee and, over the following months, continually pressed her to obtain confidential information about the personnel and working of the Censorship Section. Through Maude Ramsay, Amor was introduced to the Wolkoffs, a white Russian family that MI5 was keeping its eyes on. Admiral Wolkoff had been the Russian Military Attaché in London during the Tsarist regime and his thirty-five-year-old daughter, Anna, who had been naturalised in 1935, was a leading player in the Right Club.

She ran the family business, the Russian Tea Rooms, at 50 Harrington Road, South Kensington – not far from the Natural History Museum – and held meetings in the flat above. By early spring 1940, Amor reported that there was an inner ring of Right Club members with Anna Wolkoff at its head, which, as well as carrying out anti-war propaganda camouflaged as anti-communist, was also interested in political and diplomatic issues; Knight interpreted this as espionage.[6]

Their 'sticky-back' campaign for obstructing the war effort included sneaking out at night during the blackout and finding flat, smooth surfaces, like Belisha beacons, telephone boxes, pillar boxes, lamp posts, telegraph poles, shop windows, billboards and church noticeboards, on which they pasted pro-German, anti-Semitic posters. They used greaseproof paint to deface air-raid precaution and casualty-station posters and jeered at Winston Churchill during the Pathé Newsreels in the cinemas.[7]

Miller claimed that Knight had been told, presumably by Mrs Amor, that the Right Club was hoping to recruit someone working in the War Office. He arranged for her to be given cover as a War Office secretary and introduced to 'Mrs Amos', who she described as a cosy, middle-aged woman who reminded her of Miss Marple, Agatha Christie's famous detective. 'Mrs Amos' took Miller to the Tea Rooms, passing her off as a friend of her son who was serving in the Royal Navy, and, when Wolkoff came over to their table, told her that Miller worked in the War Office.

> The Russian Tea Rooms, with its polished wooden furniture, panelled walls and open fireplace, was the sort of café you could visit unescorted without jeopardising your reputation. Over the next few weeks I made a habit of dropping in at all hours of the day, sometimes bringing along an innocent friend to lend colour to the deception I was engaged in. The old admiral used to join me quite often at my table where he would sit reminiscing about the past in Russia. 'No nonsense like these absurd licensing laws you have in England,' he would say, when his mood was jovial. I got to know Anna too, and whenever I spoke to her I put on a show of opposition to Britain's involvement in the war and support for the Fascist cause – but not too emphatically at first, of course, but more openly as time went on. I invented a pre-war romance with a Nazi officer to account for these aberrant views. Anna, who was as wary and suspicious as a wildcat, listened to all this without giving anything away. When I insinuated that her experiences must have left her with strong opinions on these matters, she only smiled. I could sense that she approved of what I was saying though. (I was learning.)[8]

Amor arranged for Miller to attend a meeting with some of the older women in the Right Club and introduced her as having a good deal of common sense about political matters and finding working at the War Office a bit of a bore. Miller told them that she found the war a bit of a bore too and that it was a disaster for Britain to have embarked on it. She deplored the decision to jettison appeasement. She blamed the government for its wrong-headed revulsion over Germany's imperialist ambitions and complained about feeling cut off from the sense of being morally in the right that made things tolerable for everybody else.[9]

The women were suitably impressed and Miller was invited to join the organisation. Unlike Fifi, should she ever have needed it, Knight showed her a trick from his childhood days in the Gorbals in Glasgow – putting pennies between her fingers, making them into a fist and hitting hard. He also gave her a leather-covered cosh and a stocking gun, but she never mentioned having to use them. Like Fifi, she was expected to produce character reports. Whether the details she included in her book were her own or from what she had read in the office is unknown.

> Anna Wolkoff had been born in Russia in 1902 or thereabouts, into a privileged family; and this made her the right age to suffer the fullest effect of enforced exile and impoverishment, with stories of Bolshevik atrocities to keep her indignation active. After 1917 the Wolkoffs found themselves among the numerous other White Russian families dispersed all over Europe. They were never in a frame of mind to relish the colourful reversals of fortune that overtook so many of their compatriots, refusing to have any truck with a system that could allow a grand duke, for example, to wind up as a gigolo or a waiter. Anna found as much solace as she could in politics, becoming a right-wing agitator and crypto-fascist. If it hadn't been for the war she might have gone on in this way, unedifying as it was, without ever finding herself in a position to do much damage. But in the particular conditions that prevailed in 1940, her pro-Nazi sympathies acquired a very dangerous outlet.
>
> She was short and dark-haired, not very impressive in appearance, and displayed the intensity of manner which is often associated with those of a fanatical disposition. She took herself and her causes very seriously indeed. It was difficult to get close to her as she was filled with mistrust, but, once she'd accepted you, Anna was capable of impulsive and generous acts. In spite of her upbringing she was a good cook and this skill, I imagine, helped to keep the restaurant in business; dressmaking, however, was her principal occupation (one of her clients was the Duchess of Windsor). She owned the flat that served as the headquarters for the Right Club, as well as another one in Rowland Gardens.[10]

Some accounts of the double-cross criticise Miller as giving herself a role in the game when Knight credited Amor and Munck but made no mention of her role in his account. Perhaps this was because he deliberately omitted her role to protect her from being identified and perhaps hounded by the media. She had left him in late 1943, after confirming her suspicions of his obsession with homosexuality. She also admitted that he had an interest in black magic and was good friends with Aleister Crowley and Denis Wheatley. Crowley, the occultist, magician, poet, painter, mountaineer and heroin addict, had offered his services to the Naval Intelligence Division but was refused. Wheatley, an Oxford don famous for his 1935 occult novel *The Devil Rides Out*, was married to a driver for MI5; a chance meeting led to him spending the war years working with London Controlling Section to devise military deception schemes.

By late February 1940, Amor reported that Wolkoff had become acquainted with an official employed in the United States Embassy on Grosvenor Square. She also learned that Anna Wolkoff had a contact in the Belgian Embassy, Jean Nieumanhuys, the second secretary, who allowed her to use the diplomatic bag to communicate with William Joyce – Lord Haw Haw – who was broadcasting pro-German propaganda to Britain. She gave letters from Joyce to Nieumanhuys, addressed to the Comte or Comtesse de Laubespin, an official at the Belgian Foreign Office in Brussels who was one of her friends.

To avoid too much responsibility falling on Amor, Knight thought it wise to infiltrate a second agent, Hélène de Munck, a young, convent-educated Belgian woman who had known Admiral Wolkoff since 1936. Given the symbol M/1, she was told to convince him that she had many contacts in the diplomatic world. In a chat with the admiral at the tea rooms, she lied about having a friend in the Romanian Legation. When his daughter was informed, she asked Munck if it might be possible to use her friend to get a letter to Germany by channels other than the ordinary post, as Duc del Monte, her friend at the Italian Embassy, was ill. When Munck told her that her Romanian friend had access to their country's diplomatic bag, Wolkoff asked if she could get a letter through to William Joyce in Berlin.

Once handed over, Munck passed it to Knight, who had its contents photographed and then returned it to Munck. She told Anna on 10 April that all the arrangements had been made for it to be sent. Wanting to add a post-script, Anna visited Munck's flat on the following morning, was given the letter back, opened it and used Munck's typewriter to add a note in German. At the bottom of the note she drew an eagle and snake and signed it 'P. J'. The eagle and snake were symbols of the Right Club and the letters stood for 'Perish Judah'. She then re-sealed it and gave it back to Munck. Knight had the addition copied and made arrangements for the resealed envelope to reach Joyce, to find out what acknowledgement he made and to explore their future communications.[11]

As the contents were in code, Miller reported travelling with Knight to Bletchley Park to get the message deciphered and having to wait all day until one of the pipe-smoking boffins told them that actually it was an easy code to crack. They had spent ages looking for a more difficult one. It included a commentary of Joyce's broadcast and advice to stick to plutocracy and avoid making disparaging remarks about King George VI, as well as items of political news.[12]

Knight later acknowledged how important it was for an agent to be capable of correctly summing up a person's character and temperament, and stressed how dangerous it was to neglect to include in the suspect's file some note of their personal characteristics, strengths and weaknesses. In his account of Anna Wolkoff, he described her as having the Russian trait of being extremely superstitious.

> ... she was interested in spiritualism, clairvoyance, astrology, and in fact anything to do with the Occult. This fact was known to us quite early in the investigation. Now it so happened that the second of the two agents, Miss Z [Munck], was interested, from the academic point of view, in similar matters,

and she possessed to a remarkable degree the ability to read characters from hand-writing. Whether or not those who read this account share a belief in this ability is beside the point: the following facts will show that such a situation can be profitably exploited.

Miss Z. was instructed to engage Anna WOLKOFF in conversation on the subject of the Occult, and gradually to introduce her own interest in character-reading. She was told to elevate her ability from the fairly material level of the formation of hand-writing into the realm of psychic phenomena. Anna swallowed this bait avidly, and it was not very long before Miss Z. was invited to give a 'reading' of Anna's own character. Here, of course, was a splendid opportunity for Miss Z. to cement her friendship with WOLKOFF, for the latter was extremely susceptible to flattery. Miss Z. produced, on her own initiative, an extremely accurate character-sketch of WOLKOFF, which was suitably edited and embellished by ourselves, before it was presented to Anna herself. This met with such success, that Anna asked Miss Z. to perform a similar service with others of her friends. Some of these friends were purely social, and had little or no connection with the case, but among the persons submitted for readings there were those who were definitely involved in Anna's political work.

So impressed was Anna by Miss Z's abilities, that it was possible for her to increase Anna's confidence in some of her colleagues, and to decrease it in respect of others, according to the way in which we wished to direct her feelings. On one occasion we were lucky enough to have submitted a specimen of the hand-writing of Miss A. [Amor], the first agent (at that time not known to Miss Z. as anyone but a person closely involved in Anna's activities). It was at this stage that one of the principal operational problems of the case arose (referred to later). However, it was possible to give Anna WOLKOFF a reading of Miss A's character, which caused Anna to repose still further confidence in her to the subsequent great advantage of the Department.[13]

The problem was that Knight had ensured that neither Amor nor Munck knew each other. He wanted to ensure that Amor's character analysis improved Anna's estimation of her and that if Munck had known her, she might have written with more honesty. Although Knight argued that agents not knowing each other was important, valuable time was wasted when they both reported on each other.

With Anna impressed with Munck's work, Knight instructed her to talk about her family in Belgium and her plans to visit them in the immediate future. This was about a month before the German invasion. About the middle of April, Anna told Amor that if Munck went to Belgium, she wanted her to contact Guy Miermans, the Right Club's principal agent in Belgium, in order to get some translations of a Russian document. She also wanted her to visit de Laubespin to find out how trustworthy Nieumanhuys was and how successful anti-Semitic and other propaganda was in Belgium.

Wolkoff gave Munck a list of typewritten questions in inferior French, which she was expected to learn off by heart and then destroy. She translated what were requests for information on the progress of 'our work in Belgium' and encouraging news about how the Right Club was developing in Britain and passed them to Knight. He arranged her trip and she left on 16 April, having memorised Wolkoff's instructions. Returning on the 20th, she assured Anna that her contact was loyal and, presumably Knight's idea, Nieumanhuys' suggestion that she ought not to involve Munck in such a devious and dangerous game. She reported to Knight that she was convinced that Nieumanhuys was a German agent and both he and de Laubespin were alarmed at the extent to which the Wolkoff's activities were being pushed in England.

Although Knight had used the Special Branch to tap phones of the Right Club members, little useful evidence had come to light; phone tapping was known to be being used so people were cautious over what they said. Instead, he came up with an idea of getting a tape recording of Mrs Ramsay incriminating herself. Ramsay had invited Miller to have tea with her in Onslow Square, South Kensington. As it would be difficult to get permission to bug this flat, Knight used a friend's flat in nearby Pond Place as an alternative. Miller rang Ramsay to rearrange the appointment, telling her that it was her day off and she was looking after a friend's flat for the day. When Ramsay agreed to the change of plan, Miller arranged with Special Branch to send two men to wire the sitting room, clear one of the cupboards and hide inside with their ear phones, machine and shorthand writing pads. When they tested the microphone, the noise of the traffic coming through the open window meant they could not pick up anyone having a conversation in the room. Miller closed it and the men hid.

Despite it being a swelteringly hot day, she refused to open it when Ramsay arrived, fanning herself with a theatre programme and asking her to let some air in. Miller told her that her friend's cat might jump out and escape. Even opening it two inches was refused as the cords holding the sash window were faulty. As well as the meeting getting off to a bad start, Miller was unsuccessful in directing the conversation towards political topics and the bait was not taken. After she left and Miller had provided tea and apologies to the police, they said, 'Not giving much away was she? You won't catch that old bird in a hurry.'[14]

When Ramsay's invitation was repeated, Miller had no alternative but to go. This time, Ramsay thoroughly incriminated herself, but there were no witnesses. Leaning forward, she asked Miller if there was any chance she might be able to get her hands on 'hush-hush' material. Agreeing to what Miller described as 'preposterous plans', she told her that she would apply for a transfer. A few days later, Knight had arranged a temporary transfer and supplied Miller with a spate of information, which she passed on to Mrs Ramsay. It started as not very valuable, but became increasingly significant in an attempt to reel her in.

In the middle of May, Miller reported that she was ordered to change her task of collecting intelligence on the Right Club members and instead

to devote my time to keeping tabs on Anna Wolkoff, who was now suspected of rather more than run-of-the-mill subversion. MI5 was in possession of evidence suggesting that some highly confidential communications between Churchill

– then First Lord of the Admiralty – and [American President Franklin] Roosevelt had fallen into the hands of the German ambassador in Rome. It was of the utmost importance that these documents should have been kept secret; if it had been widely known, for example, that America enjoyed certain privileges with regard shipping, other countries might have claimed similar concessions, with chaotic effects. A possible source of this disastrous leakage was the Italian Embassy in London, where an associate of Anna Wolkoff was employed. But how had the carefully coded telegrams been deciphered. By this stage everything pointed to a code and cypher clerk at the American Embassy – Tyler Kent, whose duty it was to transmit in code alll telegrams handed on to him by his ambassador, Joseph Kennedy.[15]

Knight reported in 1945 that the intelligence was not concerned with the United States' domestic affairs, but that if it fell into German hands it would have been of great value to the enemy and have done incalculable damage.[16] Miller was more specific. She reported that Kent had been at the United States Embassy in Moscow for five years before being transferred to London in October 1939 and that, at that time, he appeared strongly anti-communist and pro-fascist in his views. She acknowledged that Nigel West – the pen-name of Rupert Allason, the journalist and MI5 historian – argued otherwise. In a 1983 newspaper article in *The Times*, he claimed that Kent was working for the Soviets and that his pro-Nazi attitude was a façade.[17]

Having deciphered certain documents, Kent believed strongly that President Roosevelt's foreign policy had taken a disastrous turn. Having promised the American people that he would stick to the isolationist policy and keep America out of the war, the documents proved that he was actively planning to support the British and join the conflict. Kent copied the relevant proof he needed and kept the documents in his flat until the time when he could supply the isolationist movement with the evidence they needed to defeat the president in the next election. He allowed Wolkoff and Captain Ramsay to read them. Sanctioning the theft of diplomatic messages was one of the subsequent criticisms of Ramsay, who, for his own reasons, chose not to bring them up in the House of Commons. Wolkoff, on the other hand, borrowed them from Kent and arranged to have a Russian photographer called Smirnoff copy them. According to Miller, the prints were never accounted for.

By the middle of May, Knight had passed all this intelligence to Kell. It came at a difficult time; Hitler had ordered the Wehrmacht to invade Norway, Denmark, the Netherlands, Belgium, Luxembourg and France, and the Luftwaffe gained air supremacy over most of Western Europe. Mussolini brought Italy into the war and the Right Club was expecting an imminent German invasion.

Miller recalled being consulted by some members who were compiling a hit list of prominent anti-Nazis and pro-communist supporters who would be publicly hanged from lampposts once the Germans took control. She did not think she made very sensible suggestions. They were very keen that an example should be made, to give the rest of the British population a foretaste of what strong measures they could expect.

Wolkoff had given Miller an expensive, blue Chanel dress, which she really loved, so having to spy on a woman she had some admiration for put her in a difficult position, However, Knight had instilled in her the rule that 'if you are going to tell a lie, tell a good one and above all stick to it'.

On 18 May, Kennedy, the American ambassador, was asked to waive Kent's diplomatic immunity. Although it was granted, he expressed disquiet that he had not been informed earlier, as he would not have allowed him to work in the code room for so long. Knight's argument was that, by leaving him in place, he implicated others.

Two days later, Knight and two Special Branch police officers raided Kent's flat. Although he refused to let them in, they broke in to find him in bed with his mistress. He put up no resistance and the search of the premises revealed a brown leather briefcase with about 1,500 stolen embassy documents. He was arrested and taken into police custody. The documents were neatly sorted and filed to be used as evidence.

On the same day, Anna Wolkoff was arrested and interned under Section 18B of the Defence Regulations. Captain Ramsay, Oswald Mosley and other members of the Right Club and the British Union of Fascists were arrested on 23 May and later interned. Subsequent investigation identified the photographer and enough evidence was available to have Wolkoff and Kent tried at the Old Bailey, charged with offences under the Official Secrets Act and Defence Regulations. Because of the secret nature of the case, it was held in camera. Miller recalled having to give evidence, and when Wolkoff saw her she started shouting abuse, including a threat to kill her once she got out of prison. Kent received seven years and Wolkoff ten. Knight's overview of the case included a number of key points.

From the point of view of Intelligence Officers, there are certain lessons to be learned from this case: the first is that during war-time, there will always come a point in an investigation where an agent must be sacrificed in order to achieve satisfactory results; and the Intelligence Officer in charge of the case must face the responsibility of deciding the exact point at which such sacrifice must be made.

The second lesson is that in the collection of information about suspects in the form of agents' reports, it is impossible to over-estimate the importance of distinguishing in each report which material is useless for evidential purposes.

The third lesson is that when any search of premises is conducted, and documents are taken away by an M.I.5 officer, the greatest care must be taken to see that these are properly listed and recorded, for one can never tell when a document which appears to be unimportant at the time may become vital at a later stage in the case.

The fourth, and by no means the least important lesson is that when investigations have reached the point when proceedings are contemplated, it is absolutely essential that the senior officers of the Police in the Force concerned, should be taken fully into the confidence of the Intelligence Service; for it is the Police who have to make the arrests, who have to prepare the evidence for the Director of Prosecutions, who have to take statements, and perform a number of functions outside the scope of an Intelligence Officer. Therefore, to have any reservations with the Police is not only short-sighted, but may be disastrous from the point of view of the case.

With regard to the 'affair' of KENT and WOLKOFF, the most complete co-operation existed between ourselves and Special Branch; and a great measure of the success of the case was due to the work of the Police Officers concerned.[18]

Although there were no members of the public present at the court, Miller felt that she would be well-known amongst the accused. Having her cover blown meant that Miller spent the next few years based in the office. Mrs Amor went on to be employed in another variation of provocation. She agreed to be imprisoned with the women who had been interned as enemy nationals or members of the extreme right or extreme left. Described as a 'stool pigeon', she spent time with interned female prisoners, befriending them and encouraging them to talk about what they had been imprisoned for. While it is possible MI5 had 'bugged' prisoners' cells, her job necessitated remembering the details of their conversations, as in the Russian Tea Rooms, and writing up reports.

Munck was also allocated another provocation role. With the extreme right broken, MI5 focussed on the extreme left. They had already infiltrated agents into the Communist Party's Headquarters at King Street, Covent Garden, and were tapping their telephones. One intercept hinted that there was a deed box hidden under Rajani Palme Dutt's bed. He was a well-known Indian lawyer, Stalin supporter, general secretary of the Communist Party and contributor to the *Labour Monthly*. Miller was allocated the task of examining them. After special training by Post Office staff in opening and resealing letters and a safe-cracker showing her how to open a locked trunk, she broke into Dutt's flat and examined the contents of the deed box, while accompanied by Guy Poston, an MI5 officer. Although it revealed nothing, she acknowledged being filled with aversion at having to go through other people's belongings, especially when she knew those involved.

This aversion led her to decline the offer of searching a flat belonging to Krishna Menon, an influential Indian intellectual. He was the Labour councillor for St Pancras, a fervent Indian nationalist and left-wing agitator, who MI5 considered extreme enough to target. Miller was sent to attend some of the political meetings where Menon spoke very strongly against the British mishandling of Indian affairs. She claimed that his ranting against the British Empire discouraged her from getting any further involved, so Knight gave the task to Hélène de Munck, who had worked so well in the Kent-Wolkoff case. According to Miller,

She was an excellent choice, being the sort of girl who could creep into a red-hot political meeting and remain unnoticed, but also someone who never failed to make a good impression when she wanted to. With Krishna Menon, she didn't have to overcome the initial disadvantage of being English. A convent background and moderate attractiveness added to the trustworthy effect she created. She handled the job very efficiently, feeding us with relevant information and keeping Krishna Menon satisfied at the same time. Unfortunately he fell in love with her and this led to a number of complications. Helen, unknown to us, was in the throes of a reckless affair with her case officer; stress, perhaps caused by Krishna Menon's attentions on top of this, made her give in to a craving she'd indulged in before: drugs.[19]

On some weekends Knight took Miller to Worplesdon, another large country house, on the golf course near Guildford in Surrey. It belonged to Ian Menzies, whose brother, Sir Stewart Menzies, became head of MI6 in 1939. Wanting for nothing at this sumptuous home, Miller described it as 'having no single tasteless item. Weekend parties at the house were full of Greek shipping magnates, middle-aged, lecherous and wearing pure silk shirts. Gambling for high stakes would go on after dinner'.[20]

She admitted feeling out of place at Worplesdon, especially with Ian Menzies's exceptionally beautiful wife, Liesel, an Austrian who had come to London in 1937. She had worked as an au pair, then in the London Casino, where she gained fame posing seemingly nude but wearing a body stocking and standing perfectly still in a large sea shell. Any movement at that time would have led to her arrest.

7

John Masterman's Double Agent 'Gelatine': Friedl Gartner

While at one of Menzies' weekend parties, Miller met twenty-eight-year-old Friedl Gartner, sometimes written Gaertner, who was Liesel's older sister. Born Friedericka Stottinger in Roitham, Upper Austria, she worked as a stenographer in Vienna before marrying a German Orthodox Jew and emigrating to Palestine. The marriage did not last and she came to England in March 1937. Whether this was just a visit is uncertain, as some documents state it was April 1938, a month after the Anschluss, the German annexation of Austria.

During her interrogation, MI6 found nothing incriminating against her. She was described as a beautiful Austrian singer whose father had been in the Nazi party. Through her sister's connections, she was provided with work as a part-time research assistant for Dennis Wheatley, 8 St John's Wood Park, NW8. For several months she supplied him with background information on Nazi leaders, which he used in his Gregory Sallust novels. In subsequent documents, she gave Wheatley and her brother-in-law as referees.

When Knight met her, he persuaded her that her knowledge of German and her new social circle would be useful for him. On his instructions, she obtained a German passport, joined the Nationalist Socialist German Workers Party and mixed with the German colony in London. Mary Berbier, who researched Knight's undercover operations against the British Nazis, suggested that Friedl's reasons for giving up her Austrian passport and working as a spy were 'to evade detention as an enemy alien and to live an exciting life operating in certain social circles as a double agent working for the British while pretending to be loyal to Germany'.[1]

Allocated the symbol M/G, she did a few jobs for Knight. The first was to report to him on what she picked up from the weekend parties at Worplesdon and other social events she was invited to or managed to gatecrash. She had to keep her eyes and ears open and report on café society, where gossip was rife, find out who was sleeping with whom and any examples of influential military, political or economic figures not being as secure in their talk or behaviour as they ought to have been.

According to Miller, who must have read or had to transcribe Friedl's reports, 'Ordinary senior officers, through simple openness and forthrightness, in most cases, I believe, were often not very security-minded, in spite of the enormous array of posters plastered on every available space, some bearing slogans and some in deadly earnest, urging caution and discretion on every British Citizen.'[2]

Friedl's romantic involvements were many, and she would have developed a relationship with Knight, except she discovered he was already going out with Miller. 'For Friedl, falling in love was as natural and unmomentous an activity as breathing.' She won the heart of Billy Younger, Knight's deputy, who planned to marry her until he invited his mother, Joan Wheatley, to lunch to discuss buying an engagement ring. When she left, he had a string of cultured pearls to give her, instead of a ring, which led to the engagement being cancelled.

By infiltrating the British Union of Fascists and the Duke of Bedford's British People's Party, between 1939 and 1941 she was able to generate detailed reports for Knight on the Nazi front organisations, pro-Nazi sympathisers, the Right Club and the communists, which were helpful in their subsequent detainment under Regulation 18B. These reports can be seen in her file.[3]

The most notable was the case of Benjamin Greene, secretary to the Hemel Hempstead Labour Party; he resigned in 1938, arguing that it was being infiltrated by communists. He joined the fascist British People's Party, spoke out on the threat of Jewish and American capitalism and attended anti-war demonstrations. MI5 considered him a target for their investigation and Knight gave Friedl the task of finding out about him. She was introduced to Harald Kurtz, one of Knight's agents, who, like Marjorie Amor, had agreed to be interned, sometimes for months, with British Union of Fascist and similar extreme-right-wing prisoners to help MI5 identify those who had pro-Nazi sympathies. Those with extreme views were detained for longer.

On one of Kurtz's releases, he arranged a sting operation with Friedl, who used the cover name of Fraulien von Binzer. Pretending she wanted to contact her fiancé, who had a high position in Austria, she wanted Greene's help in getting a message to him, as it would be embarrassing for him to receive a letter from a refugee in London. In April 1940, she made a statement at Paddington Police Station acknowledging her age as twenty-nine and herself as being a German subject of Austrian origin.

My sympathies are wholly and completely on the side of the Allies, and in April 1938 I offered my services to the British Military Intelligence Department. Since that date I have been employed by this Department in connection with counter espionage work.

On the 22nd April 1940 I received instruction from the officer under whom I was working to co-operate with another agent in connection with the investigation into the activities of Mr Ben GREENE and his associates.

I was given to understand that the ground had been prepared for me to be introduced to Mr GREENE by my colleague as a person whose sympathies were really on the side of Nazi Germany.

On Sunday 18th April I went by invitation to 147 Ebury Street, where I was to have dinner with my colleague, Harald KURTZ, and where Mr Ben GREENE was to be my fellow guest. For purposes of subterfuge I was introduced to him as Fraulien Gartner.

During the early part of the evening, conversation was largely general and Mr GREENE spent a considerable time trying to explain his own views in relation to the war and National Socialism.

He stated that he was a strong believer in National Socialism, but was [illegible] to point out that he did not agree with everything that Hitler had done, particularly with respect to the Jews. [Illegible] he stated that he had interviews in Berlin with Dr Goebbels and Dr Colijn, and that on his return Sir Samuel Hoare had taken an interest in his report and suggestions. He also said that he had been to see Lord Rothschild, who however had only made use of his report as anti-Nazi propaganda.

He also made a reference to his conviction that not all refugees were really anti-Nazi, and I formed the impression that this fact gave him considerable satisfaction.

On the subject of the war, Mr GREENE was definitely defeatist. He was convinced that in a year's time there would be practically nothing to do in England, and that German soldiers would be marching through London. He thought that only National Socialism could save the British Empire.

Mr GREENE claimed that he did not want to see his country ruled by anybody but Englishmen, and said that Hitler did not want this either. He thought that Hitler preferred the British Empire to the possibility of Russia, Japan or America taking the empire over, and that this was why Hitler had never attacked this country in any way. He said that he personally would not fight in the war and would do everything possible to keep out of it. He went on to say that if his country had actually been attacked, he would have been prepared to fight for it, but as the situation was now he considered that such action as had been taken by the Germans against Great Britain was only a reprisal for what we had done in Germany, and therefore he would take no part in it ...

At some time during the evening, I am not quite sure when, Mr GREENE told us that he had a few months ago seen in London a man whom he recognised as being a member of the German S.A. [Sturmabteilung – Hitler's storm troopers, known as 'Brownshirts'] This man Ben GREENE had actually seen in Germany at the time of the handing over of the Saar, and he had been the first German to cross the bridge on that occasion. When Mr GREENE saw this man in London he was sure that he too had been recognised, but that neither of them said anything to each other.

This incident alone struck me as remarkable, for had Mr Ben Greene been a loyal British subject he should have reported such an incident to the authorities at once. It was clear that he had not done so, and so one can only conclude that he was quite content to see a man about whom he should have been highly suspicious walking about at liberty in England after the outbreak of war.

I would like to conclude this statement by saying that the whole course of the evening's conversation left me in no doubt whatever that Mr GREENE was perfectly prepared to help people whom he must quite clearly have imagined to be Agents of the country with whom Great Britain was at war.[4]

As all loyal British citizens and residents in Britain during the war were expected to report to the police any suspicious characters, MI5 used Greene's pro-Nazi views extolled to Friedl and his failure to report on the 'Brownshirt' to have him arrested on a charge of treason.

Knight acknowledged that Friedl also helped in the Wolkoff case. Notes in her file indicated that he had sent her to the Russian Tea House to collect intelligence:

Re Anna WOLKOFF

A very reliable source who has been in touch with Admiral WOLKOFF reports that the Hon. Mrs STOURTON [probably wife of the person of that name in the list of Right Club members] used to be a very close contact of Anna WOLKOFF. Before Anna's arrest this lady used to be a very frequent visitor to the restaurant, but since her arrest she has never been seen there. Admiral WOLKOFF has been puzzled about this and has even suggested that Mrs STOURTON may have given Anna away to the authorities.

If old WOLKOFF has any reason to think that Mrs STOURTON would know anything about Anna that would be sufficient to give her away, then Mrs Stourton would obviously be worth interviewing. Mrs Stourton is described as being very pro-German. B5b.[5]

Re ADMIRAL WOLKOFF

The following conversation took place between M/G and Admiral WOLKOFF at the Russian Tea Rooms, owned by the latter, on 28.6.40 between 8.30 p.m. and 10 p.m.

M/G reminded Admiral WOLKOFF that he had previously told M/G that he had heard over the German Radio that General NOGUES and MITTELHAUSEN were going to give in and that, since Syria had refused to fight on with the Allies, the Admiral must have heard right.

Admiral WOLKOFF said that yesterday, 27.6.40, he had been listening to the NEW BRITISH BROADCASTING STATION [German propaganda radio] and had heard the plan of how the Germans would invade England and send over 40,000 aeroplanes; and that they would not just land their forces at one single point but at points all round the island.

M/G then asked how one could get the N.B.B.S.

Admiral WOLKOFF replied: 'You get it at 9.30 or 10.30 on 25.08 metres'. He then said he hoped nothing would happen to him because he wanted to see the day when he could spit in the faces of the English.

M/G is prepared to swear to this conversation in court.[6]

When Anna Wolkoff's court case was over, in May 1941, Knight released her from his investigative work to allow MI5 to utilise her talents more productively as a double agent. She was taken on by the Double-Cross team, whose aim was to deceive the German's intelligence services.[7]

The Abwehr and the Sicherheitdienst, the Gestapo's intelligence service, are claimed to have infiltrated about 115 agents into Britain during the war by boat, submarine and parachute. The early arrivals were caught, imprisoned and hanged at Pentonville prison with great publicity. Many gave themselves up, including some who had agreed to work for the Germans to reach Britain, and others were caught having made elementary mistakes. Miller claimed that despite having courage and optimism, a number of Abwehr agents had poor English skills or awareness of English life and customs.[8]

Once the scientists at the Code and Cipher School at Bletchley Park broke the Germans' Enigma code and other ciphers, the British knew when but not exactly where the agents were due to arrive. Except for one who committed suicide, they were interrogated by Lieutenant Colonel Robert Stephens at Latchmore House (Camp 020) in Ham, near Richmond. Those who refused to be 'turned' and work for the British were hanged at Pentonville prison or the Tower of London. This was the work of MI5's BI(a) section, run by Sir John Masterman. He was the chairman of what he called the Twenty Committee, a pun on the Roman numerals XX, meaning twenty, but also a double cross. He and other members of the Intelligence Corps set in place a counter-espionage and deception system with a long-term plan to defeat the Nazis. The deception scheme was run by Major Thomas Argyll Robertson, known by his initial 'Tar', with Major William Luke, known as 'Billy', as his deputy. They and their team of intelligence officers successfully double-crossed the Germans, transmitting British-inspired messages. Friedl was one of a number of women employed in the Double-Cross deception scheme whose stories are largely unknown.

When Luke learned that Friedl had been in touch with the German secret service representative prior to the outbreak of war but had never been asked to do any work for them, it was decided to introduce her to twenty-eight-year-old Dusko Popov at the New Year's Eve party at Worplesdon.

Popov, a wealthy, unmarried and handsome Serbian businessman, arrived in England in December 1940. He had been recruited by the Abwehr when he was studying law at Freiburg University, with a mission to collect intelligence on French politicians who might be helpful to the Germans. However, he revealed his role to the British Passport Control officer in Belgrade, who informed MI6 in London.

Instead of being interrogated at Camp 020 like other Abwehr agents, he described in his autobiography, *Spy Counterspy,* being questioned by MI5, MI6, Naval Intelligence, Air Force Intelligence and Cavendish Bentinck, the chairman of the Joint Intelligence Committee, at the Savoy Hotel. Tar took him out for Christmas Day dinner at Quaglinos restaurant and then billiards at the Landsdowne Club in Berkeley Square. After dinner and champagne back in the Savoy and a nightclub, they were in excellent spirits. Introduced to Stewart Menzies, the head of SIS, at White's gentlemen's club in St James's Street, he was invited to Worplesdon for New Year.[9]

As soon as Popov saw Friedl, whom he described as the most glamorous woman he had clapped his eyes on since arriving in Britain, she was his target for the night. He was reported as needing to be prized off her so that

Menzies could talk to him. Miller described him as the archetypal 'playboy' counterspy, who 'embodied the recklessness, insouciance, shrewdness, high courage and luck which so many writers of fiction have ascribed to the secret service agent'.[10]

His import-export links with Lisbon led to him being cultivated as a double agent – with the code name 'Tricycle', as he liked three in a bed – while Friedl was given the code name 'Gelatine' because she was said to be a jolly little thing. Miller reported having to call occasionally at Bow Street Magistrates' Court some mornings to bail Friedl out of gaol. Going to parties that proved exciting meant she often stayed out beyond the curfew time that had been imposed on foreigners. Many people walked home at night, as getting a taxi, especially during the blackout or an air raid, was difficult. 'On several occasions Friedl was picked up by the police and bundled into a van with a lot of street walkers. The police rule for these ladies was, I think, "No explaining, no complaining" – and make your excuses to the Bow Street magistrates in the morning. It really was necessary to dispel any doubts they [the police] might have entertained, for Friedl, after a night in the cells, looked uncommonly like a prostitute. The clothes we wore in those days were very tarty; dressed up for the evening at the Berkley, and dirty and dishevelled into the bargain, Friedl was in no position to affect surprise over the way she'd been treated. Actually, she was able to make a good story of her prison experience.'[11]

Before Popov was sent to Lisbon to report to his Abwehr controller, it was suggested that while he was overseas, some of his work in London could be given to trusted deputies. MI6 came up with Dickie Metcalfe, code-named 'Balloon', who was falsely rumoured to have been dismissed from his regiment following some discreditable behaviour, and Friedl, who had become one of Popov's lovers. She was tasked with supplying British-inspired political intelligence to the Germans, 'a task she performed with great competence and keenness right up until the end of the war playing an important role in what was called the "Yugoslav Ring" which carried out the instructions of BI[a]'.[12]

She was provided with accommodation at 18 King's Court, King's Road, London SW3, and her first task was to use the contents of the following four news items in letters which, when translated into German, were given to Popov to hand over to Ludovico von Karsthoff, the cover name of the Abwehr chief in Lisbon. How much of it was true is unknown. One of the names and addresses she used was Mrs Ivy Trevallion, 88 York Street, London W1, which explained why subsequent German messages about her referred to her as Ivy. She told them that she would be able to send them political intelligence in return for a payment of £50 a month to cover her expenses.

1. In the recent case where an Admiral's wife (see press) was prosecuted for offences against the state and was found guilty. The woman is Mrs Nicholson who was a member of Captain Ramsay's Right Club. She is thought to have attended several of the Neuremberg [*sic*] Rallies and has met Herr Hitler. The fact that she was found 'not guilty' seems to be more to the minute snobbery of the British middle class jury than to say lack of proof or to a tendency towards

anti-war feeling on the part of the jury. The British find it very difficult to believe that an Admiral's wife can do any act toward National Socialism. I have heard that Miss Michbos was a friend of Anna Wolkoff (sentenced with a man called Kent some time ago for offences under the Defence Regulations) and it is said in quarters which ought to know that the two cases were connected.

2. The prolonged internment of Sir Oswald Mosley is having a very bad effect on the morale both of himself and his followers. Sir Oswald is degenerating in Prison and has lost his personality and inspiration and this has had the effect of discouraging his men who are interned with him. As for those of his organisation who have not been interned, these are falling away in their activity and this is due partly to lack of leadership and partly to the fact that each succession of Air Raids on cities in England produces a powerful war of anti-German feeling. Without the presence of their leaders the members of the British Union will not undertake propaganda work. Their National Socialist ideals are not thought to have ever been very sound and this information seems to prove this.

3. There is a very definite anti-Hungarian wave of feeling at the moment. Several have been arrested. One of them Lady Howard of Effingham whose former name was Manci Guther [?] is well known to me. She has many contacts in foreign Embassies and Legations – chiefly the Brazilian, Swiss and Hungarian. I am also known to some of her contacts as a friend of Lady Howard and I could myself contact these people if desired.

4. I met some time ago at a hotel at Sanderstand in Surrey a Colonel Rousselet. This officer seems to be some kind of Vichy Consular official. I became quite friendly with him and formed the opinion that he is very anti-British. I could easily re-establish my contact with him.[13]

On Luke's suggestion, a subsequent letter included a reference to Rudolf Hess, the deputy Führer of the Nazi party, who arrived on a solo flight in Scotland on 10 May. He hoped to arrange peace talks with the Duke of Hamilton, whom he believed was a prominent opponent of Churchill's government. Arrested on arrival, he was taken into custody. A week later, Luke provided Tar with details of his plans for Gelatine, who acknowledged them as good ideas and gave them his go-ahead.

GELATINE

With TRICYCLE and GELATINE I went down to see Major Knight in the country yesterday, and we discussed with him GELATINE's position. I expressed the opinion that it would be very unwise to continue any investigation work as long as she can usefully be employed as an 'agent double'. Major Knight entirely agreed with this view and informed me that she was absolutely free to undertake these duties and had in fact no other work to do. He said that he thought her contact with the Germans could be used very effectively at the present time in connection with the arrival in this country of HESS, that she could give information as to the effect the incident had had upon the people of influence in this country in the social circle in which GELATINE associates. I told him that I thought there might be difficulties in the way of her passing information over to the enemy in connection with the HESS incident because obviously the policy was one which would have to be dictated from the highest sources and before we could send anything out we should have to see more clearly how to turn the event to our advantage.

Major Knight considered that GELATINE's information to the Germans should be more of a political nature than military, that she would in fact be their link with people of a high state of society in their country. He did not consider that she should provide information as to the whereabouts of aeroplanes, the movement of troops, or the designs of aircraft, but that she should concentrate on providing information more of an Intelligence variety. Her contacts through her brother-in-law would give her the opportunity of picking up a great deal of extremely valuable information of this kind. I told him that I quite agreed that this course should be adopted and mentioned that I thought it would be advisable for TRICYCLE to inform the Germans that although she was willing to do everything she could for the Fatherland, it would be impossible for her to obtain the fullest amount of information unless she received from them some contribution towards her inevitably heavy expenditure. Her position in peacetime vis-à-vis the Germans was that she received no payment but was doing the work out of loyalty for her country, but at that time she had got a good job as secretary to Mr. Dennis Wheatley, a fact of which they were aware and also she had the advantage of a sister who had made a successful marriage. While she is still enjoying the hospitality of her sister she is no longer working for Mr. Dennis Wheatley, although she is still on the very best of terms with him, a fact which must interest the Germans in view of the important and confidential work which this gentleman is undertaking at the present time. While she will spend much of her time in dining out with her men friends and others, obviously she will have to do some entertaining herself the cost of which she is not able to bear, therefore the Germans must try and devise some method of paying her. I told Major Knight that I thought it would be better not to have any definite scheme for effecting this payment as if the task was left to the Germans it might lead us to another of their contacts in this country which might be very interesting, moreover TRICYCLE was not instructed by the Germans to find a means of paying her. If 'Plan Midas' is adopted he can strengthen the attraction of the scheme from the German point of view by mentioning that it would provide a means of paying GELATINE.

At a previous meeting which Major Robertson, TRICYCLE and I had with GELATINE, on May 13th, it was decided that GELATINE would write a preliminary letter with ordinary ink which TRICYCLE would take over to the Germans amongst his papers if he goes as a courier or his own Legation. (A copy of this letter is attached.) It is TRICYCLE's intention to ask KARSTHOFF to send it to Frau AHREFELD [*sic*]. At the same time he will ask KARSTHOFF to send a memorandum on his behalf explaining that they will have to communicate with GELATINE and give her indications as to the information which they are seeking. In other words that the correspondence must be on both sides and not a one-way affair. He will explain that he has told GELATINE how to develop any letters which they write to her in secret ink. The address to which these letters are to be sent is: 18 Kings Court, Kings Road, Chelsea, and I think it would be advisable for us to take out a H.O.W. [Home Office Warrant] on all letters sent to her at this address which have been posted abroad. I do not think in the meantime however that we should interfere with her correspondence in this country.

My idea is that GELATINE should write not more than one letter in 10 days, and that she might look for expenses of about £25 a month. It was agreed by us all that GELATINE should be run as an entirely different agent from BALLOON, the only connecting link being through TRICYCLE himself.

From the purely domestic point of view, I emphasised that any information which GELATINE has to send over to the Germans should pass through this office for approval and that the letters should be written in the presence either of one of the B.2s officers or at any rate under their auspices. Whilst no mention of the subject was made by Major Knight it is fairly clear that as long as she is used as a double agent it is desirable that GELATINE should become a B.2a agent and responsibility for the payment of remuneration may have to be transferred to B.2a.[14]

Popov took her letters with him when he flew to Lisbon on 13 June and, according to his brief, told the Germans that he had met Friedl socially and at first they had expressed themselves as being strongly pro-British, but it gradually became apparent that they were in fact pro-German, and apart from this bond between them they had formed an attachment for each other and were on affectionate terms. He suggested that they probably knew all about her as she had a mother and another sister still living in Germany. Whether he mentioned her sister-in-law being married to the brother of the head of SIS is unknown, but he was supposed to have told them that Friedl had diplomatic and military contacts, especially amongst the American Military Mission.[15]

His introduction worked, and by 8 June Friedl was established with the Germans. With the agreement of Tar, Knight arranged for her to send political and general intelligence in secret ink on the back of each letter. The dead letter box for her correspondence was Maria Ganzalves de Ezevedo, Calcada de Destero 5IIc, Lisbon, and cover names and addresses she used included Molly Curlander, 26 Conduit Street, London W1 and Mrs Nora Channell, 7 Park Lane, London W1.

Translations of the following letters were drafted and, after being checked by MI6, were sent in secret ink on 26 June.

MORENO [?] said on Sunday that the fighting between Germany and Russia would, he thought, have a bad effect in the Argentine, as there are many pro-Ally propagandists there and also many Left Wing refugees who would be made use of.

I am in a position to contact certain White Russians in London who are always playing with politics. These people are delighted at the war with Russia, and have already started to discuss the possibilities of getting Britain to help restore the old regime. It may also be possible for us to check up on any statements made by these White Russians (who are usually liars) from my 'relatives.'

Lady Howard was a close acquaintance of mine from the time when she was almost without means and then later when she became the friend of a man named Weissblat. Weissblat got suddenly into money on the pretence of producing motor torpedo boats, but in my opinion he was trading in arms. The French paper 'Gringoire' accused him in an article in either 1937 or 1938 of being a Soviet Agent in connection with some supposed arms traffic with Spain during the Civil War. My attention to this article was drawn by a supposed cousin of L.H. [Andre d'Antal]. I know this man to be a communist and he was very emphatic to present the accusation against W. as ridiculous. D'Antal is now in British Army. He visited me on his last leave in March 1941, he was full of complaints about the difficulty of getting a Commission as apparently the authorities had heard of his 'political past'. In the right hands this man could be made use of.

After some careful enquiries amongst my 'friends' I found my opinion regarding Weissblat confirmed. He was suspected to be a Russian Agent and through him L.H. All the same, I was told it was not so easy to get her arrested as she has a great number of influential friends, spec. amongst the Diplomats and aristocracy. Some of them are known to me personally, i.e. Sima (Hungarian Press Attaché); Maris de Fries (late of Brazilian Embassy London, now back in Brazil) and the Turkish Ambassador in London. Another friend of hers at the Brazilian Embassy whose name I cannot recall, I have met several times. Other intimate friends of hers whom I have met are: Col. Unassay (Hungarian Military Attaché) and his wife Barbara; Prince Lotfallah. A very intimate friend of L.H. with whom I am acquainted is Baroness Poncracz, a Hungarian in London who might be used as she has very good contacts. Another woman who knows more about L.H. and her private life than anyone is Mrs Ebe Weiss, wife of a man named Norman Weiss. The husband is a diamond dealer, alleged to be crooked. The wife is known to take drugs. I know both these people.[16]

Friedl provided Knight with more details about Mr d'Antal. 'Information has been received from M/G which may be regarded as completely reliable. This information is to the effect that ever since d'Antal's last interview he is still continuing to propagate extreme communist opinions. He has even gone so far as to endeavour to convert the wife of a close personal friend of his, and in doing so has created a great deal of quite unnecessary domestic trouble.'[17]

Another letter sent in mid-July included the following news.

From a conversation my relations had it was possible for me to make out the following story.

About a month ago a man was in Warsaw, called Cook, who had a British passport. Apparently this man is not British but a Polish Jew called Janowitz. As far as I can make out from the conversation he had been in London before the war and had difficulties with the authorities because of his aliens' registration.

It seems to me peculiar that this man could leave England unless he has been given a false passport. It is of course possible that the man is nothing but a crook, but from remarks I heard it seems possible that he is working for England.[18]

The explanation of this deception was revealed in Luke's letter to Major Felix Cowgill, the head of MI6's Section V, counter-espionage, in which he stated that Janowitz, 'an awful blackguard', really was in Warsaw, that 'we should be very glad if we learned that the Germans had cut his throat. He is a crook who obtained a forged passport' and that he was suspected by MI6 of trying to get money out of Russia posing as a British subject. 'If the Germans check him up, they can only do so 100%, as he will tell so many lies that they will not know whether he is playing true or not. It seems to me that GELATINE's message can certainly do no harm and is just the kind of story she would be passing over.'[19] He continued,

> With reference to our discussions the other day about GELATINE, I am rather inclined to think that the best way of dealing with her, if you agree, is as follows:
>
> That you and she should continue to write up the stories which are sent over as I think she is much more likely to work on these matters between with you than with us. I should at the same time like Bill Luke to keep in close contact with both of you and GELATINE on these matters as it may be that he has one or two suggestions to make.
>
> With regard to her pay I am perfectly prepared to take over the whole of this and to pay for any extra expenses which she may have. However, if this presents any difficulties from your point of view, I am perfectly prepared to leave the payment of her salary and such other payments as you make to her in your hands and I will merely pay her expenses. If she receives any money for her efforts from the other side, we will handle this as all this money, under the present arrangements, is paid into a special account at the Bank of England. Out of this money however, we will be able to keep her case going and give her extra money.
>
> I am rather anxious that she should be in a position to entertain more freely as she will be able to increase the value of her information but I do think this would be unwise until such time as we receive some sort of remittance.
>
> As I have said before I am most anxious that she should not do any other kind of work so long as she is doing this special work. I think you will agree with me that this point is most important.[20]

Luke agreed that she ought to be given £5 a week and half of whatever the Germans might send her, up to a maximum of £500 per year. 'If the Germans lose contact with her and she ceases to be of any value to B.2.a, it would be understood that Major Knight would assume once again the responsibility of paying or pensioning her.'[21]

She was then involved in Operation Omnibus, a clever deception plan against the Germans in Norway. In early March 1941, British commandos raided the Lofoten Islands in Northern Norway as part of Operation Claymore, successfully sinking 18,000 tons of enemy shipping. A second raid was planned and she was one of five double agents engaged in making the Germans believe that another invasion was imminent. Masterman described the threat as being

> created by a number of unrelated reports all suggesting that a force was being

created and trained to invade Norway. These messages were sent concerning refugees from Norway, special training of troops in Scotland, advertisements for fishermen with knowledge of the coast of Norway, inspections by the King of Norway in Scotland, and personal suggestive remarks by officers who were supposed to be about to embark on some new enterprise.[22]

On 31 July, at Masterman's request, Friedl met W. E. Duke at the Berkeley Hotel at 6.30 p.m., where Flight Lieutenant Cholmondeley and Colonel Thornton had arranged to meet a Major Tudor Smith. She was left alone with the Major, who revealed that he was very busy working at the War Office, sometimes into the early hours of the morning; that the last time he was as busy was just before the Lofoten raid; that he was always busy before an impending raid; that he was on the Lofoten raid; that he was shortly going abroad; and what was the best strategic point for Britain to invade Norway. With Duke's help she wrote the following letter in secret ink on the back of a friendly letter to Maria Ganzalves de Ezevedo in Lisbon, the cover address for her Abwehr contact, signing it Mrs Susanne Batt, of 11 Avenue, W.4,

> At a cocktail party I met a Major who sounded like 'Truder', he is a professional soldier, 33 years old and seems to drink more than is good for him. He seems to be going on embarkation leave shortly but at the moment has been called to the War Office to settle some detail.
>
> Later I had the opportunity of talking to him, and he told me he had been in Norway, Lofoten and Iceland and that he was a very bad sailor. Somebody had told him that it is possible to cure seasickness with barley sugar 'which he is going to do as soon as he gets back to Scotland.'
>
> Later on another man joined us and the conversation turned to fishing and he told us about his experiences in salmon fishing in the 'Southern Fjord'. Truder seemed greatly interested in this and asked a great many questions regarding the conditions in this district and said finally, 'Come round to the War Office tomorrow. I believe your knowledge can assist us to clear up some difficulties.' This conversation in connection with my aforementioned one made me think that there is something in the air.
>
> As you will have seen from the papers, Lady Howard is free. I had dinner with her last week. Are you interested in her?[23]

Lady Howard, dismissed from Cambridge University because her father was a German, was a supporter of the Spartacus League, a Marxist revolutionary movement, and had helped Germans who fled from the Nazi regime in the 1930s and 1940s. There was no evidence that the Abwehr showed any interest in her.

Operation Anklet was carried out at Christmas in 1941 with British and Norwegian commandos, but this was a diversionary tactic; Operation Archery, a much larger raid, took place on 27 December at Vaagso, further south on the Norwegian coast, without the presence of German naval and air forces. Friedl's letter is thought to have helped persuade the Germans to defend the wrong location. Despite heavy Allied losses, Hitler was forced to employ 30,000 troops in Northern Norway in the belief that the Allies would invade, to put pressure on Sweden and Finland.[24]

When she met Luke on 15 September, he reported her telling him that Knight had told her that if you trust someone, you may as well tell him everything. 'I tried hard to convince her that the particular work she had now undertaken was of such a secret nature as to make it desirable that no-one should be told about it unless it was absolutely essential that we should do so. While she was quite prepared to accept our decision about this, it was plainly obvious that she did not agree with it. From the interview I also gathered that she had intended to ask the Germans whether she should obtain information from [redacted] and I pointed out that this hardly seemed to be necessary since obviously she would be expected by them to get whatever information she could discretely obtain from any friend.'[25]

On 15 October she was reported to have been delighted when an unusual telegram came from Popov, who had been sent to the United States in August. Superficially, it was interpreted to mean that Maria Gonzalvez de Azevedo was no longer functioning as a dead letter box so that it was useless for her to continue writing to her at that address. There was also the hint that she would be sent some welcome additional income. However, Luke was more suspicious and addressed his concerns to Major Robertson.

Assuming Gelatine to be a real German agent; she receives a telegram from the Germans informing her that 'Aunt Mary had died and that she would receive details of the legacy by letter'. Gelatine's first reaction to this telegram was that the address she had been given was no longer available and she would receive another one by letter. If she was real and sincere she would obviously accept this as an order not to write to this address again and, as she does not know what has happened at the other end she would hesitate to disobey this order as she might cause trouble to her friends by writing again. Nor would she want them to think that she was so stupid as to misunderstand such a telegram.

I personally do not think that the Germans would laugh off any disobedience to their orders nor would they themselves take the blame and think that their telegram was not worded clearly enough for her to understand. They would merely consider her to be either stupid or unreliable.

I do not think that Gelatine, being merely a German agent and knowing little of their methods would jump to the conclusion that the Germans by their telegram were paving the way for a remittance to her. Why should they do it in such a way? Gelatine would hardly believe that she is the only agent the Germans have in this country?

Another point raised by Mr. Luke was, that the Germans might have been unfortunate in their choice of the name of 'Aunt Mary', thus conveying that it referred to 'Maria', whereas that actually meant that she could expect some money and if they had called the aunt 'Jane' this might have been clear. An agent in the ordinary way trusts the people he is working for and it would never occur to him that such a stupid mistake could have been made.

It is possible that the Germans are trying to stop Gelatine writing altogether, but then why do it in this way? If that address is still available there is no particular reason why Gelatine should not go on writing to it, as they have nothing to lose by it and might possibly gain some useful information. She might get very annoyed if she hears nothing from them and possibly inform the British about Tricycle. But if they worried about that possibility they would not merely send her a telegram such as she has received and do nothing further as it might make her equally furious.

I merely felt that if Gelatine wrote a letter with secret writing at the present juncture, ignoring instructions and possibly causing the Germans difficulties, her chances of being used further by them would be very small, whereas if she waits another four weeks little is lost and a lot might be gained. If after that period she still has heard nothing and if she then writes an open letter as drafted by her, with no secret writing on it but containing the threat that she is going to write secret ink letters twice a month to that address, she might get a reaction, particularly if that address is really unsuitable and possibly dangerous to the Germans.

Although the Germans are bound to have their doubts about Gelatine, if they trust Tricycle they can hardly believe that Gelatine is run by the British and it might be dangerous to give them any such ideas by Gelatine not behaving true to the form of a loyal German who, although very annoyed at not hearing from them, would not go out of her way to make things difficult for them, at least not just yet.[26]

As Balloon had the same cover address and had received a similar telegram, SIS made enquiries in Lisbon. Their response indicated that the wrong address had been given and that there was no Maria with the name given. However, on 27 January 1942, Friedl was 'delighted' to receive a letter from 'Mary' in Lisbon and anticipated funds to be transferred to her account. She wrote an open letter to the Germans and, as she had nothing else to do, she was told to start collecting political or military information 'such as could be obtained by an agent of high social standing in the West End of London'. Any expenses incurred would be reimbursed on her production of receipts.

On 10 February, a letter arrived from Lisbon giving her the new contact: Jose Augusto Vieira, Rua Marques da Silva 87, Lisbon. A few weeks later, Luke noted that he had discussed the recent developments in Gelatine's case with Cavendish Bentinck at the Foreign Office and explained that she could hardly be able to collect relevant information on her social visits as her contacts and friends were not as good or as numerous as the Germans had been led to believe. With MI5's consent, she had contact with Fraulien von Ahlefeldt, the secretary of the London-based Nationalist Socialist German Workers Party, who was able to provide monthly information, but ideally she needed 'a special friend' in the Foreign Office. Bentinck volunteered, but Luke commented that to put him in the position of Friedl's boyfriend was 'going a little close to the knuckle'. Instead, Mr Eden's private secretary, 'an extremely good-looking young man', was chosen, but his name was not revealed.[27]

As the Germans had not paid her anything for her work, Knight increased her pay to £7 a week and covered the expenses of her Chelsea flat, but revised the amount she should receive from 'the other side' down to 5 per cent.

In a lunch with Luke and Friedl in early March, Bentinck dropped what were thought to be suitably indiscreet remarks which she could use in a subsequent letter of disinformation.

> Amongst other things he said that the Germans from their own point of view are making a great mistake in employing the present German ambassador in Barcelona and would do much better if they sent Ribbentrop. He also said that Viscount Kano was in this country and was enjoying liberty, and that he had been left here as a sort of insurance policy by the Japanese who would no doubt wish to negotiate for peace possibly before the end of this year. They regarded him as a person who would be acceptable in this country and who would be able to arrange for terms which would be advantageous to Japan. He expressed it as his opinion that Japan was quite prepared to negotiate a separate peace, and was entirely out for her own ends, and that she would not hesitate to leave Germany in the lurch if it seemed expedient.
>
> He mentioned that many Italians were getting over to this country, fugitives from their own regime, and he suggested that conditions in Germany were much more serious than our papers made out. Their losses in the Russian campaign having been enormous. He said reading newspapers in this country the public comes to the conclusion that the war is going very badly for us and very much in favour of our enemies. Whilst this was true as far as Japan was concerned, he felt convinced that people in Germany were becoming very anxious and that morale was not nearly as good there as it is in this country.
>
> He did not think that Japan was in a position to invade India, and it was his opinion that they would fight shy of territory of this size.
>
> He compared the war position today with that of the early Spring of 1918 when the British people began to face the possibility of defeat at the hands of the Germans, remarking that history had a habit of repeating itself. He inferred that it was quite possible that Germany would collapse towards the end of this year. Mr Cavendish Bentinck knows GELATINE's sister and brother-in-law quite well.[28]

When Kano Hisaakira, head of the Yokohama Specie Bank and leading member of the Japanese community in London, was interned following the United States' declaration of war against Japan, Masterman decided that Friedl ought not to mention him. In fact, there were a number of people who were beginning to question her usefulness. Bentinck, in correspondence with Luke about her work, commented that he was not favourably impressed. Her mentality, he told him, was that of a 'night club hostess'; she was not by any means an intelligent woman, but her chief wish was always to be on the right side at the right time. He did not think that she was double-crossing the British, because that would not have been in her interest, but 'she was definitely frightened, indeed she had a "holy terror" of the Germans and especially what might happen to her if they won'. Her sister, he thought, was being supported by Lady Holford, her mother-in-law, and 'the Greek'.[29]

Ian Wilson, one of the MI5 officers with responsibility for Friedl's case, was of the opinion that she was incapable of obtaining information on her own and that, as the Germans were showing no interest in her, he was 'inclined to let her case die altogether and not write again if her case stood by itself, but in view of the interlock with TRICYCLE's case it may just be worthwhile writing one further letter on the lines suggested to try and keep GELATINE alive'.[30]

Wilson then repeated his concerns about her, commenting that he thought it pointless to keep on paying her when she was not generating any valuable information. He suggested requiring her to come into the office once a fortnight and write down a dictated letter for them and that 'if Knight had any use for her, then he ought to employ her, providing she was available for secret writing'.[31]

In the middle of April, following Popov's report that the Germans had told him that they had lost contact with Gelatine, she was asked to write an open letter to Vieira enquiring about why she had had no response to her earlier letters. Masterman arranged for the Post Office censors to open the envelope and treat it in such a way as to give the impression that it had been tested for secret writing. However, when a telegram arrived in May from New York with evidence that the Germans suspected Tricycle and Balloon of being under Allied control, it was decided not to send the letters.

As there had been no replies to the letters sent to Vieira, SIS in Lisbon was asked to investigate. They reported there was no building with such a number on that road. Popov then provided an alternative contact: Lucilia Martens, 164 Rua da Rosa, Lisbon, to whom Friedl wrote the following open letter and signed it 'Mabel Walters, 168 Dora Road, London, SW19'.

I received a letter from P. [Popov] yesterday with this address. I cannot understand why this took so long, his letter was dated March 21st. I cannot imagine what you think you are doing with me. Since months I have been writing to Maria, no reply with the exception of an almost meaningless telegram. At last in February I received your news with Vieira's address in which you promised me immediate instructions after you received my reply. I wrote to Vieira but received no instructions and two weeks later I wrote again an open letter. Aren't you getting my letters? I would like to help my fatherland but you must at least tell me what you want from me. I will write some information tomorrow which I have heard from very influential people. But you must let me know if it is of interest to you. I do not see why I should risk my head without doing anything useful. I shall therefore not write again until I hear something from you.[32]

The following day, she wrote the following letter in secret ink:

Lord Beaverbrook refused to join the War Cabinet if it included Sir Stafford Cripps. Well informed circles in London were never confident about the Cripps mission to India. He is very popular with the public.

I heard that General Wavell would hand in his resignation should he not receive sufficient reinforcements and supplies this time.

The Japanese allowed Prince Kano to remain here as it was thought that he would be a suitable person should it come to peace negotiations between England and Japan.

The working classes here take every opportunity to humiliate rich people. No effort is made to give the right position and work to the right people. A young professional pianist was told that 'music is only a luxury'. She is now working in a munitions factory and her hands are ruined.

The people here are somewhat worried about the friction between England and Australia.[33]

On the same day, Flight Lieutenant Cholmondeley reported on Operation Tribage. This was three double agents, Tricycle, Balloon and another called Bicycle, who were reported as compromised. The Federal Bureau of Investigation had intercepted Popov's messages to Lisbon, revealing he had two agents operating in England. The Americans were playing their own game by sending their own messages to his cover address, attempting to learn the identity of his agents.

Cholmondeley argued that the Germans should be supplied with the relevant facts, which would confirm in their minds what they would like to believe. 'At this point we must review the traffic. GELATINE's traffic can be disposed of as being practically useless. On the other hand, the TRICYCLE – BALLOON traffic sent from England, which can for this purpose be considered as one source, has provided the enemy with a considerable amount of accurate and interesting details. The only deceptions to which this traffic has been made party are Plan MACHIAVELLI (which failed), Plan OMNIBUS (to a very slight degree), Plan MIDAS, PLAN BIRD WATCHER and "Anson in the Far East".'[34]

Wilson decided to wait for a fortnight before sending Friedl's last letter to give the Germans the impression that Gelatine had been arrested and that Balloon was being used as a double agent. She was told that the letters weren't sent because they had learned from the Americans that the Germans suspected that Popov had been turned and that it was therefore okay for her to work for Knight.[35]

At about the same time, she received a subpoena to appear in court regarding a case brought by Ben Greene against the Home Secretary for wrongful arrest. To avoid her identity exposing her to possible retribution, MI5 took measures to ensure that her name did not appear in the press identifying her as a British agent.[36]

She seemed very anxious to re-establish contact with the Germans and put forward various suggestions, such as that she might visit Ireland and get in touch with them from there. Wilson declined her offer, claiming it was unfeasible given the state of play with Popov.[37]

The situation took another turn when Popov sent her a questionnaire of instructions and a new address for her letters: Sousa & Campos Ltd, an antiques shop at 162a Rua da Rosa, Cunhal das Rolas in Lisbon. The Germans' renewed interest sparked an enquiry, the result of which was Tar informing Harry Kimball, the head of American Counter Espionage, that

GELATINE moves in good social circles and ought to be in a position to get good information from well-placed friends in military, Government and diplomatic circles. In fact she has proved a complete failure in providing good information on her own and now that her case looks becoming more active we will have to provide her information for her.[38]

Given the difficulties she had had with Wilson, Masterman allocated her a new case officer, Gisela Ashley, the most senior woman in B1a, who was a German-born expert on Nazism and whose cover name was Mrs Susan Barton. Before meeting Friedl, she queried with Masterman a few points about helping her write the letters.

1. I do not know whether Gelatine knows you, but I feel that it might be advisable if she was told by you that I will in future deal with her case. I have no idea what Gelatine thinks I am doing and such an explanation would certainly make my position easier.

2. As Gelatine is supposed to be getting £200 now, is there any arrangement by which she receives a certain percentage of this money, like the other agents?

3. I do not know how her incoming letters are developed now, I only saw the Photostat copy of the last one. I take it, however, that they are developed by heat and not by chemical process?

4. In order to get traffic, would it be possible for me to work with Mr Mills on this case, provided he is not too busy and is agreeable to doing this?

In view of the fact that Gelatine seems to have misunderstood the instructions given her, only to write on the back of her letter, in fact on the blank page, we should have to carry on like that for a short time, until she was either reprimanded or else had the sense to get herself larger sheets of note-paper. I am only mentioning this in case of a come-back from the other side.

I would like to discuss with Gelatine ideas of how to make her letters real, try and rouse her interest and obtain her collaboration, in fact make her do a good deal of work also. I take it that she is not working for anybody else at present and that there will be no objections from other quarters. By the way, I gathered from a remark she made that she tells Major Knight everything.[39]

This was arranged by John Marriott, Tar's deputy, who argued that Mrs Barton would be needed to ensure that all Friedl's letters read like they had been written by a woman. However, there was an issue, as she had run out of secret ink. An alternative source was suggested, a styptic pencil, which men used to staunch bleeding after shaving. Chemists determined that it was made of alum, which, when dissolved in water, produced secret ink.

1. Get a 'shaving stone' {Alum, colour of no importance).

2. Scrape some off with a knife.

3. In one tablespoon of water dissolve so much of the powder as will leave a small residue after three minutes' stirring with a toothpick.

4. Write only with a toothpick very lightly, taking care not to scratch the paper. Write only on one side and in block capitals, crosswise to the open text of the letter.

5. After writing, allow to dry for at least half an hour, then steam both sides of the paper over a kettle for about half a minute.

6. Lay the paper flat on a glass plate or marble table top with a piece of white blotting paper on top of it and a large book on top of the blotting paper. Add further books to increase the weight.

7. When the paper is dry, rub it hard with another piece of paper of the same kind with a circular motion.

8. Now write the open text on top of the secret text.

9. Thick paper is most suitable.[40]

Once a suitable supply had been acquired, with Barton's input, Friedl began her letter writing again. One such letter, written in November, told the Germans that there was a difference of opinion between Churchill and Sir Stafford Cripps, a member of the War Cabinet whose radical proposals had failed to win India's support for the Allies' efforts.

> Cripps had handed in his resignation, that [Anuerin] Bevin was trying to calm everybody down but that Cripps was tired of being in the Cabinet. In view of today's news that Cripps is out of the Cabinet the Germans ought to feel very pleased with Gelatine, and in view of the fact that this information was written nearly 5 weeks ago there can hardly be any suspicion of double-cross.[41]

In appreciation of her efforts, the Germans transferred £211 17s 4d to the Midland Bank, from which she was given 10 per cent, not the 5 per cent that Knight had suggested. The writing continued over the winter of 1942, but by early Spring 1943, the Germans expressed concerns about the poor quality of Friedl's information; Tar wrote to Wilson, commenting that

> I am most anxious, as you know, to provide Mrs. B. with a considerable pool of traffic which she can use and thus keep the GELATINE case going without having to submit the tripe which she is at present forced to submit for approval owing to the fact that she has nothing better to put forward. I should be very glad if you would make it your personal business to see that everything possible is done to attain this object.
>
> I have heard from Maxwell Knight that GELATINE has complained that the traffic which she is being allowed to send over is of pretty low grade.

> I told Mrs. B. that I had spoken to you about helping in the provision of traffic and that you would be responsible for providing as much traffic as possible. I pointed out to her at the same time all the snags in putting forward traffic to the approving authorities and getting approved in a hurry. I said that it always took a long time to get traffic back from the approving authorities unless one could persuade them to approve it on the spot which happened very rarely.

> Bevan is providing me with an Order of Battle of American Forces all over the world with names of Commanding Officers. When we get this we should be able to use a good deal of this for GELATINE.[42]

Friedl came up with the idea of telling the Germans that she was going to get married and go to Northern Ireland, where she might be able to obtain useful intelligence. Initially, Barton thought that it would be 'a grand idea' if she married an IRA man, but, having second thoughts, she told Tar,

> A woman is supposed to marry for love, even in German ideas and particularly when it comes to changing your nationality, and once she marries her loyalties, certainly to start with will be with her husband.
>
> I do not know the details of this plan, of course, but unless she marries somebody rather peculiar I do not see how it will work. I am afraid the Germans would think it much more likely if she became the mistress of somebody <u>fairly high up</u> who went to Northern Ireland and took her with him, if only for a short period.[43]

When Tar told Barton that he had no objections to this plan, she identified a potential target, General Fuller, a contributor to the *Evening Standard* who she claimed had gone on the war path again, encouraging the government to launch an invasion. She queried this option with Tar.

> I therefore feel it might not be a bad thing if Gelatine mentions him once or twice in her letters, showing that she sees a fair amount of him. (She mentioned him to the Germans in connection with the North African campaign). I am not suggesting that he gives away any military secrets at present, but he might have said to her, for instance, that he is endeavouring with his constant criticism and with his suggestions to influence the Government against its will and force it to undertake larger offensives.
>
> He might possibly even say to her, being a very vain man, that he feels he is entitled to a fair amount of the credit for the North African undertaking as he advocated such an undertaking months before it was carried out. If I remember rightly he actually did write an article along such lines a good many months ago.
>
> This last remark has certain dangers though, for supposing the Government is contemplating an offensive somewhere and General Fuller has the same idea and is allowed to write about it, it would be a pity.
>
> Quite apart from this, however, I think General Fuller would be very useful as a supposed contact for Gelatine ... If you approve I would like a few personal details about General Fuller and we might ruin his character a bit at the same time. I am not suggesting that Gelatine becomes a Mata Hari, but the Germans would think it most natural if a bit of sex came into the picture and they would expect [illegible] would ever believe that General Fuller might not be persona grata with the British authorities if he can write the way he does.
>
> P.S. The above suggestion is made on the assumption that General Fuller is not in direct contact with the Germans.[44]

Tar considered that it would be useful for Barton to collect Fuller's articles from the *Evening Standard* but, in view of the Germans' request for military intelligence, he would not be an ideal contact.

Later that month, there was a further twist in the story. Wilson suggested to Tar that to avoid any suspicion falling on Popov, Friedl's case should be brought to an end. He argued that she was asking for more money and that Mrs Barton agreed that

> it would be logical for GELATINE to lose interest, especially when things appear to be going not so well for the Germans.
>
> She has recently asked for money for expenses, and if this, as probably will be the case, is not paid by the date on which she asked for it, she would naturally write less and less frequently and take less and less trouble to obtain information.
>
> It is suggested therefore, that GELATINE should gradually slacken off without meanwhile altering the character, as distinct from the number of her letters. I see no reason why, during this slowing down process, GELATINE should not use the story about General FULLER on the lines indicated in the attached note from Mrs Barton.[45]

A four-page MI5 'appreciation' of Fuller, a previous member of the British Union, was included in Friedl's file, with the conclusion that the best way of keeping him quiet was by leaving him alone. However, it was agreed that Barton use the information. Having studied it at length, she decided that her plan of Fuller falling for Friedl would not work. Instead, she arranged for Friedl to meet Mrs Fuller, who had similar pro-German views, and to tell the Germans that she had been invited to their home in Oxted for the day. A further letter would narrate how impressed Friedl was with the general and tell them that she had found a really good contact.

The German's response to her letter posted on 24 March included an offer of more money and an interest in Fuller. This prompted Wilson to reopen her case and 'use her as a channel to pass over deceptions about Commandos and/or invasion, using FULLER as her informant. Her next letter included a paragraph about gliders being towed to Norway and a newspaper report about a headquarters of parachutists at Hardangervilla [*sic*]'.[46]

Following a request from the Germans in March, she included a fictitious report on what preparations the British were making for gas warfare and about new gas-mask filters being issued to the troops and population in various parts of Britain. In another letter, she reported meeting a 'very cock-a-hoop' Greek naval commander and lieutenant commander at a cocktail party, describing how good Greece was in early summer and that they were about to be sent to Cairo.

Learning that the Germans had transferred £238 16*s* 1*d* into her bank account on 2 April must have pleased Friedl, even though she was asked to give MI5 a cheque for 90 per cent of it. As her previous letter had asked them for payment, she was ordered to apologise in her next letter for pestering them.

On 10 June, Barton was given the go-ahead for Friedl to include the following in one of her letters.

> Gelatine told me the following story which I thought might possibly be of interest to the Section concerned.

Paul Riebenfeld, a member of the Jewish World Executive, told her that he doubted all these frightful atrocity stories the Poles told about the Polish Jews. Although he knew that many were killed, he thought that it was very likely that the Poles told these frightful stories about the Polish Jews more for propaganda purposes than anything else and in order to gain sympathy for themselves at the same time. He therefore went to the Polish Government the other day and asked them to interrogate some of the prisoners of the Afrika Korps to find out what these prisoners knew of these atrocities in order to get some sort of idea of the truth. The Poles, however, firstly refused to do this, which confirmed his opinion.

Gelatine put the above story to me as traffic, and although I told her that I thought it doubtful that it would be approved, I did not say that I had no intention of using it. She also said that as she did not know whether Riebenfeld had told this story to anybody else, she would like it treated confidentially as she would not like him to think she had repeated anything he told her. Riebenfeld is a good friend of hers.[47]

At the end of June, Barton commented that 'Gelatine was getting a bit dissatisfied with her idle life and finally talked to me about it'. She did not want work with ammunitions and thought canteen work with officers rather than workers might be possible, but was told that her German passport meant it was out of the question. When she expressed an interest in gaining British citizenship, arguing that Knight had already helped people who were working for him, Barton suggested she took some Red Cross courses so she could help in post-war reconstruction work. While she did not tell Friedl, she told Robertson that she did not feel Friedl wanted to become British out of any love for Great Britain, but rather because it would be more convenient.[48]

By this time, Friedl was in a relationship with Donald 'Don' Calder, a promising, young American diplomat. Because the United States government would not allow him to marry a German citizen, she was considering being naturalised. When Wilson was asked his opinion, he informed Tar that he agreed with Barton in that Friedl was not 'a worker, and therefore I do not see how we could recommend her to any prospective employer. On the other hand, she would make a fuss and her highly-placed relations would no doubt intervene on her behalf if she was given some menial work. If she really wanted to work I am sure she could find an occupation for herself'.[49]

Her domestic situation was rarely commented on in her file, except that she spent some time in 1943 in a nursing home recuperating from a broken ankle and attending the christening of her niece, for whom Popov was the godfather.

There was a tense time in November 1943 when it was learned that Friedl's letters were being intercepted by the Post Office Censorship Board. It appeared that they had been informed by the Portuguese post office that a British spy was sending letters with secret writing to Sousa & Campos Ltd antiques shop in Lisbon. This was Gelatine and Balloon's dead letter box. The owner had died and the person who took over his premises continued to work for the Germans, but as the war looked like it was going the Allies' way, the Portuguese post office informed their English counterpart. Although there was a worry that the Germans might have suspected Friedl's identity would be revealed, Hugh Astor, another MI5 officer, arranged for Friedl's mail to be opened and the secret writing developed and left to fade out before it was sent. His idea was that it would convince the Germans that her mail was being opened. An SIS investigation revealed that the shop had been used as a dead letter box for German agents in England, the United States, South America and Axis-controlled countries.

The Germans' response was to supply Popov with new addresses for Friedl's letters, which he delivered when he next arrived in London. He also brought £430, £30 of which was to cover the cost of a microscope she needed to be able to read the 'duffs' – the micro-photographs – he gave her. As part of her agreement, she only got 10 per cent of the rest.

The technology of secret writing had improved in early 1944; she was using a silver-nitrate pencil to write once a fortnight to addresses in Lisbon. Even though Most Secret Sources, dated 3 March, revealed that the Germans thought her first February letter was 'not uninteresting', MI5 considered closing her down. Barton admitted that

> Gelatine's letters since January 1944 have not contained any very good information, partly because I was unable to get the stuff and partly because no definite policy had been settled. Her last letter of 1 March contained one or two bits which should interest the Germans. Her letter of 12 March containing the Norway deception, was also partly in the nature of a build up as it would clearly have interested the Germans. It was worded carefully enough so as not to let too much blame for wrong information fall on her, and she could have made up for it again later with other information.[50]

The Norway deception was part of the planning for D-Day. To reduce the German defences at Normandy, one of the plans put in place was to give the impression that an invasion of Norway was imminent, thus keeping German reinforcements out of France.

When it was learned that the air-mail service to Lisbon had been cancelled in March, Wilson took the decision for her to carry on writing, explaining that they would take longer to arrive. What the content of her letters were is unknown and there was no indication in her file that they played any role in the outcome of D-Day.

On 7 June 1944, when the future of the letter-writing agents was discussed, Masterman was told by Bentinck that he would like to see Gelatine's case continued, 'so long as we had fair reason to suppose that she was believed in by the Germans'.[51] Barton's opinion had been tainted on learning from Mrs Jones, one of Knight's staff, that an American professor she met at a party had asked her what secret work Friedl was engaged in, intimating that she had already told him, and that he thought her to be anti-British and having rather a lot of money. Knight agreed that she needed 'a bit of a shock to keep her on the straight and narrow path'. Ironically, she had fallen for the same sort of trap that Fifi laid. The American professor was described as 'a very charming man who might easily invite a girl's confidence and that she might have said more than she intended. If this is so, Gelatine obviously slipped up, she will know in whom she confided and it will be a lesson to her not to do it again. Up till then she seems to have been very discreet'.[52]

As to her expensive habits, Barton decided to examine Friedl's bank account but nothing untoward was revealed. Given Bentinck's wishes for her to continue to provide political content in her letters, he agreed that he would act as her contact in the Foreign Office and for her to say that she met him at a social event in Worplesdon.

However, Barton acknowledged that the real difficulty was getting 'up-to-date or advance political information, whether home or foreign. Perhaps the F.O. have some ideas of what they would like the Germans to believe, whether it is true or not.'[53]

Despite the fact that the last letter from the Germans had been in April and there was the possibility that they had lost interest in her as her last two letters had requested money, it was decided that she would send one more. It would point out that the military course of the war made it futile for her to keep sending military information, demanding more money and saying that she would try to get work with the United Nations Refugee Relief Agency in an attempt to return home.[54] The draft written the following day read,

Coutinha,

This is definitely the last letter I am going to write to you, as it seems quite obvious that you are no longer interested in me. I cannot help feeling that I have deserved better treatment than just being dropped without a word. After all, I ran the risks, and not you. If that is the way everybody who has worked faithfully for the cause [fatherland] is being treated, now that things are not going well, all I can say is that the future looks pretty gloomy to me.

What I told you in my previous letter about some of the plans made in Canada has been confirmed to me by another source, so it seems to be true. But even that is probably of no interest to you. I simply cannot understand your attitude. Do please write to me.[55]

The letter was sent thinking that it would close her case. MI5 decided to offer her £100 as a parting gift and asked her to leave the flat, but, contrary to expectations, she received a reply, which revived their interest. The 'duffs' it included contained requests for more information to be sent to two new dead letter boxes in Lisbon. Barton was told to ensure Friedl mentioned that the focus of activity had shifted from England to the Continent, where practically everyone she knew had been sent.

She can say, if you like, that she has so far found no trace of the Uranium Research Institute. She might put in some piece as the following: 'A curious thing has happened. In order to get information about acetone works I mentioned to a business friend the fact that British Industrial Solvents Ltd. is, as reported by you, at Hull, and he replied that the factory is not working any longer at Hull. He said nothing about any other factories.'

We have no idea whether this is true or not, but if it is not it cannot do GELATINE any harm and if the Germans believe it is it provides quite a good foundation for GELATINE failing to give any information about any other factories since it will appear that the Germans have misled her.

Anglo-American feeling. We suggest something as follows: 'I will make a study of this. My impression is that there are a great many squabbles between the British and the Americans but that these are almost all over unimportant matters or relate to post-war affairs. The sorest point is civil aviation. General Critchley's violent speech about post-war competition in the air caused ill-will on both sides, but what he said got a good deal of support from many Englishmen.'[56]

Over the next five months she sent regular letters, in return for which the Germans sent her a platinum bracelet with 'brilliants' to a cover address at 68 Old Compton Road in Soho. In her file was a transcript of the Abwehr communication between Lisbon and Berlin relating to Ivy, which may well have been obtained from Most Secret Sources. Although the first few lines have been redacted, the rest cover the period from 10 March 1942 to 10 April 1945. The following cover the period from November 1943, and help to explain the Germans' generosity.

5.11.44 Berlin – Lisbon. 29. Secret. HIOB Junior to FORROS for HARRY. Your mag. 109 ref. IVY (ISBAA 4398). Address of 1943 known here: reads:- LONDON, CHELSEA, 18 KINGS COURT, KINGS ROAD.

1.2.45 Lisbon – Berlin. 65. BABETTE for MATE. V Link IVY reports from LONDON by letter: At about 18 hrs. on 14/1 a V2 projectile came down in SYDENHAM, another one landed in TILBURY on the afternoon of 13/1. FORROS HYON.

29.3.45 Lisbon – Berlin. 718/ To SIBELIUS. V. IVY reports by letter from LONDON posted 10 March received in LISA 25 March. A naval officer stationed on the East Coast said that the V.1 was 'easy meat' [anglice] for the US A.A. and were shot down so easily that the triple defence line of aircraft, guns and balloons (the last in the eastern suburbs of LONDON) was almost superfluous. There have been V.2 hits in BALLINGS, KINGSTON, ISLINGTON, SOUTHWARK, and BERMONDSEY, SHOREDITCH, HACKNEY and BLOOMSBURY. KING's CROSS STATION is very badly damaged. FORROS HYON.

31.3.45 Berlin – Lisbon. 139. For FORROS for HYON. Subject: IVY. Ref/ your FS 178 of 29/3 (ISBA 7410). Reports of hits are value less unless exact location be given, for example, the name of the street. Can IVY [verb missed] hits, giving exact place and time separated. [Remainder missed.]

27.3.45 Berlin – Lisbon. For FORROS HYON. Ref. [3 corrupt] assignments for V IVY and EVA [12 corrupt] recce. At present of priority: Regular reports on English and American divs., armoured divs. or inf. Divs. Transfer of divs., bdes, or rgts. To the continent, or new arrivals, perhaps by asking officers.

Description of totems on uniforms and vehicles, names of commanders of bdes, or regts. With present quarters or changes of quarters. BABETTE SIBELIUS 12093/3/45 of 26/3/

9.4.45 Lisbon – Berlin. 774. SIBELIUS. V contact IVY reports by letter from London on ¼. ADMIRAL LOUIS HAMILTON if First Lord Naval Member of Commonwealth Naval Board.

10.4.45 Lisbon – Berlin. SIBELIUS 777. V link IVY reports by letter from LONDON ¾. I have learned from an informed source that the TUC leaders wanted to be officially represented at the YALTA conference, but that this was refused by EDEN. To square matters EDEN assured them that a TUC official should go to SANFANCISCO as an official British delegate, provided that the opposition permitted this. FORROS HYON.

10.4.45 Lisbon – Berlin. 780. SIBELIUS. V link IVY reports in writing from London ¾. 1]. T 0940 hours on 14/3 a flying bomb fell in GREENFORD. 2]. At 1000 hours on 25/3 a V 2 fell in the Speakers' Corner in HYDE PARK and damaged the CUMBERLANDS Hotel which is nearby. FORROS HYON.[57]

In March 1945 an issue arose when she informed MI5 that she had been offered a job as a part-time translator for the Americans. Knight recognised that this could cause problems. If they found out that she was a German spy working for MI5 they might think that she had deliberately been planted on them by the British. A meeting with the American ambassador was arranged to facilitate her employment; however, it proved unnecessary. She had turned it down as she realised that it might jeopardise her impending marriage to Don Calder, who was then working in Sweden for the American Ministry of Economic Warfare.

Knight pointed out that she had been unofficially engaged to Calder, a promising young American diplomat, for two years. Because he was not allowed to marry a German citizen, he was prepared to give up work to marry Friedl, but if the British granted her naturalisation, it would be considered a reward for her contribution to the British Intelligence Service.

On 16 June 1945, she was officially told that she was no longer needed and that MI5 would do what they could for her. She was given £51 pay and £100 'severance' pay. When asked if she had been happy with how she had been treated, she said yes, and the only question she asked was whether the Americans would be informed of her wartime role. They did not tell her that they already knew, but told her that if she decided to tell them then she was to contact Knight first. Finally, she had to sign the Official Secrets Act. This was completely the opposite of all the agents taken on by the SOE, who signed theirs at the beginning of their training.

When she left MI5, she applied for naturalisation. Knight wrote on her behalf pointing out 'the very particular disabilities under which this girl is suffering, and which can solely be attributed to actions taken by her on our behalf'.[58] As he had instructed her to get a German passport to assist in his plans for her undercover work, she was now in an awkward position should she want to travel in Europe, especially if there was an active Nazi underground who wanted to exact revenge on double agents. Her request for naturalisation was refused. The Home Office's response was that there were 15,000 applications to process, some of whom had applied before the war, and that they did not want to give her preferential treatment.

What happened to her after the war was not revealed in her files.

8

John Masterman's Double Agent 'Treasure': Nathalie Sergueiew

Another double agent was thirty-year-old Nathalie Sergueiew, sometimes written Natalia Sergueiev, who was known in England as Lily or by her code name, 'Treasure'. She arrived at Bristol Airport in England, using the name Dorothy Tremayne, on 5 November 1943, and was immediately driven under police escort to Nightingale Lane in Clapham, London. Although MI5 knew a lot about her already, MI6 wanted to ensure that she was not a German agent. Transcripts of her interviews with Mary Sherer, the twenty-nine-year-old MI5 officer in charge of their female agents, revealed that she was born in Petrograd in 1912. Her Russian parents fled St Petersburg after the 1917 Russian Revolution and settled in Paris, her father working as a car dealer. Her grandfather was the last imperial ambassador to Yugoslavia; her uncle, Lieutenant-General Eugen de Miller, commanded the Russian Fifth Army during the First World War and she had other relatives living in Turkey, Portugal, Shudpain and England. She finished her studies at the École Villiers and the Convent de l'Assomption before studying painting at the Academie Julian. Fluent in French, English and German, she visited Sweden, Yugoslavia and England.

> A London friend of her mother described Lily then as being 'a minor celebrity'. She had sent her first exhibit to the Salon that spring and it was accepted and become the picture of the year. She was, at that time, fat and plain with mouse coloured hair and no idea how to dress and her mother obviously thought her a phenomenon and a pity. She was intelligent, however, and was profiting by her initial success by writing free-lance articles for the press.[1]

In 1930, she walked through Germany to Warsaw, returning via Denmark. While in Berlin she stayed with Felix Dassel, a journalist friend who provided her with useful contacts. In summer 1934, she cycled with her cousin Bessie – Dr Elizabeth Hill, a lecturer at Cambridge University – to Czechoslovakia, Austria and Yugoslavia, and returned on her own through Italy. She admired the Nazi ideology and their striking personalities and, with Dassel's help, had managed to interview Herman Goëring, who founded the Gestapo and in 1935 commanded the Luftwaffe. He told her that he could get her an interview with Hitler.

Nathalie, known to her friends as Lily, got an article published in *Le Jour*, and the editor, keen to get the interview with the German chancellor, asked her to go to Berlin. Although unsuccessful, Dassel persuaded her to go in his place to Czechoslovakia and interview three ministers about the Small Entente. He then paid her for her articles, which were published in *Figaro*. After this she had articles on interviews with Balkan politicians published in *Le Petit Journal*. As a surprise for her, her father published her letters to him as 'Mon Voyage a Pied' in *Editions des Portiques*. While they did not extol the Germans, they were not unsympathetic.

Unable to get a visa to visit Spain to interview Spanish Republicans during the Civil War, she compensated by interviewing returning French soldiers and reporting their stories to Dassel. In early 1937, Dassel confided in Lily that he was working for the Abwehr and suggested she might like to join. He argued that she would collect anti-Bolshevik intelligence, but, concerned that she might be used in Germany's plans against France, she refused.

In 1938, following the disappearance of her uncle, General de Miller, her investigations led her to be arrested and interrogated by the Gestapo. Wanting to escape the increasing tensions in Europe, she planned a cycling, writing and painting trip to Saigon in Vietnam. Unable to get advances from the newspapers, she persuaded tent and bicycle manufacturers to sponsor her for the advertisement value. Setting off alone in September, she cycled through Italy, Yugoslavia, Greece and Turkey and reached Syria, where the British invasion halted her progress.

In her autobiography, she described being unable to accept the news that France had been defeated. 'My brain refuses to visualise Paris crowded with Germans; field-grey uniforms strolling along the Champs-Elysées or sitting at the café-tables; the Swastika flying instead of the French Tricolour. Up to now, I have not hated them, but the thought of Germans parading their mastery about Paris makes me shake with powerless rage and hatred.'[2]

Her humanitarian instinct led to her giving up her onward travel and she volunteered to train as a nurse with the Croix Rouge Francaise with the intention of joining the Allied expeditionary force to the Balkans. In March 1940, she passed her exams, but, rather than go to Greece, a romance and the offer of private nursing kept her in Beirut.[3]

By November 1940, she admitted that she had been no use to the war effort and decided to return to France. Her plan was to take up Dassel's offer, get enlisted in the Abwehr and then help those in France who were carrying on the fight against the Germans. She did not know exactly how she would do this, but was prepared to try.

It is possible that the romance in Beirut was with a Frenchman, Lieutenant Jean van Meriss, who acknowledged after the war that he had known her in Syria and that, during the war, she helped people escape from France. She made no mention of this in her interviews with MI5 or MI6.[4]

Maybe she was in desperate need of money, as she decided to tell Dassel that she was planning to return to Syria in the hope that he might renew his offer to work for the Abwehr and then, thinking that the British would pay her as well, would offer the British all the information about her mission. She recorded in her diary telling Babs, her pet Bichon Frisé, 'It's a fine game, it's a grand game but, you know, if we lose it, we'll lose our lives ... or mine at any rate.'[5]

Dassel met her at Maxim's restaurant in Paris and asked her first what her attitude towards the British was. When she told him that they had let the French down badly and intimated that she had no love for them, he told her he had come specifically from Berlin to ask if she would be willing to join the Abwehr and return to Syria. She accepted straightaway, but first Dassel arranged for two German instructors to teach her secret-writing skills in Berlin, using what was called 'pyramidon'. When she returned to Paris she tried to get a visa to Syria, but the French government refused. Frustrated at this turn of events, she used her new secret-writing skills to let Dassel know that she was considering leaving the country.

She was then contacted in June 1941 by Yvonne Delidaise, who was already collaborating with the Germans and whose brother, Richard, was working as one of their wireless operators. Yvonne introduced Lily to Emil Kyllburg, her Austrian lover. This was the cover name for Major Emil Kliemann, the second-in-command of the Abwehr in France and chief of air intelligence section who was based in Hotel Lutetia in Paris. He enquired whether she knew any potential wireless operators who would be prepared to operate in France should the British invade. Needing the 3,000 francs a month Kliemann offered, she volunteered to train, but, as he was slow in making arrangements, she expressed her concerns to Dassel.

Eventually, Kliemann contacted her and suggested sending her via Russia to Australia, where one of her uncles lived; however, when she visited Berlin in late June to discuss the plan, the Abwehr officers were too busy to discuss it with her due to Operation Barbarossa, the German invasion of the Soviet Union. She returned to Paris in disgust and when she heard no more from the Germans she wrote to Dassel asking to be released from all her obligations.

Unknown to Kliemann or Dassel, during this time Lily had written to Dr Elizabeth Hill, her cousin who lectured at Cambridge University, stating that she had been invited by 'the new owners of the place where we spent the summer together' to work for them and that she did not want the job but that it might be useful to 'her people'; she did not know how to get in touch with them and asked them to contact her. Nothing came of it.

Yvonne Delidaise convinced her that the Germans would contact her and, when they eventually met her in September 1941, they suggested she went to Dakar in Senegal. Unenthusiastic about tropical Africa, she told them she had an aunt in Madeira and another in Lisbon who might be able to help her get a visa to work in Portugal. She also told them she had a friend, Mrs Mary Coate, who lived near Bristol; an English cousin, Dr Hill, who lived in Cambridge; and a Polish cousin, Jan Tomaszewski, who was working for the Polish Government in London. Having a friend near Avonmouth, where the

American convoys were bringing troops, water material, supplies, etc., helped get Kliemann to agree to send her to England.

Over the next few months, while discussions took place about how she might get there, the Delidaises, Herr Graf and M. Vogel, trained her in wireless telegraphy, ciphers, intelligence gathering, identifying Allied uniforms and equipment and further in the use of secret inks. In Sherer's transcripts of the conversations she had with Lily, she reported on her training.

First Method

1. The first time SERGUEIEW was taught to write in invisible ink was on the occasion of her first visit to Berlin at the end of January 1941, when she was shown how to make use of [redacted but Lily described it as 'antipyrine']. As this event took place 2 years ago SERGUEIEW cannot remember in detail the 'formula'.

2. From what she remembers she was to take half a tablet of [redacted] and dissolve it in a tablespoon of 45% alcohol. She was then to take a wooden toothpick or, failing that, a sharpened piece of wood, round the point of which she was to wrap cotton wool. Using this as a pen she was to write her secret letter. Once the writing was dry she was to protect it by bathing the sheet of paper in alcohol (she cannot remember the exact strength of the alcohol to be used for this). She could use any paper except that with a shiny surface. Once again when the paper was dry, on the other side she was to write her cover letter. No code was to be used for the invisible writing.

Second Method

3. The second lesson in secret ink writing was given to SERGUEIEW by Yvonne DELIDAISE in the spring of 1942 in the Place du Palais Bourbon. Yvonne DELIDAISE showed her two different methods. For the first she was to use a wooden toothpick and cotton-wool as a pen, and an already prepared, light amber coloured, transparent liquid as ink. Yvonne DELIDAISE did not tell her to protect this writing.

Third Method

4. For the other method shown her by DELIDAISE, SERGUEIEW was to take what looked like an indelible copying pencil and with it scribble on a sheet of paper so that one side of it was completely covered. This sheet of paper was then used as a carbon. It apparently left no trace on the sheet of paper underneath.

5. Yvonne DELIDAISE took away SERGUEIEW's experiments in both these methods of secret writing, saying that she would have them developed. SERGUEIEW, however, never saw the results and can give no more information.

Fourth Method

6. The final method of secret writing in which SERGUEIEW was instructed was that given her for her mission to this country. For this she was to use the pellets given her by KLIEMANN before her departure from Paris. She was instructed in their use in the flat at 29 Avenue de l'Opera.

7. A pellet was to be heated in a clear flame which would not discolour it.

When the pellet was melted she was to take a wooden toothpick and dip it in the liquid. When it was dry she would re-dip it and continue doing so until all the liquid had been absorbed and a new pellet reformed on the end of the stick. This could now be used as [a] pen for her secret writing. She would then take a sheet of paper (non-shiny surface) and rub the paper evenly with cotton-wool. On the side she rubbed she was to write her cover letter in ink or pencil, preferably the former. Her letter in invisible writing was then to be written on the same side of the paper but at right angles to the visible text. If SERGUEIEW used a double sheet which entailed 4 written sides, the invisible writing was only to be done on the first and third pages.

8. Her cover letter was to be signed 'SOLANGE'. It was left to her as to whether she made use of the code for her invisible writing, but this was considered unnecessary.[6]

As Agent SOLANGE, she agreed to be sent to England on an intelligence-gathering mission and to send her reports back using the above methods. Her other instructions included

(a) How to describe an airfield, its layout, situation and details of its construction – how it was guarded and whether the airfield was mined.
(b) How to describe aircraft. GRAF actually bought SERGUEIEW a book of aircraft silhouettes of which he asked her to learn as much as possible by heart. A point which apparently interested the Germans in connection with aircraft was the letters which appeared after the 'cockade' on the fuselage.
(c) SERGUEIEW was instructed in British and American Army ranks and also the formation of a British and American Army division. She was also shown how to recognise the arm in which a soldier was serving, i.e. whether he was an infantryman or gunner, etc. In the American Army this would be seen by the badges, and in the British Army by the coloured flashes.
(d) How to describe unit signs seen on military vehicles.

Relating more to the general questionnaire which she was given, in her reports to the Germans SERGUEIEW was told to supply the following:

(a) Locations of military headquarters in London.
(b) The exact addresses of buildings destroyed in air-raids.
(c) Information on what the Germans call the 'strategic geography of England'. She states that by this they meant the principal rail junctions.
(d) Any modifications in the coastal defence zone limits. It was also to be specified to what categories of people the zones were open.
(e) Restrictions in rationing and any information about food supplies generally. Those foodstuffs which were being imported by ship were to be specified.
(f) If SERGUEIEW was in Cornwall she was asked to try and find out if there were any modifications to the transatlantic telephone cables which start from there.
(g) In order that she could indicate any modifications to factories, she was given, just before leaving, a list showing the location of the principal industrial centres

and what was manufactured in these centres. Thus, should she be in any vicinity which she knew to be an industrial centre, she would know what was of interest and what to look for there.

She was to specify the source of all the information she sent in order that the Germans might gauge its reliability. At the end of these instructions SERGUEIEW was given a detailed questionnaire by GRAF, which she copied, using lemon powder as invisible ink.[7]

While she worked as a nurse in a hospital in Paris, during her spare time she had lessons in espionage. To cover her travelling expenses she was given 2,000 francs. She was provided with papers identifying her as a German army interpreter and told to create her own cover story as close to the truth as possible, leaving out any contact she had had with the Germans. When she jokingly told Kliemann that if she heard that her parents had been hurt, she would start to work for the British, his response was that if he heard she was working for the British the lives of her parents would be at stake. The trust he placed in her was surprising for an Abwehr officer; she was given no security check to include in her messages to let him know if she was operating under British duress and told that he would understand that if he received no messages for a few months it would be because she had had to lie low.

In June 1942, she went to Vichy in unoccupied France and spent weeks trying to arrange an exit visa. While waiting, she took the opportunity to visit her younger sister Maria, known as Bimbo, who was working in Algiers. While there she was introduced to Lieutenant Pierre Jourdain, the French husband of her sister's best friend and a naval officer who had resigned in disgust over the collaboration of the Vichy government. She confided in him her plans to defect to the British and he recommended her not telling the French authorities, but to go to the British Embassy should she ever get to Madrid.

When she returned to Paris, M. Vogel, a German wireless technician, gave her three-hour daily lessons in wireless transmission in an apartment on Rue de l'Assomption in the sixteenth *arrondissement*. Getting a visa to get into Spain proved complicated, as she had to apply for it in Lyons. As the Germans had taken over the south of France in November 1942 following the Allies taking control of north-west Africa, Kliemann got her the pass to travel to Lyons. However, her French passport had expired so the Spanish refused to issue her a visa.[8]

Kliemann's messages to Lisbon on her behalf were picked up by British wireless listening equipment and decoded by Bletchley Park staff.

SERGUEIEW's name first appeared on MOST SECRET SOURCES on 24.9.42 in a message from Paris to Lisbon. This message requested Lisbon to despatch immediately a telegram to Nathalie SERGUEIEW chez CHOLAY, Finances Exterieures, Charlton, Vichy France, purporting to come from her Aunt Louise, asking her to come immediately because her aunt Marie Therese was very ill. The message ended by saying that the telegram was only to serve as a basis for the issue of a French passport and exit permit.[9]

She did not detail to Sherer what else she did in Lyons, but, returning to Paris in early February 1943, she tried unsuccessfully to get Kliemann to recruit van Meriss; however, his excessive shyness did not convince the German of his espionage potential. By this time, her expertise was considered good enough for her training to be reduced to only one hour a day.

Once she picked up her new passport, in April 1943, she went on another trip to Lyons to arrange the visa for Spain. According to Sherer,

> SERGUIEW was now anxious to leave as soon as possible, pointing out to KLIEMANN that if she waited until just before her visa expired she might attract the attention of the British authorities. KLIEMANN persisted in his dilatory ways and finally in May 1943 SERGUEIEW rang up Yvonne DELIDAISE and said she was through. This provoked KLIEMANN into making a rendezvous with her, but still nothing was fixed. Meanwhile SERGUIEW was writing a book on her bicycle trip to Syria, and KLIEMANN obtained permission for it to be published.[10]
>
> About 1.6.43 KLIEMANN introduced SERGUIEW to a certain GRAF at a flat at 29 Avenue de l'Opera. GRAF was to instruct SERGUEIEW concerning matters in England which were of interest to the Germans. She was instructed by GRAF daily for the next nine days. At the end of her instruction GRAF gave her a detailed questionnaire which she did not have time to memorise, so she wrote it out in secret ink which she made from lemon juice and later handed it over to P.C.O. [British Passport Control Office] Madrid.[11]

After nearly two intensely frustrating years of dealing with German, French, American and Spanish red tape, she acquired the relevant French exit papers and Spanish entry papers. On 23 June 1943, she took Babs with her in a first-class train compartment to the French border and then on to Madrid, quite expecting to be able to take him with her to England. In her autobiography she admitted questioning herself: 'Am I right? Only the future will tell. Whatever happens, I regret nothing: if I must die, I accept death, for I have not undertaken this work blind to its risks.'[12]

There followed several months of tense negotiations trying to convince the Germans and Spanish that she was pro-Nazi and the American and British that she was pro-Allies. While she had to maintain contact with Kliemann, she sent him messages using her secret ink. She also contacted Colonel Stevens, an American friend, confiding that she was working for the Germans but wanted to work for the Allies.

Details of her time in Madrid meeting Portuguese, American and British Embassy officials and Hans, her Abwehr contact, are detailed in her personnel file and autobiography. Her plans to travel to Lisbon, where she would pick up the wireless set and proceed to England, were thwarted when the Portuguese authorities refused to issue her with a visa unless she showed them an entry visa for England. When she arranged this, they refused to issue her a transit visa on the grounds of her Russian origin.

On 17 July, she plucked up the courage to visit Kenneth Benton, officially the Passport Control Officer in the British Embassy, but unofficially the MI6 representative, and told him of her intention of going to England and working as a spy for the Allies. To prove her story, she handed over the questionnaire.

Macintyre's research into the Double-Cross scheme revealed that when London asked Benton to describe Lily, he reported her as self-dramatising, intelligent and, like many Frenchwomen, 'made up and dressed to kill'. He mentioned her speaking in Russian to her dog and doubted her suitability, wondering if she was 'first and foremost a self-server'.[13]

Masterman was equally wary and advised Benton to be cautious about agreeing to her being accepted as a double agent. 'She ought to be thoroughly interrogated and a full account obtained of her activities before we decide we can use her.'[14]

MI5's Section V, its foreign-counter-intelligence section, wanted Lily brought to the UK for further interrogation and allocated the task of checking her credentials to Mary Sherer, who gave her the code name 'Treasure'.

Most Secret Sources revealed that the Abwehr communications about her between Paris and Lisbon mentioned that 'a message of 29 June 1943 asks whether she has reported by telephone and given special information. This certainly gives the impression that she has been working for the Germans and collecting some sort of special information for them'.[15]

It is unknown whether Lily had any contact with Virginia Hall, an American OSS agent who was operating in the Lyons area, as Hall gave her name to the American assistant in Madrid. He sent London a note stating that Lily 'is strongly anti-Communist. Miss HALL has known the family ten years and considered SERGUEIEW as out to make as much money as possible. She confirmed that SERGUEIEW was in Syria and stated the family had gradually changed to become strongly pro-Nazi'.[16]

To check her story, Sherer interviewed Anthony Blunt, the personal assistant of Guy Liddell, the Deputy Director-General of MI5, who was said by Macintyre to have known her slightly. Blunt described her as 'a White Russian with slightly left views'.[17]

Sherer also interviewed Dr Hill in August, who admitted receiving letters from Lily asking for assistance in getting her a visa and sending her a telegram agreeing to be her sponsor. She thought she was 'something of an adventuress, but an exceedingly clever girl'. When asked what she thought her cousin would have been doing in France during the war, she suggested that she would have been pro-Allies and working with the French Resistance. Sherer reported that this would have delighted Kliemann and decided that Lily would make a suitable double agent.[18]

Madrid she described as being 'a place of menace and intrigue; a place where everyone is plotting, betraying, bribing or selling themselves. What at first appeared so easy, now seems to be full of difficulties.'[19] When Benton told her that she had been given full security clearance, that she would be of great assistance to the Allies, that they would be delighted to have her and that she had done extremely well so far, she accepted, adding that she would accept no payment but wanted him to arrange for Babs to accompany her. Even though Babs had been vaccinated and Lily had his anti-rabies certificate, Benton told her that the dog would have to stay in quarantine for six months.

She insisted on taking him as part of the deal and Benton promised to arrange it. To emphasise how serious she was about it, she reported in her autobiography telling Benton to

> be absolutely sure to tell them that I will not leave without Babs. If my work is important it is worth this exception; if it isn't worth that, then it isn't worth my going to England. You probably think I'm ridiculous ... You can't see the sense of making such a fuss about a dog. To you, it's just a dog but to me, it's Babs, and worth more than a million pounds. Just tell your people in London that.[20]

As well as the worry about her dog, there was also the stress about whether the Germans knew what game she was playing. She admitted 'beginning to feel the nervous strain. This double game, the alternating visits to one side and then to the other, this constant change of personality without any let-up when I can be myself again, is wearing me out. The slightest noise makes me start. There are times when I am with von Buch [a German officer], when I feel a sudden terror that I will confuse him with Benton. What if he turns out to be a clairvoyant? Or a hypnotist? It's stupid; I drive the foolish thoughts away, but they make it only too clear that my normal balance is upset'.[21]

Benton made the arrangements for her onward travel to Gibraltar, but her departure was deliberately delayed to give SIS officers a chance to identify and track Kliemann. On 17 September, two days before she left Madrid, he turned up, but was more interested in getting Lily's help regarding Yvonne Delidaise, his mistress. She had been in Madrid a few months earlier, trying to get a visa to Portugal, and he was so suspicious of her motives that he asked Lily to make enquiries at the Ritz Hotel about what she did during her time there. Not wanting to draw attention to herself, she refused. However, when he told her that he was considering being transferred to the Russian Front, she relented, especially as it would end the two years of effort she had made.

On informing Benton about the incident, he passed the information to Tar, who authorised a private detective to investigate. Although it was found that Delidaise had had an affair with a Portuguese banker, to keep Kliemann happy, he was provided with a fictitious explanation, which so satisfied him that he gave Lily an extra 2,000 pesetas, about £40.

Before returning to Berlin, he offered to send her a wireless set disguised as a gramophone, but addressed to her cousin in Cambridge. The one-square-centimetre micro-photographed instructions would be hidden inside. In the German Embassy was 'a very powerful and accurate apparatus which can reduce a photograph of a printed sheet of paper to the size of a dot or even smaller. To read such a micro-photo one has to fix it onto a glass slide and look at it through a microscope. To the naked eye, a micro-photo of this kind looks, when it is laid on a piece of paper, like a black full stop. The micro-photos will be sent to me in ordinary letters, stuck on in place of punctuation. The German takes a few slides out of a small case. At first sight they appear blank. Then he sets up a microscope, focuses it and tells me to look into it. There, before my eyes, small but very neat, is a whole printed page. I can read every word, every letter. The German takes out the slide and hands it to me. I examine it carefully. "I can't see anything," I tell him.'[22]

When asked how she could read them in England, he recommended her buying a microscope and *The Microbe Hunters* by Paul de Kruif to explain her interest in microscopy.[23]

On 21 September, Tar wrote a memo that Kliemann had told Lily that 'one of his agents in England had reported between 8th and 10th September that the British were going to land between Cherbourg and Treport; that paratroops of the 5th and 8th Commandos were to be employed, and that the British had passed orders to the civil population to resist. TREASURE added that the inaccuracy of the report had not shaken Kliemann's faith in his agent'.[24]

Before he left he told her to send letters in secret ink to addresses in Paris and Barcelona. As well as giving her an Omega watch, which cost 1,350 pesetas, a diamond solitaire ring, which cost 95,000 francs in Paris, and a two-inch brooch in the shape of a branch with five diamonds in it, which cost 39,000 escudos, he also gave her additional instruction sheets, a list of wavelength frequencies she could use to pick up his wireless operator's transmissions and two more secret-writing pellets containing quinine. Benton forwarded the details to London, and a memo in her file reads,

We are shortly expecting a woman to arrive in this country from Gibraltar whom we have called TREASURE. She so far shows that she will be working to Paris. I think the enemy have slightly miscalculated the amount of time necessary for her to obtain a receiver to this country, and they have stated that they will commence to transmit to her from the 13th of this month. Even if TREASURE arrives here by the 15th, we shall not attempt to contact for some time, but I am sending you bare details of the information which we have so far received from S.I.S. concerning her transmitting instructions. You will no doubt be amused by the first paragraph of them.

1. Her instructions are, on arrival in the U.K. to acquire as soon as possible one of the following types of W/T sets:- HALYCRAPTER SKYRIDER, H.R.C., or R.M.E.65.

2. As from 13.10.43. KLIEMANN's organisation will communicate with TREASURE on Mondays, Wednesdays and Sundays on the following frequencies:-
(i) 5100 kcs.
(ii) 5650 ..
(iii) 6730 ..
(iv) 7650 ..
(v) 8650 ..

3. Frequencies (i), (iii) and (v) will be associated with call signs MLO, OKL and XRF respectively.

4. KLIEMANN's organisation will broadcast to TREASURE as follows: -
    MONDAY – 07.30 hours G.M.T for ten minutes on frequency (iii).
    The message will be repeated at 12.00 hours G.M.T. on frequency (v). Again the broadcast will last ten minutes.

WEDNESDAY – the same at 12.00 G.M.T. on frequency (v) and at 22.00 hours on frequency (i).

SUNDAY – at 12.30 hours G.M.T. on frequency (v) and at 22.00 hours on frequency (i).

5. TREASURE will reply using her transmitter (when she receives it) on frequencies which appear in the micro-photographs. She will of course transmit during the ten minutes following KLIEMANN's broadcast.[25]

When she arrived in Gibraltar, she followed Benton's advice and refused to answer any detailed questions. MI9 had already been informed of her arrival and her importance so proceeded to arrange a flight to take her to England. She handed over 39,000 escudos, about £390 then, and they arranged for it to be forwarded to her bank account in London.

It seems highly unlikely, but while waiting for her flight in Gibraltar, she was reported by Sherer to have fallen in love with Lieutenant Kenneth Larson, an American serviceman, who had promised to smuggle Babs into Britain. It is more likely she befriended him in the hope of ensuring a passage.

On 5 November, she landed at Bristol and was immediately involved in an incident that generated considerable paperwork. MI6 in Madrid had advised her not to answer any questions when in Gibraltar. MI9 officers in Gibraltar gave her the same advice for when she arrived in England, so that when she was unwilling to respond to the immigration officer's questions, his response was, 'We know all about you. The Germans have sent you here.' Aware that if knowledge of her double-cross spread back to the Germans her parents' lives would be in jeopardy, she had to ignore the remark and would only tell them that she wanted to work as a nurse with the Free French Forces. When Tar learned of this leakage, he was obliged to launch a major investigation.[26]

In contrast to her leaving France, she was unimpressed to be escorted to London in a crowded third-class train compartment. London was not as attractive as she'd hoped. What struck her was the shabby appearance of everyone in the street: worn-out overcoats, shiny sleeves, dowdy clothes. 'In the shop windows the dresses are straight, without facings, lapels or belts – anything remotely frivolous has been pitilessly sacrificed.'[27]

The transcription of her interview with Captain Osborne at Nightingale Lane shows that she was quizzed about her family background, her life story and the character, appearance and relationships of her Abwehr contacts, as well as their espionage methods. She explained the unique cypher that she had been taught based on pages of *Montmartre*, a French novel by Pierre Frondaie. However, the book had been confiscated in Gibraltar. She also described the methods of using secret inks. Throughout the whole of the account, there was no mention of her dog or a romance in Gibraltar.

When she was introduced to Tar, her new boss, he congratulated her on her work and told her that she was going to be his 'trump card in the Intelligence game, worth more than an armoured division'. As the Abwehr had complete confidence in her, he told her his plan for her to send them false information in the hope of deceiving them about the Allies' plans for D-Day.

With your help we can do one better than secrecy, we can go over from the defensive to the offensive and make them think that we had made our preparations to invade an area which in fact we have no intention of going anywhere near. If we succeed in this, the Germans will concentrate their troops in the worst possible places to cope with the landing when it is finally launched. You can see the value of this.[28]

While she acknowledged the value, the enormity of the deception plan frightened her. To avoid the French authorities in London making enquiries and jumping to the conclusion that she was working for the British, Tar arranged for her to be given war-refugee status. She visited their headquarters to inform them of her arrival and that her cousin, Dr Hill, would be looking after and maintaining her.

One of her first requests to Sherer was to ascertain the value of the diamond ring and brooch Kliemann had given her, but she was disappointed when they only realised £105 rather than the £400 she had been told. As she needed money, she accepted MI5's proposal of £50 a month and 10 per cent of whatever she received from the Germans, but thought the British should have had more self-respect; the Germans had paid her £250 a month.

Lily would have recognised Macintyre's description of Sherer as robust, ambitious and having a sharp sense of humour, often at other people's expense.

She spent the first part of the war in the counter-sabotage section and working for the British Security Coordination in New York, the clandestine arm of MI6, MI5 and SOE that sought to bring America into the war through propaganda, blackmail and espionage. A child of the Indian Raj and daughter of a brigadier, Mary was military in bearing, and often wore a red jacket with epaulettes which she thought made her look like a general. She walked with a long martial stride, swinging her arms, and humming little songs to herself when she thought no one could hear. In a male world, she assumed a carapace of toughness, smoking filterless Kent cigarettes and holding her gin as well as the next man. 'Mary was someone you did not want to cross, and was not quick to forgive any misdoings.' But there was also a gentleness to her, and a resolute sense of purpose.[29]

There was a plan for Lily to start a nurse-training programme in Watford, but she became ill shortly after arriving. Whether it was stress-related is unknown as there was nothing in her file that identified the cause. Although it prevented her from listening in to the first German transmissions, one imagines that British wireless operators were doing so.

She then moved to live with Mrs Coate in St John's House, Wraxall, Bristol. While this meant she could be looked after while recuperating, it also was part of Kliemann's plan as he wanted to know whether the Allies were amassing their troops in south-west England in advance of an invasion of France.

She wrote fourteen letters in secret ink to addresses in Barcelona and Sweden, but the contents were not her own; they were provided by the Double-Cross team as part of their grand deception scheme. They included bits of overheard conversation mentioning rank and badges and trains supposedly seen in stations, information meant to deceive the Abwehr into believing that there was no troop build-up in the south-west when in fact there tens of thousands. She told him that she had an American boyfriend, who was in the non-existent Fourteenth United States Army, which other turned agents were reporting on, and that American, Canadian and British forces were amassing in East Anglia and south-east England, when in fact they were not. The Allies' intention was that Hitler's powerful XV Army would remain poised to defend the area around Calais from the expected invasion.

However, when she was not writing letters she was preoccupied with what was happening to her dog. Although Tar had no objection to it being brought over, he had no control over quarantine regulations. Matters came to a head in December when she refused to send any more letters to the Abwehr until Babs arrived. Sherer was unsympathetic with Treasure's 'strike', stating she was very unreasonable, acting like a spoilt child.

> TREASURE is very upset about the absence of her dog, and has seriously threatened that if the dog does not arrive soon she will not work anymore. I think this can be dealt with but it will mean a scene. I do not quite know what we can do to help, because if we have the dog sent over here officially it will have to go into quarantine, which from TREASURE's point of view would be as bad as having it in Gibraltar. I am afraid that TREASURE's American boyfriend has let her down and has no intention of smuggling the dog over here for her. I am wondering whether we could get the Navy to help via Commander Montagu.[30]

Lily admitted that she had been very stupid, but she had fallen in love with Larson and he with her, and for some very complicated reason of her own she had told him about her being a double agent in order to see if he trusted her.[31]

How she spent the Christmas of 1943 is unknown, but her health deteriorated so rapidly that she had to be taken into St Mary's hospital in London on 29 December. When the doctors identified stones in her kidneys, a condition so bad that if she did not have an operation she would die within six months, Lily refused to allow it, saying that she had nothing to live for. She discharged herself from hospital on 5 January but changed her mind about sending the letters. She did not want to die in England and be buried in damp soil. She wanted to help win the war in France, return to see her family and write her autobiography.

Having a transmitter was considered essential for her to contact her control station known as 'Ast Paris'. Although it was not the Double-Cross team's intention to use her during the invasion operations, they acknowledged that it might become necessary to do so at some stage in the future, 'in which case it would be invaluable to have a direct channel of communication to Paris'.[32]

MI6's initial plan was for her to write to Carmen Espinosa de los Monteros, an old friend in Madrid, and ask if she would accept a package for her and keep it until a man visiting Madrid from England called and picked it up. At the same time, she sent Kliemann a letter in secret ink asking him to deliver a set to her friend's address. These letters were sent on 17 January and two days later her first message from Paris came through, but poor weather conditions meant it that it could not be transcribed clearly. It was described as an 'undecipherable'.

Her first incoming message to be received and deciphered read, 'Information very interesting – Letters arrive well – Continue. You are very charming.' However, the success at being connected with Paris faded. Three weeks after being told she was going to die, she received a letter from her sister. She had to read and reread the first sentence: 'My poor darling, I hate the pain I will give you but it's better you should know, so as not to make plans for the future: you will not see your Babs again. He has been run over.' Unknown to her, the British had sent Babs to Algiers, where her sister would take care of him.

She was devastated. While she could cope with her own death, learning of Babs's made her indifferent. 'The circle of loneliness has closed all around me; I am alone, absolutely alone ... In three months England has killed all my enthusiasm although it had survived three years under the German yoke. I had worked with a passionate zeal, but now I feel a complete indifference.' She admitted the British tenacity and powers of endurance, but could not live like them. She wanted 'to love and hate; to be live; I find them cold, uncommunicative, undemonstrative, impenetrable. I would like to see Mariya [Sherer] laugh, cry or scream; I would like to see her face express something. To me, she seems almost an automaton.'[33]

Whether it was to uplift her spirits is unknown, but an alternative plan was arranged for her to get the wireless set. Tar negotiated with the Ministry of Information to provide the cover for her to go on a trip to Lisbon. The chief passport officer agreed to issue her with a British passport and Michael Stewart, the press attaché in Lisbon, agreed to provide whatever assistance he could. The plan was considered so important in the Double-Cross scheme that Winston Churchill was informed. As well as receiving the set, it was considered imperative for her to continue her contact with Kliemann, to get more money, new cover addresses and more up-to-date instructions.

She was provided with an alternative cover story for the time she spent between leaving Madrid the previous November and arriving in London and, given the content of the information she had sent him so far, another carefully worked out cover story, expecting Kliemann to question her about her current work.

Cover story for TREASURE before leaving for Lisbon on 1.3.44

You are supposed to have been employed since the middle of January in the Enemy Occupied Territories Section of the Film Division at the Ministry of Information.

The head of the Film Division is Jack BEDDINGTON, a Jew. Before the war he was Publicity and General Manger of Shell Mex Ltd. The head of your Section and your immediate chief is Sidney BERNSTEIN, another Jew, and the owner of Granada Cinemas.

The Minister of Information is Brendan BRACKEN. He is a newspaper publisher and was Parliamentary Private Secretary to Winston Churchill from 1940 to 1941. He is very close to the Prime Minister.

The Director General is Sir Cyril RADCLIFFE, a barrister and the Deputy

Director is Eric BAMFORD, a permanent Civil Servant, at one time a Principal at the Treasury.

There are four Controllers who come immediately under the D.D.C.

The Divisions which come under the four Controllers are as follows:-

1. Press and Censorship

2. Home (Under which comes the Film Division). The Controller of Home is Sylvester GATES.

3. Overseas (Controller Kenneth GRUBB)

4. Production

In the Film Division there are about 60 people, men and women, many of whom have been in film before the war. The Officers of the Division are situated on the ground floor of the University of London which is in Malet Street, just behind the British Museum. The telephone is Euston 4321. The offices are small and overcrowded. You have been lucky enough to get a very small office at the end of the corridor to yourself.

You were put in touch with the Ministry by your cousin, Dr Elizabeth Hill, who was in the Soviet relations Section. Her successor is a Mr. H. SMOLLETT. Dr Hill doesn't think much of him and thinks he is incompetent.

You were called for an interview by Mr. WOOBURN, the Establishment Officer, seen by Sidney BERNSTEIN and offered a job as an Assistant Specialist at £350 a year. This sum is subject, of course, to Income Tax which is very high.

Your Section is concerned at present with producing documentary films of the history of the war for showing in Occupied Territories. A series of these films are being made to counter German propaganda and to give true facts in cases where the facts are distorted by the Germans. For example, the Dunkirk episode is being filmed. Your daily work consists of seeing films which have been made, and discussing them afterwards with the representatives of Allied Governments who attend, and with the representatives of a branch of the Foreign Office which looks after the Propaganda side of the work and say what they want in the way of propaganda films and the Films Division carries out the Production side. There are several theatres in the Ministry where these films are shown.

You are also engaged in translating scripts for these films. This work you are able to do at home owing to a special dispensation because you have not been well. You also have consultations with members of the Free French Government who all use assumed names.

There is a frequent contact with free-lance script writers who [...] Ministry [...] have seen James L. HODSON, the well-known [...] He was responsible for the script of 'The Des [...]

Another author whom you have met is Victor S. PRITCHETT who writes regularly for the weekly paper, 'New Statesman and Nation'.

You have lately been in charge of the administrative details involved in the production of one of the aforementioned films. This has involved quite a lot of correspondence with various Film Companies, such as the Strand Film Co. Ltd. and the Finance Section has had to be consulted and specifications put to them.

You are to tell KLIEMANN that as soon as you started work in the Film Division you saw that there was the possibility of a trip to Lisbon. You made enquiries amongst the other members of your Section and learnt that they were very short of actors in the country who could be used for making these propaganda films to be shown in Occupied Territories. You also discovered that there was a great shortage of French script writers. You therefore went to Mr. BERNSTEIN, the Head of your Section, and suggested to him that you should go to Lisbon and interview refugees to get first-hand information from them about conditions in Occupied Territories which would help you in writing the script. This idea was turned down. You will say that a week later Mr. BERNSTEIN sent for you again and said that he would like to discuss your ideas. You seized the opportunity, amplified your first idea and suggested a consultation with the Press Attaché aware of the Ministry's needs regarding actors and script writers so that he will keep his eyes open in Lisbon and if he finds a likely refugee candidate he will recommend that he should be granted a visa to the U.K. Mr. BERNSTEIN thought this was a good idea and after consultation with the Controller of Overseas Section, Mr. GRUBB, it was decided that you should visit Lisbon to carry out this work during a two week period. Mr. GRUBB has given you a letter of introduction to the Press Attaché.

You will tell KLIEMANN that before leaving you endeavoured to find out the future policy of your Division. You found the 'high-ups' vague and very secretive. You gathered that there were many discussions with the Americans and Allied Governments concerning the Policy and you understood that there had been serious disagreements with the Americans who had had a film monopoly in Europe before the war which they were very anxious to maintain.

One piece of incidental information which you picked up was that Alfred HITCHCOCK, the well-known film producer, was working for the Film Division of the Ministry of Information.

There is even a Canteen on the top floor where you can have meals.[34]

The last letter she wrote to Kliemann before her trip was a shorter version of the above, which Sherer would have ensured that she memorised. On 1 March 1944 she was flown to Lisbon, and when she met him he told her that Berlin was very pleased with her work. He supplied her with a receiver set that had not been disguised and arranged for a technical expert to give her a few days tuition in how to use it.[35]

She was also taught how to make a keyboard by taking a small wooden board, pierce it with a nail so that the point sticks out half an inch. Before you drive the nail home, you fix one wire of an electric light flex round it. You place your board down with the point of the nail upwards. On the board you put a book with the blade of a kitchen knife slipped between the pages. You attach the second wire of the flex to the blade of the knife and you plug the other end of the flex into the wireless set … You must make sure that the knife blade is held firmly in the book and that the handle-end sticks out just above the point of the nail – then all you have to do is press on the handle to make contact.[36]

Rather than carry the set herself, Stewart, the press attaché who had agreed to look after her, arranged for it to be sent in the diplomatic bag with her detailed descriptions of all the German officials she had contact with in

Lisbon. Her report on Kliemann revealed he had been ill and 'appeared apathetic about the war. He admitted to TREASURE that he considered the situation was quite hopeless and that it was only a matter of time before Germany would have to give in. TREASURE is convinced, however, that KLIEMANN is potential VERMEHREN (?). He asked (rather surprisingly since he admitted TREASURE's reports had given him a considerable build up) whether TREASURE would care to return to Paris, and promised to arrange this for her if she so wished.'[37]

She added that he had told her that his stock had gone up considerably because of her success but that it was a very worrying business running agents, because with most of them he was always worrying about whether they were double-crossing him or not. With her, in whom he had complete confidence, it made him feel bad to be sending her to do such unpleasant things and to run such risks.

Kliemann was aware of the Allies' invasion plans but knowledge of the exact location of the landing was essential. He was pleased that she had friends in Bristol as the area between there and Salisbury Plain was particularly important. She reported him telling her to listen very carefully.

> The next big move in the war will be the Allied landing. Our only chance of winning, at the moment, is to throw them back into the sea. To do that we must know in advance where they are planning to land, so that we can prepare a hot reception. It could be in Holland or Belgium, but we don't think so. We are fairly sure that it will be in France and there are two possibilities; either the Pas de Calais or Normandy. If they choose the Pas de Calais, the Allied troops will be concentrated on the Channel coast; but, if it is to be Normandy, they will move into the area round Bristol. Do you understand? What you must tell us is whether that area is peaceful or whether there is a build-up of troops and other activities, so that we can work out where the enemy is making for.
>
> 'I don't think any woman has ever had the same opportunity to alter the course of history,' he says with great emphasis, and for a while he is silent.[38]

Just before she left for England, he said that even if it meant the end of his career, if she said that she did not want to go back, he would not force her and he would let her go back to Paris. She asked him if he wanted her to go back to England and he said, 'Yes, of course,' but not against her will.

> TREASURE says that she has nothing against KLIEMANN personally, that he has always treated her very well and it makes her feel very badly to have to lie to him and cheat him. I asked her what he would do if he thought she was controlled, and I said presumably he would not tell Berlin because this would make him look such a fool. However, TREASURE was quite adamant and said that she was absolutely sure that if he thought she was double crossing him he would report it.[39]

She reported that he was uninterested in her cover story; his main aim appeared to be to use her to infiltrate more German agents into the UK. There were no details about how he intended to do this. He gave her a diamond bracelet set in platinum, for which he had paid 39,000 escudos, £300 in £10 notes (23 were later discovered to be forgeries) and 20,000 escudos. Among the photographs she brought back, there was one of her and Kliemann standing in the sunshine, but most were of Babs.

Having arranged for the cash to be transferred to her bank account, she flew back to England on 23 March and, following interviews with Sherer, her report was written up. It included a complicated code system for every British weather condition, which she had to use in her messages as Kliemann had demanded detailed weather reports. He also wanted her to supply information on

1. Everything seen in or around Bristol.

2. The exact location of Eisenhower's Headquarters. This is very important.

3. Kliemann mentioned a new aeroplane, not the jet-propulsion plane but another propellerless plane controlled by radio. She did not know what he meant and he did not appear to be able to describe it very well, but his exact words were 'Qui marche par les ondes' [walking by the waves]. He wanted to know if this plane was still in the experimental stage or whether it was in production and being used for operations.

4. More information was required about the training aerodrome at Bristol which was reported in letter No. 14. Also he asked her to try and identify a training plane which she described as a type of Lysander but with square tips.

5. The Germans are anxious to know about a device attached to reconnaissance planes which enables us to detect submarines when they are submerged. KLIEMANN thought the device was operated by radio and wanted to know what frequencies it operated. He told TREASURE that anything she could discover about this device would be of interest.

6. Any exercises that might take place for practising gas throwing or spraying.

7. The exact address of the Headquarters of Combined Operations.

8. The Germans are very interested to know if invasion barges are arriving in Bristol from America; if so, numbers.

9. When giving information she need not bother to give exact sources.[40]

Any correspondence had to be addressed to Maria Pia Leitao, Rua Luz Soriano 100, Lisbon, or Jean-François Solomon, Florissant, Geneva, Switzerland.

Unknown to Lily, her visit had attracted the attention of the Portuguese authorities, who enquired of Stewart as to how a woman of Russian origin with a French passport who had been refused an entry visa to Portugal in 1943, had arrived in Lisbon with a British passport and an entry visa issued in London. He explained that she had been sent on official business by the Ministry of Information, who had arranged her passport and visa, but that they had not found her work satisfactory so had sent her back to London.

The matter was considered serious enough for the Portuguese first secretary in London to discuss the affair with the chief passport officer. Although it was reported to have been 'smoothed over', Stewart was recalled to Britain, with the explanation that the Portuguese had described him as 'persona non grata'.[41]

When her suitcase was delivered, the lock was found to have been forced and various items were missing: three silk dresses, a green blouse, a pink satin blouse, a skirt, three shoes (not pairs), four pairs of silk stockings, four pairs of leather gloves, two dozen handkerchiefs in a red leather case, a long jade necklace, a new red leather bag and belt, another red leather bag, a set of leather cuff links, a big coloured wool shawl, a plaid rug and a small chamois leather pillow.[42] Without Tar's knowledge, she had claimed compensation of £128 2s 6d, but the delay in payment led her to mention it to him and he then had to resolve the issue. Not wanting her to build up resentment against the British authorities, she was given £50 in cash and £40 in clothing coupons.

She was provided with a furnished flat at 39 Hill Street, Westminster, where the new wireless set was installed. The Germans contacted her on Tuesdays, Thursdays and Saturdays at 1200 GMT on 8650 kcs (kilocycles) and at 2200 GMT on 5100 kcs; they were never late.

> She will call them on any day between 1200 and 1230 GMT and/or between 2200 and 2230 GMT. The daytime transmissions would be on 7550 kcs and the night-time transmissions on 4635 kcs. She is allowed to call them at any time during the half hour mentioned, and it was suggested to her that she should vary the times at which she commenced calling. If TREASURE sends a message on one day which has been received correctly by the control station they will acknowledge receipt of this during the next scheduled transmitting time by sending 'OK' followed by the initial letter of the French word signifying the day on which the message was sent, e.g. if the message was sent on a Wednesday (Mercredi) they would signal on Thursday 'OK M'.[43]

For those interested in the code she used, there are pages of examples in her personnel file. It was based on this sentence: 'Aux chevaux maigres vont les mouches', so if the message to be sent on 27 March 1944 was, 'Viennent de debarquer Bristol trois cent avions. Camp American Ashton Clifton Park change emplacement dieuz lieues plus nord,' it was explained as follows.

> The sentence contains 31 letters. These are written in alternate squares on two lines. The first 16 are written in the top line and the remaining 15 in the spaces underneath. The square in which the second line begins is determined by the month, e.g. March is the third month so the second line begins in the third square. The last letters of the sentence are put in the squares at the beginning of the second line.
>
> A U X C H E V A U X M A I G R E
> E S S V O N T L E S M O U C H
>
> The letters are then numbered according to their place in the alphabet.
>
> A U X C H E V A U X M A I G R E
> E S S V O N T L E S M O U C H
> 1 6 25 21 30 22 24 26 11 18 7 17 29 24 2 14 26 8 31 25 15 16 3 19 13 27
> 10 5 20 12 9

Then a bar is put in front of the square which contains the same number as the date on which the letter is coded. In this case 27, and all the squares behind the bar are blocked out. Similarly the squares below the square before the bar are blocked out.

Then the message is written into the grid starting in the first square after the bar and then continuing from left to right until the whole message has been written in. W. is put before and after proper names and 2 WW indicates full stop. The number of letters in the message has to be divisible by five, because in its final state the message is written out in groups of five. In this case the total number of letters is 118, so any two dummy letters, say S.L. are added to make 120.

Now some of the letters in the message are transposed.

The first line is left as it is.

Second line Es changed to Fs and Fs to Es.

Third line Es changed to Gs and Gs to Es.

Fourth line Es changed to Hs and Hs to Es.

Fifth line as it is.

Then begin again with the sixth line changing Es to Fs and so on.

Another grid is then prepared. In order not to have to write the sentence again and number the letters again it is convenient to prepare the second grid underneath the first. The second grid is prepared in the same way as the first, except the blocking out of the squares is only done horizontally, not vertically.

The message is now written into the second grid, reading gown from column 1, then column 2 and so on.

The coded message, ready for transmitting, is now written down in groups of five, beginning with column 1, reading downwards as follows:

WOTNT SFIIW KBETS WFQDU SWVEM
IMTHC SAIUE NESLT CFIWH WGAAD
TCXFP IAREH PIBER LOVRRFLNNW
RNRLA SNSAC LDNCCODWAP RCATU
NOAAN NHOHM FPMWN LUWGI

When starting to transmit TREASURE begins KA, then gives the number of groups, then a dash and then the date of ciphering, e.g. 24 – 27.[44]

Partly to satisfy Kliemann's desire for her to visit Bristol regularly, but also to escape the city life and be looked after, she spent several days each week with Mrs Coate. The cost soon mounted up and she asked Sherer if she might be better compensated. It was pointed out that MI5 had deducted £4 10s a week for her flat, but that its rent was much more than that. The War Office was paying the difference. She commented that she found it difficult not to smile.

I figure it out myself: the weekly trip to Bristol, with taxis and tips, costs me four pounds, which makes sixteen pounds a month; about ten shillings a day for meals makes fifteen pounds a month; to this I have to add telephone, laundry (six shillings a week), electricity – let us say three pounds. No that won't do: I'm two pounds short!

'I'll have to go begging,' I say sadly.[45]

She became ill back in London, which prevented her from sending her first transmission on 6 April. Her first 'blind' message was sent on 13 April and the third incoming message was received almost a week later. Two-way traffic was not established until 10 May, just in time for further British-inspired deception plans to be included in her outgoing messages. She claimed that she sent six messages a week describing imaginary journeys to Salisbury Plain, Cambridge and 'to places which I did not know existed, and from which I bring back rich harvests of information; the extent of which frightens me! In this world of fiction, I spend my time in trains, clubs, messes, canteens. I transmit a hotch-potch of descriptions of badges, vehicles, tanks, planes and airfields, garnished with conversations overheard, from which the Germans cannot fail to draw the right conclusions'.[46]

One imaginary source was a high-ranking general staff officer who, as he regularly drank too much, told her that the Allies had no intention of being the first to use gas. 'But they are quite ready to retaliate by using it in vast air attacks should the Germans start it up. Allied airpower is so much superior to the Luftwaffe that it should make the Germans think twice.'[47]

A further complication arose when the OSS reported that the British Secret Service had sent a Russian woman to Lisbon in March who had made contact with a German agent, told him the name of the head of the British Secret Service, returned to London and was still in contact with this agent.[48] A report in Lily's file stated that Buecking, one of the Abwehr agents she met in March, had met Eitel, another German official, when he got back from Berlin on 22 April 1944. Being rather drunk on whisky, he told Eitel about meeting a Russian woman in Lisbon in March who he had known before the war and who was working for British Intelligence. She had told him that her British chief in England, whom she named, had sent her to contact a certain person in Lisbon and she had given him the name and address. Through her he had learned a considerable amount about the British Secret Service. 'She was a dark, good-looking girl, but he was afraid he could not mention any names. She had left Lisbon with the undertaking to keep in touch by mail. EITEL did not dare to question him more closely, and BUECKING went on to tell his agent that he would never make good in the Abwehr unless he got a really worthwhile contact like this woman'.[49]

MI5 decided to ignore this warning, arguing that it should have read the British Information Service, i.e. the Ministry of Information, and that Lily had not had enough time to write to Lisbon. Another reason was that, a week before D-Day, Denys Page, the assistant director of the Government Code and Cypher School at Bletchley Park, wrote to Masterman telling him that

> I should like you and Robertson to know how much we appreciated the assistance you are giving us in respect of TRAMP/TREASURE and BRUTUS/HERBERT traffic. I have discussed the matter again this morning with the people actually on the job, and I find that about 30% of our success with

the whole French network has been due solely to TRAMP and HUBERT: experience in using the material will certainly raise this proportion even higher.

It is seldom that we get such a stroke of luck in this job, especially with traffic so valuable as our French network: so I thought that you should know what a high degree of importance we at this end attribute to BRUTUS and TREASURE. [50]

At the beginning of June, she admitted to Sherer that she had not told anyone before but she had agreed with Kliemann to omit a control sign in her messages to indicate that she was operating under duress. In revenge for the death of her dog, which she held MI5 responsible for, she had planned to get the set working properly and then omit the signal, but had changed her mind about 'blowing the case'. However, she refused to divulge the signal.

When Tar was informed, given that D-Day was imminent, he took the decision to allow her to keep transmitting, but not to include anything of a deceptive nature. He also allocated another wireless operator the task of learning her 'fist' – her unique style of typing the Morse messages on her transmitter – so that they would be able to copy it without the Germans being aware.

On 5 June, the day before D-Day, she reported ill again and was taken into St Mary's Hospital after making a final transmission. A week later, her set was in use again, but not operated by Lily. She released herself from hospital on 14 June and in a 'tumultuous' meeting with Tar was told that her services as an agent were no longer required. It is unknown whether he was aware of how valuable Bletchley Park had considered her services. He considered her unreliable on account of the story of the control signal and that she had arranged a private method of communication with the Abwehr while in Lisbon. She flatly denied this and was reported to have been very upset when told that her set was being operated by someone else.

Yesterday I saw TREASURE at 39 Hill Street in the presence of Miss Sherer.

I said that I had come to deliver a very serious talk as I had, during the past few days, formed definite opinions with regard to her case. I said that we had already taken over the transmitter and were imitating her and that in future she would not be required to assist us in this way. I pointed out my reasons for coming to this conclusion were two-fold:

[1] that I had heard from Miss Sherer that TREASURE had been to Lisbon and had fixed up with KLIEMANN a signal or signals which would appear in her messages indicating whether or not she was working under control, and

[2] that from a reliable source it had been reported that while in Lisbon she had fixed up a means of communication with a German Intelligence Officer without this coming to our notice.

I pointed out that it was quite impossible for me to place any confidence in someone who behaved in this manner.

I then said that we would pay her £5 a week as from Monday next, and that if she decided to have an operation [?], we would undertake to pay all expenses. At the same time we would clear up all outstanding doctors' bills. I also said that we would endeavour, although I made no promise whatever, to send her at some future date, either to her sister in Algiers or to her family in Paris, if conditions made this possible.

I pointed out, however, that if I had any cause to think that she was being indiscreet or was in any way acting contrary to the Allied cause, I would at once take severe action and either put her into prison or hand her over to the French authorities who would no doubt deal with her pretty severely. I also said that naturally any allowance in the shape of money which I was making to her would cease. In addition, I said that we might occasionally wish to consult her over some point in connection with the traffic and that I expected her to give us every assistance. I also asked her to make arrangements to leave 39 Hill Street within the next fortnight.

Before leaving, I made quite certain that she understood what I had said and asked her if she had anything to say. She had nothing to say except that she did not want the money. I said that she would take it whether she liked it or not, and that she could do what she liked with it.[51]

There was no indication that Tar had emphasised the enormity of the consequences of her action, potentially diminishing the successful Allied invasion of Normandy. Sherer was left to deal with the consequences.

I found TREASURE very upset as a result of the interview with Colonel Robertson. She asked me if we had really taken over the transmitter, and if we had did we realise that we had blown the case. She said she thought I had not understood about the control sign which she told me about a short time ago. I said I had understood perfectly well. She went on to say that the reason she had told me that she had a control signal was to prevent our doing the very thing we had done; taking over the transmitter and blowing the case. I then asked TREASURE to give me the control signal. She said there was no object in her telling me because Colonel Robertson had said she was unreliable and if he thought he would not believe the control signal was correct even if she gave it to me.

TREASURE went on talking in this way for some time until I had to leave, when she came out with me and walked to Piccadilly Circus. When I was just leaving her in the street, she suddenly said; 'This is the signal.' I made her write it down, and this is what she wrote: 'Don't put the dash after KA. If dash before AR do AR once. If no dash AR twice. Month starts 13, Next no dash. Following month anyhow.'

This means that the beginning of a message when she gives KA or CT then the number of groups, dash sign and then date, she never puts a dash between KA or CT and the number of groups, e.g. She always sends CT 72 – 23.

This signal is constant. She has another signal which varies according to the month. She started transmitting on 13th April, so the month starts on the 13th for the purpose of this signal. For the first month the signal is that if she puts a dash before sending AR (which comes at the end of the message) she sends AR once, if she does not put a dash, she sends AR twice. The next month she does not put a dash. The third month she can send AR anyway she pleases. The fourth month is the same as the first month and so on.

I have not yet had an opportunity of checking TREASURE's statement regarding the second control signal, with the logs, but I shall do so at the first opportunity.[52]

Lily admitted in her autobiography that she had not wanted to capitulate, but it was the people of occupied France, 'the hungry faces; fire-places without a fire; hands covered with chilblains; the dreary despair of those who have waited for four years. It's for them that I have struggled'.[53]

Tar was unsympathetic. He described her as being exceptionally temperamental and troublesome, lacking in discretion and commitment. Although her services were dispensed with, MI5 continued transmitting messages on her set until November 1944. By that time Bletchley Park had a number of other channels to the Germans, so her messages stopped with no explanation.

Ironically, the government code-breakers who monitored her transmissions and the Germans' response praised Lily, saying that she had 'absolutely saved the bacon of GC and C.S [Government Code and Cypher School, Bletchley Park] during June, July, August and September', while she described MI6 as 'gangsters'.[54]

Dwight D. Eisenhower, the commander-in-chief of the Allied forces at Normandy, commented that if the XV Army had reinforced the VII Army its sheer manpower would have crushed his forces. While Lily was not the only agent employed in the Pas de Calais deception scheme, her role was important. Field Marshall Montgomery commented later that 'we now know that we attained a degree of surprise greater than any we could have imagined'.

Although MI5 offered to send her to Algiers to stay with her sister or to Paris to be with her family, she had to give up the flat and move to Bristol. She planned to join the French army and fight on the front line, but MI5 attempted to dissuade her, arguing that, if the Germans captured her, she would be shot. On 26 June, she offered her services to Captain Vauedreuil of General de Gaulle's Free French Forces and, after going through the work she did with MI5 and explaining that she had left as her work had finished, she was accepted for work with the French Red Cross. Sherer warned her that the French authorities would question her on her activities, so she provided them with a detailed biographical account, which Lily accepted as not incriminating.[55]

With a group of French female volunteers, she returned to France in late July, where she served as a nurse in the Mission Militaire de Liaison with the Third American Army in Verdun, inoculating Russian prisoners of war before their repatriation. While there she met Major Fertig, an American serviceman, and after a three-month romance, married him and planned to live in the United States.

She was called to a meeting with the French Police, where she was cautioned about contacting anyone she had previously been in touch with who had connections with German espionage activities, and told that if she did so she would incur direst penalties. She would be treated as a spy and immediately arrested. She acknowledged 'having received formal orders to cease all relations with those whom I had been in contact during my work for the British Secret Services. I also recognise being notified that if I fail to follow these instructions action will be taken against me'.[56]

For whatever reason, she broke this promise and located Yvonne Dedilaise, who told her that she had been arrested by the French authorities, interrogated and then, surprisingly, released, after admitting that she had given them some but not all the names of those she had worked with. Lily told her that she had bluffed the British, that after her arrival in England she had lost everything, including her wireless set, in the bombing and had joined General Leclerc's 2nd Armoured Division.

She also met Van Meriss, her friend from Syria, whom she had kept in contact with during the war. As he had joined the Bureau de la Sécurité Militaire, he thought she might be helpful in identifying and providing details about collaborators, particularly those already in prison. She refused, claiming she wanted nothing to do with Kliemann's associates. Following the liberation of Paris, Kliemann was located and, from a note in Lily's file, it appears that he offered the British his fullest services. Over thirty Abwehr agents scattered all over France were arrested and all their secret wireless stations identified.

Having had a number of her books published before and during the war, she talked about publishing her memoirs. Given the British government's opposition to such a publication, as she might reveal the names of the people she worked with, on 3 November Tar wrote to Mrs Linda Barton, one of the women Lily had got to know in England, hoping she might be able to help. He told her that this 'wretched woman' had been given 'a fairly substantial ticking off' by the French and that

> she will always be a source of trouble for us, no matter what restrictions we impose on her – short of imprisonment for life.
>
> In writing back to her, I don't know whether there is anything you can say which might appeal to her better nature, if she has one, but I am inclined to think that if you do so, you will find yourself placed in the category of 'gangsters.' I think probably it would be better if you endeavour to get on the right side of her. You might suggest, however, that you would very much like to see the manuscript of her book before publication, as in doing so you might possibly assist her in some of the details and advise her in connection with possible prosecutions which might arise as the result of published indiscretions.[57]

Malcolm Muggeridge, an MI6 officer in France, was given similar instructions to see if he could dissuade her from publishing it or at least get hold of a copy to be able to identify which sections ought to be redacted. How successful he was has yet to come to light.

Following her learning that her sister had been murdered, she emigrated to the United States in 1946. Worried that an American publisher would be interested in her story, Tar contacted the American Embassy. They told him that the FBI had no details of her activities or intentions but they would attempt to discourage her from revealing such sensitive information. Lily died in 1950 and her wartime autobiography, *Secret Service Rendered*, remained unpublished until 1968.

John Masterman's Double Agent 'Bronx': Elvira Chaudoir

Another woman involved in the British deception scheme was Elvira Concepcion Josefina de la Fuente Chaudoir, the daughter of a Peruvian merchant living in Paris who had made his fortune exporting guano, phosphate-rich bird droppings. Research by Ben Macintyre revealed that, after an expensive education, she married Jean Chaudoir, a Belgian stock-exchange representative for a gold-mining firm, when she was twenty-three. She found life in Brussels to be 'exceedingly dull', so, after four years of marriage and a number of unsatisfactory love affairs with both men and women, she ran away to Cannes with her best friend, Romy Gilbey, the wife of the gin manufacturer. Not caring about losing their ex-husbands' money in casinos in the south of France, they fled to Britain in an open-topped Renault when the Germans invaded.

Arriving on 3 September 1939, they were interrogated by MI6 at the London Reception Centre and allowed to stay. A note in her file indicates that Elvira was considered by SOE but they turned her down.[1]

Research by the *Telegraph* reporters Neil Tweedie and Peter Day revealed that, based in a flat on Sloane Street, twenty-nine-year-old Chaudoir spent her evenings drinking at the bar of the Ritz and then gambling for very high stakes at bridge and poker tables. Her life in London followed the same extravagant pattern as 'a high society gambler who managed to run up debts at Crockford's Casino and the Hamilton Bridge Club while pursuing a colourful sex life. Weekends were spent at house parties thrown by Lord Carnarvon, with the likes of the Duke of Marlborough and Duff Cooper.'[2]

Unable to borrow money from her parents in France, she tried to join de Gaulle's Free French but was considered unsuitable. Although she did some translating work for the BBC, she complained at the Hamilton's Club about not having an interesting job. Overheard by an RAF officer, he passed her name to a friend in military intelligence.

Mr Masefield, the cover name of Lieutenant Colonel Claude Dansey, the deputy head of MI6, met her at the Connaught Hotel, having previously investigated her background. Hugh Trevor-Roper, a fellow intelligence officer, described Dansey as 'an utter shit, corrupt, incompetent, but with a certain low cunning'.[3] Macintyre described him as 'a middle-aged man in a rumpled suit with a bristling white moustache and the eyes of a hyperactive ferret'.

> Dansey was a most unpleasant man and a most experienced spy. They made an odd couple: Elvira, tall and overdressed, with a sweet, rather innocent face, her auburn hair arranged into question mark over her forehead; Dansey, small, bald, bespectacled, and intense. Elvira rather liked this fizzing little man, and as the conversation unfolded it became clear that he knew a great deal about her. He knew about Mrs Gilbey and the unsuccessful evenings at the bridge tables; he knew her father had been appointed Peruvian chargé d'affaires to the collaborationist Vichy Government in France; he knew what was, or rather what was not, in her bank account. 'I realised he must have been tapping my telephone. There was no other way he could have learned so much about me and my friends,' she later admitted.[4]

His investigation of her finances revealed that she had gambling debts of almost £1,000 (almost £30,000 today) and had borrowed large sums to cover repayments. The small allowance from her father covered the rent of 5 guineas a week that she paid on a furnished flat at 12 Hertford Street and although her divorced husband had promised to pay her 338,000 Belgian francs over seven years, it was not to start until 1947. She needed a regular income.

Dansey knew that her Peruvian passport and an influential father would make it easy for her to visit France and he proposed what in spy language was called 'coat trailing'. He was prepared to pay her well – how well was not stated – to go on a long holiday to Vichy, stay with her parents and report back to him on any political intelligence she might pick up. While mixing in top social circles, he expected her to be picked up by one of the Abwehr officers in Paris and asked to spy for them. Aware of her financial dilemma and the prospect of a well-paid and highly stimulating job, she agreed. According to Macintyre,

> The MI6 assessment of its new recruit was blunt: 'Attractive in appearance. She speaks fluent French, English and Spanish. She is intelligent and has a quick brain but is probably rather lazy about using it. A member of the international smart gambling set, her friends are to be found in any of the smart bridge clubs in London.' Surveillance revealed that her 'tastes appear to be in the direction of the "high spots."' Police reported 'hilarious parties' at the Sloane Street flat, with 'rowdy behaviour, singing and shouting late at night, and the arrival of drunken men and women in the small hours.' Deputy Chief Constable Joseph Goulder noted, with disapproval and some understatement, that Mrs. Chaudoir 'favours the companionship of women who may not be careful of their virginity.' Though Elvira might have come across as some dizzy-headed socialite, in reality she was bright and resourceful, and with a cast-iron cover: a good-time girl with no interests beyond the next cocktail, the next bed partner, and the next bet. She

was also attractive to both sexes and hungry for cash, qualities that might come in useful. As Dansey knew from a lifetime of espionage, even the most intelligent and discreet of people will tend to indiscretion if they think they are talking to a foolish and beddable woman.[5]

One of MI6's instructors taught her how to use secret ink using a match head that had been dipped into a chemical powder. The idea was that while in France she could write 'apparently innocuous letters' to an innocent address in Lisbon, but between the lines she could write her intelligence report in invisible ink. Once received by MI6, their technicians could dab it with cotton wool that had been dipped in a chemical solution, which would expose the writing; they could then transcribe her secret message before it dried and disappeared. Her instructor reported her being a swift learner. 'She is very intelligent and quick to grasp essentials.'[6]

However, her career in espionage almost came to an abrupt end when a naval officer reported overhearing her at Crockford's Casino telling Gilbey, her friend who she had come to England with, that she was being taught a secret-service code in the neighbourhood of St James's and that she was shortly to be sent to Vichy to contact British agents in France. The code was said to be something to do with music and lyrics. Called into the office for a meeting, after she was severely reprimanded, she promised to be more discreet in the future and avoid divulging any intelligence that she might pick up to anyone except Christopher Harmer, her MI6 handler.

Harmer described her as 'a typical member of the cosmopolitan smart set and, though possibly lazy, is not unintelligent. At the present moment she is living in a flat in Hertford Street, Mayfair, and there is some reason to believe she is living with a man who has a flat in the same house. It is not known whether she is continuing with her lesbian tendencies'.[7]

While in the south of France, as Dansey had hoped, one of her friends who was collaborating with the Germans introduced her to thirty-five-year-old Helmut 'Bibi' Biel, a tall, black-haired Abwehr officer. He was one of Herman Goering's agents, and was thought to have been one of the economic experts engaged in unoccupied France on behalf of the Armistice Commission in Wiesbaden. After a good deal of 'entertaining', Masterman described him as an alcoholic; she was said to have formed a 'personal relationship' with him, but whether this had been at Dansey's suggestion is unknown.[8]

She reported on her return that he had a diplomatic passport, with a visa allowing him to visit Madrid. She was not interrogated at any length and, once her personal details had been checked by Berlin, he suggested that she would be a useful agent, providing him with any economic intelligence she might find in Britain. He told her that he already had one agent in Britain who was being paid £1,000 a month, but all their other agents had been captured. All he wanted her to do was to read financial magazines and write a resumé, stressing that it would not harm Britain. All her intelligence had to be sourced with the name of the magazine or the name of any contacts she made who provided information. If she was to contact the British Intelligence Service and get information from it, he would be prepared to offer a lot. He suggested that her cover should be as a journalist, writing anti-Axis articles for publication in a magazine. The way she would send her intelligence was to write an ordinary letter and then write the information using secret ink. One imagines that she showed complete ignorance when he gave her the instructions.

> You take a sheet of paper, not too thick, not too thin, white, and rub it carefully with a piece of dry cotton-wool to make it less slippery. Then you write your message in block letters, separating each word from the next with a little line, in telegraphic style on the front side of your sheet if it is single, on pages 1 and 3 if it is double, never on the back of where you have already written. You hardly caress the paper with the little match; you write so lightly that the point hardly touches the paper. As soon as you press even a little the writing can be seen by strong light. (He proved this to me later on in my room.) You write in the long sense of the paper so that you can write another cover letter on top in the short sense (the normal letter-writing one). You write your cover letter in PENCIL or TYPEWRITER but never in ink. To read our letters you dissolve the powder I give you in 50 grammes of water so that it has the appearance of milk and you add ammoniac until the liquid becomes clear gain. You keep it in a bottle of YELLOW glass and each time you get a letter you wet a piece of cotton-wool with it and wash the BACK of our letter with it (the contrary of the side you write on) and you copy our letter quickly because the writing soon vanishes.[9]

His letters to her would be addressed to the Peruvian Legation and signed 'Mireille', 'Henri' or 'Guilette'. She was given a bottle of the latest secret ink as well as a developer with a promise of £100 a month, more if she required it, and told that it would be paid from Switzerland into her London bank account and she could claim it was part of her husband's divorce settlement. The questions he wanted her to find answers for were:

> What is the production of such and such a factory?
> How many people does it employ?
> Where does it stock its production?
> Do I know of any factory shutting down? Or changing place? Or opening up?
> What does such and such a shop store?
> What products are becoming rare?
> Where do foodstuffs arrive?
> How is their distribution organised within the country?
> What are the wages of factory workers?
> Any possible information about arrivals of war material of same etc.[10]

MI6 paid her the same £100 a month but tax free, plus expenses for any trips they expected her to make. She also agreed to share fifty-fifty any bonus the Germans might pay her, given that it was all going to be as a result of British-inspired intelligence.

However, as they were not completely sure that what she had told them was the full story, it was considered 'essential to keep her under the closest observation, and that her contacts and activities be watched'. All her mail was opened and her telephone was tapped from 26 October until 3 December 1942, but this procedure was cancelled when only irrelevant details of her social life were revealed.[11]

Accommodation was provided at 15 Clarges Street, Westminster, and, as writing letters was not considered a full-time job, Dansey arranged employment for her as a Spanish translator in the BBC's Foreign Language Service. To explain her meeting a wide range of influential people, she was given cover as a journalist, like Fifi, researching articles for the *Sunday Graphic*. Her first contribution, enhanced by her MI5 officers, read,

A few days after my return from France I dined at a well-known London Club. After two excellent courses the maid gave us a choice of several puddings, but a man sitting opposite me said he would rather have cheese. However when the cheese was produced he said he couldn't possibly eat it without butter or celery and as both these things proved unavailable he pushed the cheese away with a martyred look on his face. The following evening a young officer friend of mine left a dinner party grumbling: 'Oh! Dear! What a bore! the eleven o'clock train has been stopped so I have to catch the ten forty back.'

Exactly two months before this I had arrived at Toulouse one August evening feeling very hungry and very tired. The train that had taken me from Madrid to the border had done so in twenty-two hours, although it was an express and the journey normally takes eight or ten hours. Of course I had missed the only daily connection to Pau and had to spend the night in the station. It then took me the whole day to reach Toulouse, which is one of the nearest towns to the Spanish border. When I got there I spent two hours trying to get a room in which to spend the night, but this was quite hopeless; there were crowds of people at every hotel begging to be allowed to sleep in the lobbies. (No restaurant had any food left either.) However, I managed to convince the waiter at the station buffet to let me have dinner. Nevertheless he asked to see my coupons and then reluctantly gave me a thin vegetable soup, some cold tomatoes and boiled beans. I told him how hungry I was but he said that was the menu and they just didn't have anything else. There were already lots of people sleeping on the floor of the station but I felt too exhausted to face such an ordeal and I must have looked rather pathetic because I finally obtained permission from a hotel manager to spend the night in the hall. I got up at dawn in order to catch the only train to Vichy, which was packed and stopped at every station on the way so that I did not arrive till dinner time.

Already by then I realised what a state France was in and how little we know in England of their misery. All night I was haunted by pictures of the poor crowds in Toulouse, aimlessly wandering about, in old shabby clothes, searching the floors for some cigarette stub. I have little space here to give in detail any experiences but I shall try to give a rough idea of the situation. Most meals consist of vegetables and fruit only. The meat ration provides three slices a week and the cheese ration for a month is smaller than ours for a week. The bread is hard and uneatable. There are no potatoes, no eggs, no oil, no tea, no coffee, no rice, no macaroni, no biscuits and hardly any sugar. Even salt is running out. And of course, one can get nothing at all without coupons, even at restaurants. Men get a tobacco ration of two packets of twenty bad cigarettes every ten days. The clothes coupons are about half the number we get here. There are no leather-soled shoes, only wooden ones; no stockings so that women go bare-legged even in winter, and no wool. Soap is replaced by a substitute which leaves your hands as dirty after they have been washed as before. In summer there is no hot water even in the best hotels and in winter only once a week; as for central heating, it no longer exists and as gas and electricity are severely rationed there are no other ways of heating. Travelling is made almost impossible: there is generally only one train a day from town to town, which means it is always packed and it stops at every intermediary station so that the journey seems unending. The local buses work on charcoal and are invariably slow and crowded. There is also a noticeable lack of indispensible things such as cotton wool, hospitable bandages, iodine and Vaseline, all of which even the sick have to go without.

Personally I was very lucky as I was staying in the Hotel des Ambassadeurs, which has been commandeered for the Diplomatic Corps and provided with a few exceptional favours. On the night of my arrival, as there was no room free and our Minister was away I occupied his room. Great was my surprise to find I could hardly move about his bathroom for electric stoves, pots and pans, boxes of sardines, apples, potatoes and other food-stuffs (most of which, I subsequently heard, had come all the way from Peru). The bedroom was in the same condition and so, apparently, were the rest of them. And the dining room resembled a scene from a comedy: everyone walked in carrying preciously some mysterious little dish privately prepared to supplement the meal; some South American ambassador was content with rice, while Mrs. Tuck, the wife of the American Charge-d'Affaires, had managed to find a corn on the cob and the Rumanian Minister had just received caviar. There seemed to be little diplomatic courtesy amongst them as no-one offered even their most precious Ally a share of their specialty, but nothing kept their amicability to a lot of bowing and smiling, though of course the Italian Representative haughtily ignored the Americans sitting at the next table and the Japanese glared in cold anger at the Chinese opposite them. After dinner some people vanished to their rooms to make coffee while others had it brought down and occasionally could afford to offer a cup to some French friend who had come to ply bridge with them in the hall.

Even at official luncheon parties every course had been provided by the host, generally from stores sent from his own country in the diplomatic bag, or from excursions into the surrounding farms. For the French, however, even those belonging to the Government, there are no such facilities and it was heart-rending to see queues of hungry, tired people waiting at the doors of empty shops.

Of course many people will compare my picture with that of a still luxurious South-of-France. I went there too. Yes, I saw people who get more or less all the food they want, who wear lovely clothes and who, though dancing is forbidden even to them, spend their nights gambling in the Cannes and Monte Casino casinos. There exists a minority of people with enough money to buy the others out of their share, to organise and use a scandalously expensive black market which provides them with a decent meal for the equivalent cost of several pounds, and with a packet of cigarettes for a pound. Most of them are on holiday from Paris and from their own testimony, this fabulous black market is even more flourishing in countries such as Italy and Belgium, where it is organised by the army of occupation itself for the benefit of its own individuals and of those who collaborate with them. It strikes me that under the National Service order the mass of the population lacks the essential, while a small majority is provided with all the refinements of pre-war times. It has been the German system everywhere to try and buy the services of a few leaders, political industrial and intellectual who carry out their schemes, bearing the unpopularity themselves and save the Germans a great deal of re-organisation difficulties. It is worth their while to pay any price and so they have formed, and sustain a small class of unscrupulous millionaires. With the terrific war on their hands they must contrive to minimise their task in the occupied territories. They must have a Laval, to whom to say; 'We need a hundred and fifty thousand workers by the fifteenth of October. It's your business to find them; use your own police if necessary; If you fail perhaps Doriot would succeed ...' There are also factory owners to whom they can likewise talk: 'We need so many tanks by such and such a date; we shall guarantee an enormous profit but it's your own affair to manage your workers. If you refuse we shall take over your business, or send your employees to our own factories in Germany (a threat they would rather not have to carry out)'. And unfortunately there are writers too, and journalists to whom they have succeeded in dictating their propaganda. Actually it's almost the only kind of literature left as the paper shortage gives a reasonable excuse for keeping everything else out of print. The papers receive no news that is not German-inspired and weekly magazines such as 'Gringoire' have adopted the grossly insulting style of [?] mentioning anything or anyone the Germans may disapprove of. I was particularly amused for instance by the violent attack made on the jews by papers such as Leon Bailby's 'L'ALERTE' whose editor is a man who covers his typically jewish name by a bogus title. However it seems that propaganda has already outlived its short hay-day and that even the most uneducated see through it all. I was having my hair done one morning in Cannes, the news-seller walked into the shop, screaming with delight: 'No papers this morning; for once some bit of truth has escaped the censor's eye and so the papers have been stopped.'

Although it is forbidden to do so, many people listen to the British and Free-French news.

It remains that France is in a pathetic state of misery, both materially and morally. She is lost and discouraged. Only those of her leaders who have been bought are allowed to speak openly and guide the mess. She has a guilty conscience which has developed an inferiority complex and which makes fairness of judgment very difficult. She hates company but she is cold and hungry and afraid and the enemy sits at home, overpowering with military processions and machine-guns. French workers stand on the roofs on the nights when the R.A.F. come and destroy their own homes, thinking of the factory next door which is crumbling too, which will save them for some time from working for the detested occupant; but they also have a desperate longing for the day when the same heroes will come and deliver them for good, bringing them arms so that they may fight to deliver themselves. They want to fight now; they want to kill with all the rage of accumulated pain and hatred.

The British people, who have deservedly gained the world's admiration for their unfailing calm and courage throughout the battle of Britain, and for their heroism in the face of incessant danger, have suffered enough to sympathise now with those across the Channel who are living another episode of misery and despair. The Government here has made all restrictions as light as possible and has seen to it that one and all have their fair share, but it will have to ask us for more sacrifices before we can put an end to the war and, when we have to make them, maybe it will help to think of those over there who are really starving, to remember that the sooner we make these sacrifices the fewer children will die for lack of milk. Germany is no longer the one who will pay for famine. Until we take her place she will help herself to the last crumb of bread in stricken Europe.[12]

The suggested titles were 'A Neutral's Impression of France' or 'A Peruvian in France'. One imagines that, should Biel have read it, he would have been suitably impressed by the anti-Axis sentiment – excellent cover for his agent. In fact, he trusted her so highly that she sent ninety-six secret messages over a two-year period. It would have been more, but the planned messages to France were shelved following the German take-over of the unoccupied zone in November 1942. The majority of her correspondence was sent to cover addresses in Lisbon and Madrid, including Antonio de Almeida, the general manager of Espirito Santo Bank, who was friendly to the Germans, and Henriquetta de Oliveira.

She was given the code name 'Bronx' and was sometimes known as Cyril. A file entitled 'SUMMARY OF CHAUDOIR TRAFFIC 03/11/1942 – 24/11/1944' includes all her British-inspired messages, which were part of Operation FORTITUDE, the Allies' plan to deceive the Germans into believing that their invasion site was on France's western Atlantic coast. As her German salary was not always paid into her account regularly, she often included demands for more money to cover lodging, food, clothes, dentists, medicines and amusements. She was provided with a carefully selected range of white, grey and black intelligence, white being true and from a reliable source, black being completely false and from a fake source. It was reported to have been gleaned from weekend parties at the homes of influential military and political figures, soldier friends, contacts in various industries and personal observations made on her travels around the country. Initially it was economic intelligence, but in order to enable her to play a role in the deception plan, it later became more military and included results of bombing raids, aircraft production, troop movements, naval movements, etc.[13]

One message Tar wanted her to write confirmed the action of another double agent operating in North Africa. He wrote to Colonel A. H. Robertson, another Double-Cross officer who helped generate her reports.

We shall be very grateful if you could see your way to helping us in the following matter:

Our representative in Algiers has a double agent in the sabotage branch. This man has been very useful to us. We wish to build him up and encourage the Germans to think he is efficient and truthful.

In July he was given bombs and instructed to blow up the petrol dump at SENIA station (3 miles west of ORAN). He was told at the same time that if he succeeded he would be given further bombs and assistance in blowing up the pipe line running to the TAFAROUI aerodrome.

In conjunction with G.2 an explosion and fire were staged at SENIA on 26th July at 23.30 hours. We are not certain whether the Germans believed their assignment had been carried out, but a message in our Most Secret Sources dated 19.8.43 my refer to the incident.

It has occurred to us that if you could confirm the incident through one of your agents in this country we should reap useful advantages.

Would you consider whether it would be possible for BRONX, for instance, to report that at a dinner party she was placed next to a naval officer who had one arm in sling. She had to dissect his chicken, or shall we say grouse, for him. She asked him whether he had been in action; he replied in a disgusted way that his wound was not the result of action against the enemy but of an explosion – in fact German sabotage carried out by a German sabotage agent at SENIA (outside Oran) at the end of July, or words to that effect. His wounds could be increased or decreased according to your pleasure.[14]

A tick underneath suggested that Tar's wishes were carried out. The Most Secret Sources referred to were 'Ultra', the decoded intercepts of German messages thanks to the work of Alan Turing and boffins at Bletchley Park breaking the Enigma machine.

There were also plans to ask Biel to deposit £25,000 in a bank account with which she could speculate on the stock exchange in order to make a lot of money. It was thought that an unscrupulous Abwehr officer might be tempted as a way of getting his money out of Germany, but after discussions, this plan was shelved.

Tar reported that on 4 March 1944 she received a message from the Germans asking her to use the following code in telegrams to de Almeida and de Oliveira asking for money for her dentist. The code was to provide intelligence on the impending invasion.

£80	means	Atlantique.
70		France Nord, Belgique.
60	..	France Nord et Biscaya.
50	..	Biscaya.
40	..	Mediterrané
30	..	Danmark.
20	..	Novége.
10	..	Balkans.

An additional procedure is specified to indicate two target areas if necessary.

Bronx is not sure of the precise meaning of Atlantique, but has written to say that she understands it to mean the La Rochelle region of France.

We have subsequently told the Germans we will use the following improvements on the original code:-

'Pour mon dentist' means the information about the target are is certain.

'Pour mon docteur' is almost certain.

'Pour mon medicin' is probable.

'Toute de suite' means landings will be in one week.

'Urgent' two weeks.

'Vite' one month.

'Si possible' date is uncertain.[15]

At one point MI6 issued a directive to case officers requiring them to have greater security control of the cover letters their agents were sending. Tar reported that

BRONX is in the habit of dashing off a cover letter consisting of completely meaningless feminine chat, which it would be difficult to control or alter; further, this text is so much in her own style (which is very far removed from anything I could produce) that in my opinion any attempt to interfere with it would be liable to show the text was written under control.

It would seem that there is no danger from allowing her to go on writing the cover letters herself, because apart from the fact that she was a British agent before she was ever recruited by the Germans, and is probably one of our most reliable agents, she writes these letters so spontaneously that there would appear to be no opportunity for inserting anything, which we could regard as offensive, as the result of premeditation.[16]

When she was asked to supply details of the effect V1 rockets were having on Britain, Tar helped her put together the following response:

Reference your rocket question: I have found that Duncan Sandys, Churchill's son-in-law, is in charge of counter-measures to the rocket. He talks quite well. Position seems to be that English are sure that main threat is rocket aeroplanes controlled not by radio but by master compass – main evidence said to be orientation of launching sites. Therefore, although they have published in the press about radio control, this is part of careful campaign to mislead Germans into thinking that they (the British) are wasting their time on radio counter-measures, while in fact their real counter, apart from bombing the sites, is to build big magnetic deflecting fields. Bombing has gone so well that Sandys is cross with technicians who led him to embark upon costly enterprise of building big power supplies and cables to make magnetic fields. Sandys is getting strafed by other politicians for having sanctioned the work.

Specific answers to your questions:-

(1) Actual operational control has been tentatively accorded to the same organisation as undertakes radio measures by Sir John Turner.

(2) Does not arise. Power stations are the sources.

(3) Energies said to be thousands and thousands of horsepower.

(4) Ideas nil. British are so confident that Germany will never again try radio control on a large scale after failure of 1940 that they are concentrating on the magnetic side.[17]

On 5 May 1944, she reported, 'Many U.S. troops in East Anglia from west; 4th U.S. Armoured Division near Bury St Edmunds.' On 13 May, she wrote, 'Definite news landing Bay of Biscay.' Two days later, she passed on information from one of her sources that there was 'to be airborne attack Bordeaux tomorrow before invasion. Next day he said, much agitated, that attack postponed for a month'. On 16 May, she wrote, 'Send fifty pounds. Quickly. I need it for my dentist.' This coded message indicating a planned invasion of the Bay of Biscay, she explained in a letter the following day, had come from a drunken officer who had told her that an airborne attack on Bordeaux was being planned. He later implored her not to mention it to anyone as it had been postponed for a month, i.e. until the 15 June. On 24 May she told them that an Armoured Division had moved from Yorkshire to Brighton at the end of April.[18]

Hugh Astor, her second case officer, shed more light on her role in the D-Day deception plans.

BRONX AND PLAN IRONSIDE

With regard to PLAN IRONSIDE, it seems to me that it might be possible to use BRONX to assist in the implementation of this scheme. So far as one can judge, she appears to enjoy the confidence of the Germans, and she has been given a telegraphic code which enables her to indicate where the targets are and probable date of attack.

I suggest that BRONX should send two telegrams to her cover address in Lisbon, the first indicating that the main attack will be launched against the north-western part of Europe, between Belgium and France. the second telegram would indicate that this attack will be followed a fortnight later by an attack against the Bay of Biscay coastline, which will be delivered direct from bases in America and the Azores.

In order to achieve our object of containing the German Panzer division in the region of Bordeaux, it will be necessary to time these telegrams so that they arrive on D-2 of NEPTUNE, as otherwise the Panzer division will probably be moving north to meet the real assault. The arrival of these telegrams in Lisbon should provoke a reaction on most secret sources

I understand that there is at present a delay of 14 days on private telegrams addressed to the Iberian Peninsula. It would be necessary therefore for the first telegram to be dated the 15th May, and I suggest that it should be in the following terms: 'If possible please send £70 to pay my medicine!' This message means that an attack will probably be launched against Northern France and Belgium on some undetermined date.

On the 16th May BRONX would send a further telegram stating: 'Please send urgently £50 to pay my dentist. This is required urgently. Please try to arrange for it to be sent within a fortnight of your first remittance.' This should indicate to the Germans that an attack will definitely be made against the Bay of Biscay and that it will take place exactly a fortnight after the first attack.

If it is thought necessary, BRONX could send a further telegram dated the 17th May, stating 'Further to my telegram of the 16th, have received confirmation that my friends will be arriving direct from America. Please welcome them on my behalf.'[19]

Astor also drafted a covering letter to give an explanation for the telegrams, which read,

Spent Sunday with Lady Carlisle [Commandant of the Air Transport Service, Southeast Command], where I met General Simmonds of the 1st Canadian Army and Colonel — of O.S.S., who arrived a week ago from America. From him I learned that an attack is being planned against the Bay of Biscay area, which will be launched from bases in America and the Azores, in the hopes that it will outflank your armies. Colonel — regarded this as a logistical masterpiece worthy of Hannibal, as the attack, which is due to be delivered a fortnight after the first assault, will have two advantages. In the first place you are expected to believe that all shipping resources available to the British will be completely occupied in supplying their armies across the Channel and will therefore be caught completely by surprise, and in the second place it is thought that within a fortnight you will have moved all your troops north to meet the threat from England.

I do hope that my telegrams reached you in time and that you will be able to interpret them properly.[20]

An estimated 15,000 crack German troops and tanks belonging to the SS Panzer division Das Reich were moved from Toulouse to defend Bordeaux instead of Normandy. When it was eventually ordered north, sabotage operations on road and rail links and Allied air strikes reduced its strength and delayed its arrival for a fortnight, by which time the Allies had successfully made their beachhead.

Despite Chaudoir's faulty intelligence, she was still trusted by the Abwehr and for the next few months she supplied them with false information about Britain's defences against V1 and V2 rocket attack. Her last telegram on 24 November 1944 read, 'Thanks for letter, but no money. Think can get return visa through Charge d'Affairs. Must have expenses paid and good bonus. Send telegram and letter by 15 December or shall stop arrangements.'[21]

As her father had been appointed the Peruvian ambassador to Spain, a trip to Madrid for Christmas was organised. Before she went, careful plans were made to ensure Biel met up with her. She was to leave a message for him in an envelope addressed to the Abwehr officer, detailing where she was staying and giving the code name Elise Dubois; this envelope had to be put inside another addressed to the German Embassy in Madrid. To ensure she did not get into trouble should Biel challenge her about the Bordeaux message, copies of her messages were brought out for her to refresh her memory of the contents. She was also briefed to be able to answer the following questions:

(a) Military: she will be asked her opinion as to the next Allied moves in the West, in the North, in the Mediterranean and in the Far East.

(b) She will be asked about airborne forces in this country.

(c) The number of American troops in this country and their rate of arrival from America.

(d) Details of the Atlantic battle, and counter-measures against U-boats.

(e) Industrial information regarding the production of aircraft, tanks, supplies of petrol and oil and food.

(f) Diplomatic relations between England, Russia and America.

(g) The attitude towards the war in England, and whether any section of the public is in favour of a compromise peace. This question has already been put to BRONX some months ago in one of her letters.

(h) The effects of V.1 and V.2 – damage and effect on morale.[22]

She was even briefed as what to say should she be asked whether Russia was planning to attack Japan. She had to keep her eyes and ears open about the German plans for peace, but she was instructed not to offer herself as an intermediary. Special arrangements were made with the Peruvian and Spanish embassies for her visas and with British Overseas Airways for her flights.

She left on 19 December and returned on 12 January 1945, but when she reported that Biel did not show up this caused consternation, as it was thought he might have suspected something. However, intercepted messages from Most Secret Sources indicated that he had been too busy in Berlin, was disappointed not to have seen her but was anxious that she visited Madrid again. The draft of her reply read,

Returned the day before yesterday. Absolutely livid about the uselessness of the journey which was expensive and disagreeable in winter, and you could well have taken the trouble to stop me before my departure, or to have arranged for one of your friends over there to telephone me in order to spare me the constant anxiety of waiting for your news. In several of your letters you insisted upon this visit to Madrid, and after my Ambassador had gone to endless trouble approaching different authorities to obtain permission you let me down.

The journey cost me £60 for the ticket and 2,500 pesetas [just over £100] at the hotel, without counting the extras. Furthermore I only made the journey because I was expecting a handsome bonus in addition to the expenses.

As a last straw I find on my return your letter complaining that my information is of little interest after I have put myself to so much trouble on your behalf. How in God's name do you suppose that I can write more often when I already have so much difficulty in obtaining the information?

As a precaution I have only kept a tiny bottle of developer which was more easy to conceal during my absence. It will be exhausted after your next letter [crossed out and replaced by last only a very short time later], and therefore please without fail tell me how I can buy the new ingredients to make fresh developer.[23]

The extras were two cases of sherry. As her father had failed to give her cash as a Christmas present, MI6 gave her £50. However, subsequent notes indicated the Germans were planning to set up a bank account for her containing £20,000. In a note dated March 1945, Astor wrote to Major Luke,

> ... it seems to me that there are many advantages of continuing this case. She is not bound by any assumed loyalty to the Nazis but works for purely mercenary motives. She is controlled from Lisbon and will be able to continue the contact after the war. Her rather bogus diplomatic status makes her an obvious person with whom the Germans may keep in touch. BRONX is prepared to make another journey to Madrid if you deem it necessary.[24]

Even in March 1945, the Germans were asking her if she could send them the anticipated dates of the Allied landings in Scandinavia. They clearly trusted her as she was asked, 'When we should expect a new invasion, either by landing or by parachute, let us know in the following code. Send. I need for my dentist ... Landing south of Sweden £30, landing in Norway £40, landing in Denmark, £50, landing in the German Bay £60, landing and parachuting in the German Bay £70, parachuting to the west of Berlin £80, parachuting to the west of Berlin and landing in the German Bay £100.'[25]

Luke suggested that she might be used to disseminate information to the Germans about the Allied Control Commission.

> ... it should be of a very general character, and should not paint too black a picture of the conditions which will prevail after Germany's defeat. The message might be something on the following lines:-
>
> 'Have picked out some information about the Allied Control Commission, one of the controllers of which is Ivone Kirkpatrick who has been in close contact with Hess. It will consist of about a dozen departments, each of which as far as possible will function through the established Government machinery in Germany. They intend to leave a very large number of German officials to carry on with their work, provided they co-operate satisfactorily. Under the Department of Internal Affairs there will be no sub-sections dealing with Social Insurance and Unemployment Relief, wages, industrial disputes and labour relations and also for housing.
>
> As far as I can gather the question of feeding the population is causing some anxiety here. I think the Americans have insisted on having control over the northern part; although this area has been earmarked either for the Russians or for the British, and they may want this to facilitate the supply of foodstuffs. It seems likely, however, that the Control will rely for the most part on the ability of the German population to feed themselves.
>
> There will also be a department for manpower and the British seem to be anxious that soldiers who are not war criminals should be directed into work near their homes. On the whole my informant gave me the impression that the British were anxious to approach the problem of government in a humanitarian way, but that they would show no mercy towards guerrillas and others who might add to their difficulties.'

It may be considered desirable only to send a part of the above first, and to give the further information if and when the Germans show any reaction.[26]

Whether it was sent is unknown, but at the end of March there was a note added to a letter from Masterman to Mr Marriot, another member of the Double-Cross Committee, stating, 'I think that at this stage of the war it would be a mistake to blow Bronx except over a major deception as although her usefulness in the immediate future appears to be limited, it is evident that her masters eagerly await her news and will probably believe any information she puts over provided that it is not childishly improbable. Her long-term possibilities should not be overlooked.'[27]

The last document in her file included a transcript of a postcard written to her in French from Lisbon, which showed that the Germans wanted her to keep in touch. Luke commented that it might be worth sending her to Spain with the idea of penetrating any German stay-behind organisation. Rather than sending her in immediately, he recommended waiting until the general clean-up of Germans in the Iberian Peninsula had taken place. As there were a number of redacted pages, for how long she continued working for MI6 is unknown, but at the end of the war she retired on an MI6 pension and lived under a false identity in a small village in the south of France.

Conclusion

While this book has shed more light on the role of women employed as honeytraps, decoys, infiltrators and in double agents' deception games during the Second World War, it has also provided insight into the mindset of their case officers, handlers and the officers responsible for the planning and implementation of their schemes. While they all can be considered to have been successful, some were much more successful than others and a number can be considered to have played a largely unmentioned but significant role in the outcome of the war.

Although these women were Allied agents operating against the Germans, there must have been other women employed in similar roles in other countries whose stories have yet to come to light. In Anatoli Granovsky's autobiography, *I was an NKVD Agent*, he admitted being given lessons in love-making in a specialist Soviet spy school outside Moscow. He was told that the directors of some important organisations in the West were women. As they were able to direct national affairs, agents or counter-agents needed to learn how to influence them. These women would not succumb to offers of money, invitations to parties or gifts of jewellery, but a young, ardent and skilled lover was an extraordinary gift.

It was explained to him that men had an ingrained habit of asking women for advice and that consequently, wives had an indirect influence over a nation's affairs, out of all proportion to their qualifications. Women could be an invaluable help to an agent in bringing a subject round to a desired way of thinking. Should the agent fail to commit himself and fail sexually, all his efforts could be nullified.

NKVD agents were expected to seduce married women and get them to encourage their husbands to have a more sympathetic attitude towards communism. It was drummed into them that they had to let the woman know that they loved them, that she excited them and they wanted her body; if they were successful in love-making, she would love them. Granovsky remembered being told that a woman's love is more passionate and less selfish than a man's in all its manifestations, except the sexual one. Not being able to satisfy a woman's sexual urges arouses her contempt and boredom. Men become tedious, even hated. Students were shown charts showing various parts of a woman's anatomy. It was purely academic, with nothing about emotional involvement.

There were also practical lessons with local girls, sometimes more than one and often with his instructor present. The point was made very strongly that emotions and weakness of the flesh had to be mastered. The mind of the true 'tchekist' had to be concentrated on the objective and how to achieve it. There had to be no preconceptions, no absolute truths, no principles and no values other than efficiency. He was expected to be the perfect servant and guardian of the State, to train incessantly until he became a 'one hundred per cent efficient human machine'.[1]

He made no mention of there being similar training sessions for Soviet women agents but it is possible, given the stories of British and American males finding themselves sexually compromised at the hands of some Russian beauty. Maybe Poles, Germans and other nationalities succumbed too. Maybe the Norwegian intelligence services, the Danish, the Dutch, Belgian, French, Italian, Polish, Czechoslovakian, Greek and other countries employed women as honeytraps, decoys and in deception games and this book will spark an interest in such research.

My aim is to ensure that Fifi's story, and those of other agent provocateurs during the Second World War, will not be forgotten.

Notes

Foreword

1   Foot, M. R. D. *An Outline History of the Special Operations Executive 1940 – 1946*, Greenwood Press, BBC Books, 1984, p. 68
2   Stafford, D. *Secret Agent: The True Story of the Special Operations Executive*, BBC Worldwide, 2000, pp. 44–45
3   http://blog.nationalarchives.gov.uk/blog/special–agent–fifi–special–operations–executive/

1 Fifi's Background

1   Simpson, W. *One of our Pilots is Safe*, Hamish Hamilton, London, 1942, p. 183
2   Ibid. pp. 184–5
3   Say, R. & Holland, N. *Rosie's War*, Michael O'Mara Books, 2011, p. 99. Noel Holland is a composite name of Noel Fursman and Julia Holland, the latter being Rosie's daughter.
4   Ibid. pp. 100–101
5   Ibid. p. 102
6   Ibid. p. 108
7   Brooks, A. M. 'Tony' Interview in Imperial War Museum, Tape 9550, reel 2
8   Ibid. p. 209
9   Ibid. p. 228

2 Background to Britain's Intelligence Services

1   https://www.sis.gov.uk/our–history/sisor–mi6.html; http://www.spartacus–educational.com/SScumming. htm
2   Yarnold, P. *Wanborough Manor: School for Secret Agents*, Hopfield Publications, 2009
3   Harrison, D. *Paramilitary Training in Scotland during World War Two*, Land, Sea & Islands Centre, Arisaig, 2001
4   Cunningham, C. *Beaulieu: The Finishing School for Secret Agents*, Leo Cooper, London, 1998
5   Communication with Steven Kippax, SOE historian
6   TNA HS7/51 Training Section 1940—1945, Industrial Sabotage Training, 1941—1944
7   TNA HS8/229

3 D/CE: SOE's Security Section and Fifi's Recruitment (1940–1941)

1   TNA HS9/1341/9
2   Imperial War Museum Sound Archive (IWMSA), Interview with Peter Lee, Reel 4
3   Murphy, C. *Security and Special Operations: SOE and MI5 during the Second World War*, Palgrave Macmillan, 2006, p. 4
4   Field Security Sections of the Intelligence Corps; Security and Special Operations; Rose & Laurel, 1984
5   Murphy, op. cit. p. 6
6   IWMSA, Lee Interview, Reel 3; Quoted in Murphy, op. cit. p. 7
7   TNA HS7/31
8   TNA HS7/31 History of the Security Section and Field Security Police
9   Murphy, op. cit. p. 8
10 Foot, *SOE in the Low Countries*, St Ermins Press, 2001, pp. 267–8, 336–7, 488
11 Ibid. pp. 120–1; Murphy, op. cit. pp. 9–10
12 Lee, Peter, IWM SA, 7493
13 TNA HS9/307/3
14 Ibid.
15 Ibid.
16 Ibid. 13 November 1941
17 Ibid. 3 December 1941
18 Ibid. 3 December
19 Ibid. 28 December 1941
20 Ibid. 6 March 1942
21 Ibid. September 1942
22 Say & Holland, op. cit.
23 Murphy, op. cit.

4 Fifi's Role as SOE's Agent Provocateur (1942–1945)

1   Ibid. 11 September 1942
2   Ibid. 16 September 1942
3   Ibid.
4   Ibid.
5   Ibid. 24 September 1942
6   Ibid. 24/25 September 1942
7   Ibid. 25 September 1942
8   Ibid. 25 September 1942
9   Ibid. 28 September 1942
10 Ibid. 1 October 1942
11 TNA HS9/1034/7; Murphy, op. cit. p. 14
12 Except it was not in her file, TNA HS9/307/3, 22 October 1942
13 Ibid. 22 October 1942
14 Pilot Officer Hugh Park, one of the Security Section officers who liaised with Beaulieu regarding their 96–hour schemes
15 Ibid. 29 September 1942
16 Ibid.
17 Ibid.
18 Ibid. 30th November 1942
19 Ibid.
20 Ibid.
21 *The Independent*, 17 September 2014
22 TNA HS9/1470/7
23 Ibid. 13 December 1942
24 www.secretscotland.org.uk/index.php/Secrets/InverlairLodge
25 Communication with Steven Kippax
26 TNA HS9/1470/7

27 TNA HS9/307/3. 8 December
28 Ibid. 12 December 1942
29 Ibid. 18 December
30 Pattinson, J. *Behind Enemy Lines – Gender, Passing and the Special Operations Executive in the Second World War*, Manchester University Press, 2007, p. 71
31 Lee, Peter, IWM SA, 7493
32 TNA HS9/1601/4
33 TNA HS9/307/3, 5 January 1943
34 TNA HS9/1369/6, 27 November 1942
35 TNA HS9/1369/6; http://operationmusketoon.com/norwegian–indep–co–1/corporal–sverre–granlund/
36 TNA HS9/307/3, 5 January 1943
37 TNA HS 9/1470/8, 12 January 1943
38 Ibid.
39 TNA HS9/307/3, 6 January 1943
40 Ibid. 10 January 1943
41 Jonathan Cole, National Archives blog, 17 September 2014, from her personal communication with Patricia Grant and Solvita Viba
42 Pattinson, J. op. cit. p. 72
43 Miller, R. *Behind Enemy Lines: the Oral History of Special Operations in World War II*, New American Library, 2002, pp. 131–2
44 Pattinson, J. op. cit. p. 72
45 Author's communication with Patricia Grant, 23 November 2014
46 Ibid. 13 January 1943
47 TNA HS 9/1370/6; http://www.rollofhonour.com/Surrey/GodalmingCharthouse SchoolWW2.html
48 Ibid. 15 January 1943
49 Ibid. 20 January 1943
50 Ibid. 21 January 1943
51 TNA HS 9/1452/8, 24 January 1943
52 O'Connor, B. *Return to Holland,* wwwl.lulu.com, 2012
53 Ibid. 21 January 1943
54 Ibid. 10 February 1943
55 Ibid. 12 February 1943
56 Ibid. 13 February 1943
57 Ibid.
58 Ibid. 11 October 1943
59 Ibid. 15 February 1943
60 Ibid. 24 February 1943
61 Ibid. 6 March 1943
62 Ibid.
63 Ibid.
64 Ibid. 22 March 1943
65 TNA HS9/595/2
66 Ibid.
67 TNA HS9/398/6
68 TNA HS9/1370/6
69 TNA HS8/832; email communication with Fred Judge, 17 November 2014
70 TNA HS9/307/3. 8 April 1943
71 Ibid. 17 April 1943
72 TNA HS9 908/1; O'Connor, B. *The Women of RAF Tempsford*, Amberley Press, 2011
73 TNA HS9/307/3, 17 April 1943
74 Ibid. 19 May 1943
75 Ibid. 29 May 1943
76 Ibid. 29 May 1943
77 Ibid. 2 June 1943
78 Ibid. 7 June 1943

79   Ibid. 17 June 1943
80   Ibid. undated but probably 25/26 June 1943
81   TNA HS9 246/2; http://www.crimefictioniv.com/Part_49.html
82   TNA HS9 246/2
83   Ibid. 15 May 1943
84   Ibid.
85   Ibid.
86   Ibid.
87   Ibid.
88   Ibid. 5 July 1943
89   Ibid. 30 June 1943
90   2 July 1943
91   Ibid. 18 July 1943
92   Ibid. August 1943
93   TNA HS9/398/6
94   Richards, L. *Whispers of War: Underground Propaganda Rumour-Mongering in the Second World War,* www.psywar.org, 2010
95   TNA HS9/307/3, 31 July 1943
96   Ibid. undated but end of July 1943
97   Ibid. undated but about 10 August 1943
98   TNA HS9/355/2, August 1943
99   Ibid. 26 August 1943
100   TNA HS9/355/2; HS9/356; O'Connor, B. *Churchill's Angels*, Amberley Publishing, 2012
101   TNA HS9/1341/9
102   TNA HS9/307/3, undated but about 20 August 1943
103   Ibid. undated
104   Ibid.
105   Ibid. 26 August 1943
106   Ibid. 27 August 1943
107   Ibid. 27 August 1943
108   Ibid.
109   Ibid. 16 September 1943
110   Ibid.
111   Ibid. 9 September 1943
112   Ibid. 16 September 1943
113   Ibid. 23 September 1943
114   Ibid. 26 September 1943
115   Ibid. 8 October 1943
116   Ibid. 13 October 1943
117   Ibid.
118   Ibid. 16 October 1943
119   TNA HS8/832 History of Security Section – List of Personnel
120   TNA HS9/505/2
121   Ibid.
122   Riols, N. *The Secret Ministry of Ag & Fish: My Life in Churchill's School for Spies,* Pan MacMillan, London, 2013, pp. 257–8
123   Ibid. p. 149
124   Ibid. pp. 153–5
125   Clare Mulley, 'Unsealed documents unravel the secretive careers of Britain's forgotten female spies,' *The Telegraph*, 18 September, 2014
126   Riols, op. cit. p. 156
127   Ibid. p. 157
128   Ibid. pp. 155–6
129   Ibid. p. 257
130   Ibid. p. 258
131   TNA HS 9/1587/3; Riols, op. cit.
132   HS9/307/3, 2 March 1944

133 Ibid. probably August 1944
134 Ibid.
135 Ibid. 19 August 1944
136 Ibid. 2 September 1944
137 Email communication with Phil Tomaselli, 2 November 2014; http://www.dailymail. co.uk/news/article–2579722/Dark–secret–life–original–M–Spymaster–inspired–007s–boss–closet–gay–married–three–women–never–slept–reinventing–childrens–presenter–called–Uncle–Max.html; http://www.grahamstevenson.me.uk; Masters, A. *The Man Who Was M: the Life of Maxwell Knight*, Grafton Books, London, 1986
138 Ibid; Twigge, S. Hampshire, E, Macklin, G. *British Intelligence,* The National Archives, Kew, 2008, p. 33; http://www.theguardian.com/uk/2004/may/21/artsand humanities.highereducation
139 TNA HS9/307/3. 4th November 1944
140 Ibid. 14 November 1944
141 Ibid. November 1944
142 Ibid. 18 December 1944
143 Ibid. 21 January 1945
144 Ibid. 27 December 1944
145 Ibid. 2 February 1944
146 Ibid. 6 February 1945
147 Ibid. 12 February 1945
148 Ibid. 8 February 1945
149 Ibid. Miller, J. *One Girl's War: Personal Exploits in MI5's Most Secret Station*, Brandon/Mount Eagle Publications Ltd, 1986, p. 39
150 Ibid. 26 February 1945
151 Ibid. 2 March 1945
152 TNA KV4/227
153 TNA KV 4/227; http://www.theguardian.com/uk/2004/may/21/artsandhumanities. highereducation; http://www.Telegraph.co.uk/news/uknews/terrorism–in–the–uk/ 6252408/MI5–and–the–sexy–secret–agents.html; 'Women make better spies – as long as they forget sex', *The Guardian*, Friday 21 May 2004
154 TNA HS9/307/3 20 March 1945
155 Ibid. April 1944
156 Ibid.
157 Ibid.
158 Ibid. 29 May 1945
159 Ibid. 21 June 1945
160 Ibid. 28 August 1945

5 Christine's Post–War Life 1945 to 2007

1 'Revealed: identity of Fifi the stunning wartime spy', *The Telegraph,* 17 Sep 2014
2 Communication with Patricia Grant, 23 November 2011
3 Magnus, S. W. 'Foreign Compensation and the Taxman', *Business Law Review,* Vol. 5, Issue 8/9, 1984, pp. 218–219
4 Author's communication with Patricia Grant, 23 November 2014
5 Ibid; http://www. telegraph. co. uk/news/11110756/Life–in–pictures–of–the–secret–agent–seductress. html
6 http://www. dzd. lv/new/
7 Ibid.
8 Revealed: identity of Fifi the stunning wartime spy, The Telegraph, 17 Sep 2014

6 Maxwell Knight's Female Infiltrators

1 http://www.grahamstevenson.me.uk/
2 Miller, J. *One Girl's War: Personal Exploits in MI5's Most Secret Station*, Brandon/ Mount Eagle Publications Ltd, 1986

3 Ibid. p. 19
4 Miller referred to her as Mrs Amos
5 TNA KV 4/227; http://www.express.co.uk/posts/view/126784; http://www.spartacus-educational.com/2WWrightclub.htm
6 TNA KV4/227
7 Miller, op. cit. p. 16
8 Ibid. p. 23
9 Ibid. p. 25
10 Ibid. pp. 23–4
11 TNA KV 4/227; Miller, op. cit. pp. 34–5
12 Ibid.
13 TNA KV4. 227, pp. 50–2
14 Ibid. p. 28–9
15 Ibid. p. 30
16 TNA KV4/227
17 Miller, op. cit. p. 31
18 TNA KV 4/227, pp. 48–9
19 Ibid. pp. 52–3
20 Ibid.

7 John Masterman's Double Agent 'Gelatine': Friedl Gartner

1 Barbier, M., 'Clash of the Titans', Arms and the Man, *Military Warfare* 68, Brill, Netherlands, p. 46
2 Miller, op. cit. pp. 86–7
3 TNA KV 2/1280
4 Ibid, undated
5 TNA KV 2/1280, 9 July 1940
6 TNA KV 2/1280, 21 July 1940
7 Berbier, op. cit. p. 47; TNA KV 2/1280, 2 August 1945
8 https://www.mi5.gov.uk/home/mi5–history/world–war–ii.html
9 Popov, D. *Spy Counterspy: the Autobiography of Dusko Popov,* Grosset & Dunlep, 1974
10 Miller, op. cit. p. 88
11 Ibid. pp. 87–8
12 Ibid.
13 Ibid.
14 TNA KV 2/1275, 18 May 1941
15 TNA KV 2/1275, 25 March 1941
16 Ibid. 26 June 1941
17 TNA KV 2/1280
18 Ibid. 14 July 1941
19 Ibid.
20 TNA KV 2/1275, 22 July 1941
21 Ibid. 20 July 1941
22 Masterman, J. C. *The Double–Cross System: The Classic Account of World War Two Spy–Masters*, Vintage, 2013, p. 86
23 TNA KV 2/1276, 13 August 1941
24 http://www.combinedops.com/lofoten_2.htm
25 Ibid. 17 September 1941
26 KV 2/1276, 13 November 1941
27 TNA KV 2/1276, 27 February 1942
28 Ibid. 11 March 1942
29 Ibid.
30 Ibid.
31 TNA KV 2/1277, 22 April 1942
32 Ibid. 9 May 1942

33   Ibid. 10 May 1942
34   Ibid. 10 May 1942
35   Ibid. 4 June 1942
36   TNA KV 2/1277, 26 August 1942
37   Ibid. 16 June 1942
38   TNA KV 2/1277, 8 September 1942
39   Ibid. 16 October 1942
40   TNA KV 2/1277 16 October 1942
41   TNA KV 2/1277, 23 November 1942
42   TNA KV 2/1277, 3 February 1943
43   Ibid. 9 February 1943
44   Ibid. 9 February 1943
45   Ibid. 20 March 1943
46   Ibid. 3 April 1943
47   TNA KV 2/1288, 10 June 1943
48   TNA KV 2/1288, 30 June 1943
49   TNA KV 2/1288, 1 July 1943
50   TNA KV 2/1288, 14 March 1944
51   TNA KV 2/1288, 7 June 1944
52   Ibid.
53   Ibid. 17 July 1944
54   Ibid. 9 September 1944
55   Ibid. 10 September 1944
56   Ibid. 20 November 1944
57   TNA KV 2/1278
58   Ibid.

8 John Masterman's Double Agent 'Treasure': Nathalie Sergueiew

1   TNA KV 2/464, 20 August 1943
2   Sergueiev, L. *Secret Service Rendered: An Agent in the Espionage Duel Preceding the Invasion of France*, Kimber, University of Wisconsin, 1968, p. 16
3   TNA KV 2/464
4   TNA KV 2/466, 15 October 1944
5   Serguiev, op. cit. p. 20
6   TNA KV2/464, November 1943
7   Ibid.
8   Ibid.
9   TNA KV 2/466
10   The book was actually published in September 1943 and is called *Routes, Risques, Rencontres.*
11   Ibid.
12   Serguiev, op. cit. p. 68
13   Macintyre, Ben. *Double Cross: The True Story of the D–Day Spies*, Broadway Books, 2013, p. 151
14   Ibid.
15   TNA KV 2/466
16   Ibid, 16 July 1943
17   Macintyre, 2003, p. 152
18   TNA KV 2/466; 24 August 1943; Macintyre, 2003, p. 151
19   Serguiev, op. cit. p. 80
20   Ibid. p. 88
21   Ibid. p. 92
22   Sergueiv, op. cit. p. 97
23   TNA KV 2/464
24   Ibid, 24 September 1943
25   TNA KV 2/464

26   TNA KV2/465
27   Sergueiev, op. cit. p. 126
28   Sergueiev, op. cit. p. 125
29   Macintyre, 2003, p. 151
30   TNA KV2/465, December 1943
31   TNA KV 2/466
32   Ibid. 12 February 1944
33   Sergueiev, op. cit, pp. 146–7
34   TNA KV2/465
35   Ibid. 14 March 1944
36   Sergueiev, op. cit. p. 175
37   TNA KV2/465
38   Serguiev, op. cit. p. 182–3
39   Ibid.
40   Ibid. 28 March 1944
41   'Attaché in border row – called home', *Daily Express*, 31 May 1944
42   TNA KV2/465
43   Ibid.
44   Ibid. 3 April 1944; Copies of the examples can be seen in the illustrations.
45   Sergueiev, op. cit. pp. 194–5
46   Ibid. p. 204
47   Ibid. p. 206
48   TNA KV2/465, 17 May 1944
49   TNA KV2/466, 28 December 1944
50   Ibid. 26 May 1944. Brutus/Herbert was Roman Czerniawski, a Polish double agent.
51   Ibid. 15 June 1944
52   TNA KV 2/466, 17 June 1944
53   Segueiev, op. cit. p. 214
54   TNA KV2/466; 29 November 1944
55   TNA KV 2/466, 4 July 1944
56   Ibid.
57   TNA KV 2/466, 3 November 1944

9 John Masterman's Double Agent 'Bronx': Elvira Chaudoir

1   TNA KV 2/2908, 21 October 1942
2   'How a Peruvian beauty stopped a Nazi tank division in its tracks,' *The Telegraph*, 5 September 2005
3   Macintyre, http://www.commandposts.com/2012/08/the–d–day–spies–part–iv–elvira–de–la–fuente–chaudoir/
4   Ibid.
5   Macintyre, op. cit.
6   TNA KV 2/2908, 29 January 1943
7   Ibid. 31 December 1942
8   Masterman, J. C. *The Double–Cross System: The Incredible True Story of How Nazi Spies Were Turned Into Double Agents*, Vintage, 2013
9   Ibid. 18 October 1942
10   Ibid.
11   TNA KV 2/2098, 26 October and early November 1942
12   Ibid. 4 November 1942
13   TNA KV 2/3639
14   TNA KV 2/2098, 10 September 1943
15   TNA KV 2/2098. 16 April 1944
16   Ibid. 6 March 1944
17   Rest of note redacted. TNA KV 2/2098
18   TNA KV2/3639; KV 2/2098, 20 March 1945; Masterman, op. cit. p. 162
19   TNA KV 2/2098, May 1944

20 TNA KV 2/2098, 20 May 1944
21 TNA KV 2/3639
22 TNA KV/2/2098, December 1944
23 Ibid. 12 January 1945
24 TNA KV 2/2098
25 Masterman, op. cit. p. 162
26 TNA KV 2/2098, 14 March 1945
27 Ibid. 31 March 1945

Conclusion

1 Granovsky, A. *I was an NKVD Agent*, The Devin–Adair Company, New York, 1962

Bibliography

Books and Journals

Andrew, Christopher, *The Defence of the Realm: the Authorised History of MI5*, Penguin, 2010

Barbier, Mary, 'Clash of the Titans', Arms and the Man, *Military Warfare 68*, Brill, Netherlands, p. 43

Clough, B. *State Secrets: The Kent-Wolkoff Affair*, Hideaway Publications, 2005

Foot, Michael R. D. *An Outline History of the Special Operations Executive 1940–1946*, Greenwood Press, BBC Books, 1984

Foot, Michael R. D. *SOE in the Low Countries*, St Ermins Press, 2001

Lee, P. *Field Security Sections of the Intelligence Corps: Security and Special Operations*, Rose & Laurel, 1984

Macintyre, Ben. *Double Cross: The True Story of the D-Day Spies*, Broadway Books, 2013

Magnus, S. W. 'Foreign Compensation and the Taxman', *Business Law Review*, Vol. 5, Issue 8/9, 1984

Masterman, J. C. *The Double-Cross System: The Incredible True Story of How Nazi Spies Were Turned Into Double Agents*, Vintage, 2013

Masters, A. *The Man Who was M: the Life of Maxwell Knight*, Grafton Books, London, 1986

Miller, Joan. *One Girl's War: Personal Exploits in MI5's Most Secret Station*, Brandon/ Mount Eagle Publications Ltd., 1986

Miller, Russell, *Behind Enemy Lines: The Oral History of Special Operations in World War II*, New American Library, 2002

O'Connor, Bernard. *The Women of RAF Tempsford*, Amberley Publishing, 2011

O'Connor, Bernard. *Return to Holland*, wwwl.lulu.com, 2012

Pattinson, Juliette. *Behind Enemy Lines: Gender, Passing and the Special Operations Executive in the Second World War*, Manchester University Press, 2007

Popov, D. *Spy Counterspy: the Autobiography of Dusko Popov*, Grosset & Dunlep, 1974

Riols, Noreen. *The Secret Ministry of Ag & Fish: My Life in Churchill's School for Spies*, Pan MacMillan, London, 2013

Richards, Lee. *Whispers of War: Underground Propaganda Rumour-Mongering in the Second World War*, www.psywar.org, 2010

Serguiev, Lily, *Secret Service Rendered: An Agent in the Espionage Duel Preceding the Invasion of France*, Kimber, University of Wisconsin, 1968

Simpson, W. *One of Our Pilots is Safe*, Hamish Hamilton, London, 1942

Stafford, David. *Secret Agent: The True Story of the Special Operations Executive*, BBC Worldwide, 2000

Twigge, S., Hampshire, E., Macklin, G. *British Intelligence*, The National Archives, Kew, 2008

Vargo, Marc E. *Women of the Resistance: Eight Who Defied the Third Reich*, McFarland, 2012

Newspapers

'Attaché in border row – called home', *Daily Express*, 31 May 1944
'Agent's devotion to her dog put D-Day in peril', *The Telegraph*, 5 July 2001
'Double agent nearly revealed D-Day secrets over dog's death', *The Guardian*, 5 July 2001
'Women make better spies – as long as they forget sex', *The Guardian*, Friday 21 May 2004
'How a Peruvian beauty stopped a Nazi tank division in their tracks', *The Telegraph*, 5 September 2005
'The Wartime Spymaster', *The Times*, Tuesday, May 15 2007, pg.4[S]; Issue 69012
'MI5 and the sexy secret agents', Duncan Gardham, Security Correspondent, *The Telegraph*, 2 October 2009
'Revealed: identity of Fifi the stunning wartime spy', *The Telegraph*, 17 September 2014
'Meet Agent Fifi, sent by British spymasters to test out trainee agents before they were sent to occupied Europe', *Daily Mail*, 17 September 2014
'Revealed after 75 years of secrecy: "Fifi" the glamorous WW2 special agent who tested British spies' resolve', *The Independent*, 17 September 2014
'"Agent Fifi" tested British trainee spies during WW-II', *Press Trust of India*, London, 17 September 2014
'World War II's "Agent Fifi" test and the history of female spies', *Newsy*, 17 September 2014
'Unsealed documents unravel the secretive careers of Britain's forgotten female spies', *The Telegraph,* 18 September 2014
'Identity of blonde Second World War spy "Fifi" is uncovered', *Western Daily Press*, 19 September 2014
'Licensed to thrill: Christine Chilver, Britain's Second World War special agent', *Sunday Telegraph*, 21 September 2014

Websites

http://blog.nationalarchives.gov.uk/blog/special-agent-fifi-special-operations-executive/
http://www.lsm.lv/en/article/societ/society/latvian-girl-was-british-wartime-super-spy.a98786/
http://www.dailymail.co.uk/news/article-2762845/Special-agent-seductress-Her-hush-hush-wartime-mission-bewitch-trainee-spies-spilling-national-secrets-Now-70-years-tells-gripping-story.html
https://www.mi5.gov.uk/home/mi5-history/world-war-ii.html
http://www.crimefictioniv.com/Part_49.html
http://www.dzd.lv/new/
http://www.palgrave.com/resources/sample-chapters/9780230002418_sample.pdf
http://www.zoopla.co.uk/property/9-nevern-road/london/sw5-9pg/23161204
http://operationmusketoon.com/norwegian-indep-co-1/corporal-sverre-granlund/
http://www.yara.com/about/history/1940-1959/glomfjord _a_new_rjukan.aspx
http://www.foreignpolicy.com/articles/2010/03/12/the_history_of_the_honey_trap
http://www.theguardian.com/uk/2004/may/21/artsandhumanities.highereducation
http://www.Telegraph.co.uk/news/uknews/terrorism-in-the-uk/6252408/MI5-and-the-sexy-secret-agents.html
http://www.secretscotland.org.uk/index.php/Secrets/InverlairLodge_CachedSimilar
http://www.roll-of-honour.com/Surrey/GodalmingCharthouseSchoolWW2.html
http://www.dailymail.co.uk/news/article-2579722/Dark-secret-life-original-M-Spymaster-inspired-007s-boss-closet-gay-married-three-women-never-slept-reinventing-childrens-presenter-called-Uncle-Max.html
http://www.grahamstevenson.me.uk
http://www.raleighspyconference.com/speaker_speeches/2009_crowdy_speech.aspx
http://www.nationalarchives.gov.uk/spies/spies/treasure/default.htm

Documents in the National Archives

HS 7/31 History of Security Section and Field Security Police 1940-45
HS 7/51 Training Section 1940–1945, Industrial Sabotage Training, 1941–1944.
HS 8/229 Intelligence (L) Sub-section
HS 8/832 History of security section: 1940-1945; list of personnel date 1945
HS 9/246/2 Euan Beresford Butler, also known as Captain Beresford
HS 9/307/3 Marie Christine Chilver
HS 9/398/6 Winifred Elizabeth Davidson
HS 9/505/2 Jean 'Alex' Felgate
HS 9/530/6 Gerald Forty (Closed)
HS 9/595/2 Paul Goffin aka Paul Quinaux
HS 9/908/1 Cécile Lefort
HS 9/1034/7 Cyril Thompson Miller
HS 9/1653 Norman Gilbert Mott
HS 9/1319/8 Rosemary 'Pat' Say
HS 9/1341/9 John Watt Senter
HS 9/1370/6 Joyce Gwendolen Skinner, *née* PRIZER
HS 9/1369/6 Tobias Skog alias Peter Larsen
HS 9/1470/8 Gunnar Tingulstad
HS 9/1587/3 – Dorothy Wicken
HS 9/1601/4 Prudence Willoughby
KV 2/464–466 Nathalie SERGUEIEW, alias Lily, codename TREASURE; Vols.1-III
KV 2/1275–1280 GELATINE (Friedl Gartner) Austrian Double Agent
KV 2/2098 Chaudoir, Elvira, Conception, Josephina
KV 2/3639 SUMMARY OF CHAUDOIR TRAFFIC 03/11/1942 – 24/11/1944
KV 4/227 Report on the work of MS (recruitment and operation of agents) during the Second World War, written by Maxwell Knight

Documents in the Imperial War Museum Sound Archive

Brooks, Anthony 'Tony' Morris, Interview, Catalogue Number: 9550, tapes, reel 2
Lee, Peter, Interview, Reels 3 and 4

Other Books by Bernard O'Connor

RAF Tempsford: Churchill's Most Secret Airfield, Amberley Publishing, 2010
The Women of RAF Tempsford: Heroines of Wartime Resistance, Amberley Publishing, 2011
Churchill and Stalin's Secret Agents: Operation Pickaxe at RAF Tempsford, Fonthill Media, 2011
The Tempsford Academy: Churchill and Roosevelt's Secret Airfield, Fonthill Media, 2012
Agent Rose: The true Story of Eileen Nearne, Britain's Forgotten Wartime Heroine, Amberley Publishing, 2010
Churchill's Angels: How Britain's Women Secret Agents Changed the Course of the Second World War, Amberley Publishing, 2012
The Courier: Reminiscences of a Female Secret Agent in Wartime France, (Historical faction) www.lulu.com 2010
Designer: The True Story of Jacqueline Nearne, www.lulu.com, 2011
Return to Belgium, www.lulu.com, 2012
Return to Holland, www.lulu.com, 2012
Bedford Spy School, www.lulu.com, 2012
Old Bedfordians' Secret Operations During World War Two, www.lulu.com, 2012
Henri Déricourt: Triple Agent (edited), www.lulu.com, 2012
Churchill's School for Saboteurs: Brickendonbury, STS 17, Amberley Publishing, 2013
Churchill's Most Secret Airfield, Amberley Publishing, 2013
Sabotage in Norway, www.lulu.com, 2013

Sabotage in Denmark, www.lulu.com, 2013
Sabotage in Belgium, www.lulu.com, 2013
Sabotage in Holland, www.lulu.com, 2013
Sabotage in France, www.lulu.com, 2013
Blackmail Sabotage, www.lulu.com, 2014
Sabotage in Greece, www.lulu.com, 2014

Index